D1140498

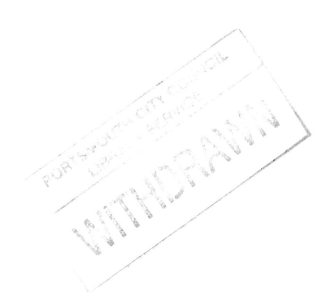

Tulisa

Also by Sean Smith

Kate

Robbie

Cheryl

Victoria

Kylie: The Biography

Justin: The Biography

Britney: The Biography

J. K. Rowling: A Biography

Jennifer: The Unauthorized Biography

Royal Racing

The Union Game

Sophie's Kiss (*with Garth Gibbs*)

Stone Me! (*with Dale Lawrence*)

Tulisa

Sean Smith

**SIMON &
SCHUSTER**

London · New York · Sydney · Toronto · New Delhi

A CBS COMPANY

First published in Great Britain by Simon & Schuster UK Ltd, 2012
A CBS COMPANY

3 5 7 9 10 8 6 4 2

Simon & Schuster UK Ltd
1st Floor
222 Gray's Inn Road
London
WC1X 8HB

www.simonandschuster.co.uk

Simon & Schuster Australia,
Sydney

Simon & Schuster India,
New Delhi

A CIP catalogue for this book is
available from the British Library.

ISBN: 978-1-84737-871-2 (Hardback)
ISBN: 978-1-84737-872-9 (Trade paperback)

Typeset by M Rules
Printed and bound by CPI Group (UK) Ltd, Croydon, CR0 4YY

To Jo
Making me happy, keeping me so

Contents

PART ONE: **TULA**

1   **The Family Business**   3
2   **One in a Million**   14
3   **Jumbo**   25
4   **The Book of Five Rings**   33
5   **Jekyll and Hyde**   44
6   **Blood on the Page**   54
7   **Drama**   66

PART TWO: **TULISA**

8   **Big Strings**   77
9   **Crying Under Shades**   87
10   **Building the Brand**   98
11   **More Drama**   108
12   **Feeling Crap**   123
13   **The Rap Sheet**   129
14   **Tulisa in Love**   138
15   **Empowered**   149

PART THREE: **THE FEMALE BOSS**

16   **Tulisa in Lust**   165
17   **On Def Ears**   174
18   **Simon Calling**   183
19   **Chavtastic**   196
20   **The Role Model**   207

21 **Tulisa v Kelly**   214
22 **Woman of the Year**   223

    Tulisa's Stars   238
    Life and Times   245
    Acknowledgements   251
    Select Bibliography and Picture Credits   253
    Index   254

PART ONE

TULA

1

The Family Business

The moment Tulisa Contostavlos filled our television screens in the opening sequence of *The X Factor* and shouted, 'What is *WRONG* with you!' she became a star. That's the power of TV and of reality programmes in particular but the great majority of the viewing public had no idea where this stunning young woman had come from.

As the weeks progressed, we warmed to her as she brought passion to her role as a judge, picking up Little Mix, the group she was mentoring, and carrying them over the finish line victorious. She called them her 'little muffins' and gave them an identity that left everyone wanting them to do well.

When they were announced as the winners, she became one too. It was a joyful occasion, a triumph for ordinary girls. But Tulisa is far from being that and her life story is extraordinary. Tulisa loves acting. It's early days in her film career but if she needed a good script opportunity she should star in a movie about her own life. It would be a modern melodrama.

The old Hollywood view of becoming a star would show the young Tulisa as a happy little girl gazing out of her bedroom window at the heavens and dreaming of bouquets and applause. The reality was a lonely child, staring tearfully at her bedroom walls, worried sick about her mum and not knowing what to do.

They lived in Belsize Park, one of the pleasanter areas of North West London, two minutes from Haverstock Hill. If you turn right, you can walk past her primary school and on to Rosslyn Hill with all the inviting boutiques and chic coffee houses of Hampstead. If you turn left, you can gaze at the prison-like walls of Haverstock School before venturing on to the grim Denton Estate in Chalk Farm and the high-rise blocks of Camden Town. Why did Tulisa turn left?

Tulisa's mother, Ann, was a singer and on good days would dance around the kitchen, serenading her little girl with her favourite songs from the forties – classics by The Andrews Sisters and Glenn Miller. Her father, Plato, was a professional keyboard player. Music was the family business just as much as if they owned a grocer's shop or a plumbing firm.

Plato, the Anglicized version of his Greek name Platon, was born in Egypt and grew up in Africa where his father, Spyros Contostavlos, had diplomatic postings in the Congo and Ethiopia. He loved the outdoor life there so much he was nicknamed Tarzan by his family.

It would have been quite a culture shock, therefore, when Spyros took up a senior position with the United Nations in London. The family found a lovely home two and a half miles from Belsize Park in Asmara Road, Cricklewood, and this is the house where Tulisa's parents were living when she was born and where her story begins.

The six-bedroom house was the Contostavlos family home for more than thirty years. Asmara Road is the sort of street – a peaceful oasis in the urban madness – that nobody wants to leave once they have found it. This is a middle-class street with million-pound houses, where 4 × 4s occupy the resident parking bays ready for a mum or nanny to speed off and collect the children from school.

Asmara Road is perfectly located for London life. It's ten minutes' walk away from the busy Kilburn High Road and Cricklewood Railway Station, while in the other direction you can stroll along Mill Lane to West Hampstead with its trendy shops and bars. Asmara, named after the capital of Eritrea, is one of a complex of local streets, including Somali Road and Menelik Road, which make up a neighbourhood known by estate agents as Little Africa.

When the Contostavlos family settled there in the late seventies, they lived opposite the street's most famous resident, Dr Joseph Rotblat, the renowned Polish-born physicist who was the only scientist to quit working on the atomic bomb for moral reasons. He was awarded the Nobel Peace Prize in 1995 for his tireless campaigning for disarmament and was knighted three years later.

Dr Rotblat was a founder of the Pugwash Conferences, where scientists and powerful political leaders would meet to discuss ways of diminishing the importance of nuclear weapons in international politics. He coined the phrase 'We have been trying for forty years to save the world, sometimes against the world's wishes.'

Such grave matters concerning the future of the world seemed far removed from Asmara Road where, to the Contostavlos family, Dr Rotblat was their slightly eccentric neighbour from across the street. The scientist probably thought the Greek diplomat's family the more eccentric, as they drove around in a large black American limousine. Mrs Contostavlos – whom Tulisa calls Yaya, the Greek for grandmother – was notorious for being the worst driver in the street. Every day she would reverse straight out of the driveway without looking.

By one of those quirks of British planning, the Contostavlos family lived in Cricklewood and the Rotblats lived in Hampstead: Asmara Road formed the old dividing line between the two boroughs. The houses on the Hampstead side had a more desirable postcode and were therefore more highly valued.

Nowadays both sides of the street live in Cricklewood, although residents – and estate agents – prefer to say they live in West Hampstead. One of the rare houses for sale in 2012 was on the market for £1.4 million despite being in a rundown state and needing a lot of modernization. The Contostavlos family sold their house for £880,000 in 2005, when Spyros decided to retire to Greece. For a terraced property, it was extremely spacious and would be worth comfortably over £1 million even in today's faltering market.

The teenage Contostavlos sons, Byron and Plato, had to get used to a life without servants. In Africa, they grew up in an environment where it was commonplace among well-to-do white families to have household staff, including a driver, a cook and someone to do the washing. Both brothers grew up to be accomplished young men who had been privately educated, spoke good English and were brilliant musicians. They had two passions in life when they arrived in NW2: music and fishing. They were best mates, and their lives and careers would remain intertwined for the next thirty years.

They took a little while to settle in and adjust to what was culturally acceptable in their new country. Soon after arriving, they went to Hyde Park for the day and were happily shooting pigeons with an airgun, as they would have done in Africa, when the police saw them. They were taken home in a squad car, deposited on the doorstep of the house in Asmara Road and given a stern warning by officers and a good talking-to by their astonished mother. Fortunately, they were able to claim diplomatic immunity and escaped prosecution.

More importantly for their futures, they watched *Top of the Pops* for the first time and loved what they saw. They decided there and then that they were going to be professional musicians. In an amazing coincidence, one of the bands performing on that first show was Mungo Jerry, whose classic 1970 number one 'In the Summertime' remains one of the great holiday anthems. The brothers were much taken with the lead singer, Ray Dorset, who in those days sported a large frizzy Afro and impressive sideburns. This was one of those weird moments of fate because Ray would play an important part in their careers over the next twenty years.

The brothers started trying to find work in the flourishing North London music scene. Their parents were not as certain as they were that there was a living to be made from pop music. Their father had worked his way up the diplomatic ladder, culminating in his final posting to London as the chief of General Services in the administrative division of the International Maritime Organization (IMO), a branch of the UN that is responsible for the safety and security of worldwide shipping, as well as the prevention of marine pollution by ships. His position must have seemed a degree more stable than an evening's gig at a pub in Kilburn. Spyros insisted that his sons learn a trade to have something to fall back on if things didn't work out. And so Byron and Plato trained as ladies' hairdressers, which, as their parents had hoped, did provide them with work and a wage when music did not.

Byron was the more outgoing of the two. He played an energetic bass guitar, while Plato became a keyboard wizard. Byron fell in with another musician, Larry Berridge, who was the bassist with Mungo Jerry. Larry was looking to branch out on his own and played some of his songs to Ray, who was sufficiently impressed to want to help. Ray recalls, 'I thought the songs were really good so I helped them with some money to get started, some rehearsal time. I wasn't really their manager, just helping them to get going.'

Larry recruited Byron, a Greek drummer called Billy Lemon and another guitarist, Terry Jenkins. They decided to call themselves Hi Fi. Byron was the bass guitarist, while Larry was the vocalist and songwriter. In those days there was no *X Factor* to help fast-track you to fame but Byron learned some of the tricks of the trade that would be so important to Tulisa's future career. The new band taped some rough demos in Terry's living room and from that unpromising start they managed to get a deal with Aura Records, a small independent label, in the old-fashioned way: by playing the demo to the label's founder, Aaron Sixx. He recorded one of the demo tracks, called 'Run, Run', which was heard by the DJ John Peel.

The radio legend liked it and invited the boys in to record a session for his evening programme in March 1979. They recorded four tracks then that you can still hear online today. One critic described them as performing 'a combination of light-hearted romantic rock music in a tongue-in-cheek new wave manner' with 'no pretensions, no aggro, no demand on brain power, just entertainment.'

Much of the impetus for Hi Fi came from Byron, who at this point in his career was calling himself Byron Con, which was much easier for would-be fans to pronounce. Larry Berridge observed, 'His enthusiasm in promoting Hi Fi wherever he could was part of his unrelenting zest for life.'

Byron Con was electric on stage. When Hi Fi played the legendary Marquee Club in Wardour Street, he moved like Jagger – all nimbleness and enthusiasm. He literally threw himself into the crowd, his bass guitar like an extension of his arm as he drove the beat forward at what seemed like breakneck speed. They played everything fast, which was the fashion of their era. Byron had charisma and the local reviewers agreed that he was 'certainly their biggest stage asset.'

The band were one of those formed in the post punk world of the late seventies, when groups like The Jam and XTC were a partial throwback to the smartly dressed mod crews of the sixties. They were a clean-cut bunch, with Byron the nearest thing to a bad boy in jeans and trainers.

Hi Fi travelled to Germany, to a studio in Hamburg, in 1979 to record their first album *Towns and Bars*, which was released in 1980. They followed it with another, *Sing Song*, the next year. Plato joined them to play keyboards on a third album, *Gringo's Revenge*, but sadly the hoped-for success eluded them and they never finished it. The band split in 1982.

Larry Berridge signed a solo deal and became successful in Germany under the name of Sal Paradise. Byron, meanwhile, still calling himself Byron Con, released a solo single called 'Chakanoori Tango' on the Phonogram label but, despite publicity photos revealing him to be blue-eyed and blond with an eighties Rod Stewart haircut, he never made the breakthrough.

Byron's and, more briefly, Plato's experiences with Hi Fi were a lesson that you can't make it in the music business on talent alone – you need an edge. In London there were literally dozens of bands playing the same pubs and small music venues almost in rotation. Like many others, Hi Fi were on the brink of a breakthrough but never quite achieved the success they deserved. One music critic, the amusingly named Robin Blind, was convinced they would make it. He saw them perform at the Nashville Club and wrote 'this group has the "x" factor'. He predicted success within a year but it didn't happen.

When you get that close to the big time – when you're almost able to touch fame – you want it more. The Contostavlos brothers wanted it. Twenty years later, when they were masterminding the careers of their wet-behind-the ears children, Byron's son Costadinos (Dappy) and Plato's daughter Tula (Tulisa). Byron, in particular, could have written a book about struggling for success in the music business.

One reviewer went to the heart of why an accomplished band like Hi Fi failed to become a household name: they had no rage. 'There's no seething anger and frustration boiling in their souls and without that I don't see any point in breakneck renditions, except of course to be in vogue.' Dappy and Tulisa had the anger Hi Fi lacked, and railed against the injustices of their young lives. When they formed N-Dubz, Byron knew how to channel their aggressive enthusiasm into their music.

Instead of headlining, the Contostavlos brothers remained in London, where they spent the subsequent years as nearly men, always finding session work in studios and gigging in various bands on the pub circuit. They would load the gear in the back of a van literally hundreds of times and set off. But, while it made them enough money to go fishing, it wasn't sufficient to support a family. They had to resume their second careers as hairdressers.

At one recording session in the mid-eighties Plato, who had started calling himself Steve Contostavlos, met a vivacious and sparkling Irish girl, a member of one of Ireland's premier music families with a tradition and history stretching through the whole of the twentieth century. Her name was Ann Byrne and, with her three older sisters, she was part of a singing group called Jeep.

Ann's father – Tulisa's Granddad Tom – was Tommy Byrne, a celebrated boy soprano in the thirties. He would certainly have won *Britain's Got Talent* today. Instead he won the Feis Ceoil (Festival of Music), Ireland's top music competition, three times – testament to his beautiful voice. He carved out a career singing on radio shows and performing at venues such as the Theatre Royal in Dublin.

He appeared with one of the biggest acts in Ireland in the fifties, Val Doonican and the Four Ramblers, and sang with them on the radio show *Workers' Playtime*. Val went on to become famous across the Irish Sea on British television, where his Saturday night variety show was popular throughout the seventies and eighties.

Tommy Byrne stayed behind in Ireland and began a family dynasty in Churchtown, a largely Roman Catholic suburb of Dublin. Years later Tulisa would recall her mother taking her on trips to Ireland, where she has so many relatives. She would sit next to her granddad while in his wonderfully pure Irish voice he sang 'Molly Malone', a timeless tune learned by children of all generations: 'In Dublin's fair city, where the girls are so pretty ...' She observed, 'That's where I get my music from.'

The Byrne house was so full of music that one of the daughters, Moira, described it as being like the von Trapp family from *The Sound of Music*, as they would gather round the piano in the evening for a sing-song. And, just as in that famous musical, all the children had beautiful voices. Moira recalled, 'As kids we were forever putting on shows for our parents.'

The eldest sons, Brian and Mick, were keen to follow in their father's footsteps. They formed The Spiceland Folk Group and were runners-up in the Wexford Ballad Contest in 1967 before joining forces with another band and becoming Emmet Spiceland. They became one of the most popular acts in Ireland.

Tulisa's uncles specialized in hauntingly beautiful renditions of classic songs. Their best known single, 'Mary from Dungloe', knocked Bob Dylan's 'Mighty Quinn', sung by Manfred Mann, off the top of the Irish charts in February 1968. They were pin-ups and attracted huge crowds of teenage girls wherever they went. They were also ahead of their time in employing modern marketing techniques to keep the band's name in the public eye.

Sir Bob Geldof remembers them: 'They did Irish music, but in a different way and they dressed like mods! They were like the f**kin' Beatles, man.'

Emmet Spiceland signed with a British label, Page One Records, but never made the same impact in the British charts as they did in Ireland. They also toured America but broke up shortly afterwards, in 1970. Brian Byrne became a successful stage performer in London's West End, where he appeared in *Hair, The Rocky Horror Show* and *Jesus Christ Superstar,* one of the earliest Andrew Lloyd Webber musicals. He married a dancer called Mavis Ascot, who went on to choreograph the original *Riverdance* with Michael Flatley and Jean Butler.

By this time some of the Byrne family had moved across the Irish Sea and settled in Bradford, where the four sisters dreamed of following in their famous brothers' footsteps. Ann, the baby of the group, and her sisters, Moira, Paula and Louise, never enjoyed chart success, but their winning smiles and close harmonies brought them much television work in the early eighties.

Their 'big break' was like something out of a movie. They were singing in the foyer of the Victoria Theatre in London before one of Brian's shows when the renowned radio broadcaster Monty Modlin heard them one evening, took a shine to the smiling Irish girls and suggested they perform on his show. Moira Byrne recalled, 'Someone heard us on the radio and signed us up and it all went from there ... For young girls like us it was all terribly glamorous.'

They weren't cutting edge – more a throwback to the days of famous harmony groups of the Big Band era, such as The Andrews Sisters. They sang cover versions of 'Chattanooga Choo Choo' and 'Boogie Woogie Bugle Boy', which were perfect for what used to be known as light entertainment. They memorably sang the former while wearing military uniforms and driving into Richard Stilgoe's television show in a US Army jeep. Tulisa's cousin Goldmund Byrne, who is Mick's son, observed, 'You haven't heard beautiful until you've heard them singing that.'

It all seems so dated now but at the time the artists they appeared with – including Cannon and Ball, Jimmy Tarbuck, Russ Abbot and Les Dennis – were among the most popular performers on television. Les always had a great rapport with Ann and thought she did a marvellous rendition of 'The Trolley Song', the classic Judy Garland number from *Meet Me in St Louis*.

Ann was proving to be the most talented of the sisters. As well as possessing a striking singing voice, she had a real talent for mimicry and impersonations – a gift she would pass on to her daughter. Her appearance on a BBC talent show called *Rising Stars* led to some work away from her sisters. Les asked her to appear alongside him in his new show *Go For It* in 1984 and she proved a great hit. She was just twenty-four.

In one sketch, Ann, sporting a blonde wig, is dressed as Marilyn Monroe in her iconic white dress, while Les, somewhat improbably, is pretending to be Boy George. As well as Marilyn, Ann stole the show with her impressions of Dolly Parton, complete with pneumatic bust, and Mae West. Quite simply, Ann was very funny.

Their careers were blossoming, but behind the scenes Moira, Paula and Louise were beginning to notice that all was not well with their vivacious sister. She had spells when she would go quiet. The first time she showed real signs of mental health problems was when they were on tour in Europe. After a particularly stressful week, they were in Monte Carlo when it became clear that Ann was struggling.

Moira told the *Daily Mail* that there were always signs of her changeable moods. Nobody realized in those early days just how bad things were going to get. Here was a beautiful, bubbly and talented young woman who was going places. How could this happen to her? At this point no proper diagnosis was made but doctors prescribed medication to help Ann keep calm.

Much later, Moira would tell her niece Tulisa all about those difficult times and her memories featured on a very moving BBC documentary entitled *Tulisa: My Mum and Me.* Tulisa explained, 'Her symptoms were that she went very quiet, very emotionless, very thin but her body was very racy yet blank.'

The other sisters wanted to get on with their own lives: Moira was keen to start a family and settle down, Paula moved to Singapore and Louise was in a serious relationship. Somehow Jeep no longer seemed to be their priority and, anyway, it was Ann who was going to be the star. Sadly it didn't work out like that: after Jeep split up, Tulisa's mother never performed in public again.

2

One in a Million

Ann Byrne was six months pregnant when she married Plato Contostavlos at the Camden Register Office in Judd Street. Ann had been living in a flat near Swiss Cottage but after the wedding she moved into the house in Asmara Road with her new husband and his parents. There was plenty of room but they were keen to start their family life in a home of their own. The world should have been at their feet when their daughter was born at the Royal Free Hospital in Hampstead on 13 July 1988. They followed tradition and called her Tula after Plato's mother and added a second name, Paulinea, in honour of Ann's mother, Pauline.

Tula is a popular Greek name with several meanings, including 'gift from God' or 'gracious gift'. The girl herself preferred the meaning 'goddess'. The name had a burst of popularity when the hugely successful movie *My Big Fat Greek Wedding* was released in 2002. The lead character is called Toula and the name became known worldwide when the film took more than $368 million at the box office. It was a pretty name but no longer distinctive. Anyone called Toula or Tula would, for a while at least, be associated with this very funny film and with all things Greek.

It was a bit confusing when her grandmother was at home, as

there were two Tulas, so her parents started calling her Tulisa – little Tula – so she would know they were talking to her. She was quite proud of being a 'mini-goddess', although she never thought for one minute she would become famous with that name. She always thought it would be as 'Lady T'.

Tulisa was just a toddler when her parents were found a place of their own by Camden Council. Ann's sisters, Louise and Moira, were living in the borough so it made sense to move near them in case Ann needed help.

Byron was also a father now. He had married a Greek girl, Zoi Agorou, known as Zoe, and they'd had a son called Spiros after the head of the family and another called Costadinos, known as Dino. They'd moved into a flat in an uninspiring block off Royal College Street in Camden Town.

Ann and Plato were more fortunate and were given a flat in Lawn Road, a pretty tree-lined street in the much more up-market Belsize Park, one and a half miles to the north towards Hampstead. It's very quiet here – one of those lovely, leafy North London streets of large detached houses with steps leading up to the front door. Many are now given over to flats but while there are still some single residences, the odd Porsche, Mercedes or Audi parked outside provides proof that there is money in the neighbourhood.

Only one small block is obviously council-owned because of the signs outside declaring 'No Ball Games' and 'Keep Off the Grass'. Tulisa's family home, however, was in a very pleasant, large terraced house. This modestly furnished, one-bedroom first floor apartment would be Tulisa's home while she was growing up.

Plato's recollection of their home is slightly different from the urban, street kid image that would later become part of Tulisa's accepted life story. The flat had high ceilings, spacious rooms and wooden floors, but they used plastic garden chairs in the kitchen. It was definitely a cut above the sort of council flat you would find in the tower blocks of Camden Town.

For some reason, the family never attempted to buy a place of their own despite both parents earning decent money before they married. Much later, Plato's second wife, a singer called Mel Vondrau, claimed the family was obsessed with claiming benefits. She told the *Daily Mail*: 'He [Plato] thought it the best thing ever to have a council flat. They were all entrenched in the benefits system. It suited them because they were so used to having things handed to them.'

Tulisa settled happily into her new home. As a toddler she had no idea of her mother's illness. She was two and too young to register what was going on when Ann started having hallucinations. Her father, Plato, whom her friends at primary school would later call Plato Potato, was splitting his time between working as a hairdresser and session musician like his brother.

In the early nineties, things looked up for the brothers when they went to The Cartoon in Croydon one Christmas Eve and Ray Dorset was performing. He was a regular at the popular rock venue in South London, which had opened in 1976. Byron and Ray started chatting about the old days and were soon laughing as if they were the best of mates and saw each other regularly. Ray hadn't met Plato before but remembers thinking he was a 'very cool guy' dressed in black leather trousers and coat.

Ray needed some musicians to accompany him to the MIDEM music festival held in Cannes every January. Everyone assumed they would be miming, as it was a showcase, but that didn't prove to be the case and the brothers were thrown in at the deep end. The live performance went so well that Ray asked the brothers to join him for an upcoming UK tour. It was the start of an enduring friendship.

They recorded an album together, *Candy Dreams*, for which the brothers did most of the production. Ray thought very highly of Plato, who was accomplished in all things technical but whose contribution to the Tulisa story is sometimes overshadowed by that of his elder brother. 'Everything depended on Plato when we were recording. He was the technology man, a keyboard player of high calibre and very good at mixing and sound engineering, creating grooves and melodies. I rated him really highly as a person and as a musician.'

The highlight of the brothers' time touring with Mungo Jerry was on a trip to Riga on the Black Sea, where the legendary singer Demis Roussos, arguably the most famous Greek entertainer in the world then, was performing. Ray had known Demis for years and introduced him to Byron and Plato, who were thrilled to chat to one of their national heroes and be invited to a concert he was giving in the city.

One of the unusual and charming traits of the Contostavlos brothers was the importance they placed on respect. Byron, for instance, would always carry Ray's bag into the hotel while they were on tour. Ray recalls, 'They had this thing about respect. If I ever protested, they would always say that it was about respect. The brothers had an aura about them. They were always very polite, very honest and very positive.'

Touring proved to be a welcome distraction for Plato, who was finding things increasingly difficult at home.

Tulisa's life changed forever when she was five and she watched, bewildered, as an ambulance drew up outside the house with its lights flashing: 'My parents were arguing and my mum was taken away to hospital. I knew something was wrong because everyone around me was upset but I didn't understand what was actually going on.' She spoke about the experience in *Tulisa: My Mum and Me*, in which she recalled, 'I just have this vivid memory of her screaming out of an ambulance.'

Her mother was sectioned and taken to the Royal Free Hospital, where Tulisa was born. She had to get used to visiting her mum in a psychiatric ward. She recalled, 'When I visited her she seemed distant, not like my mum at all.' After a few weeks, during which doctors tried to work out new and better medication for her, Ann was allowed home and life seemed to return to normal.

Unfortunately, the full extent of Ann's illness wasn't diagnosed properly at this stage. She was thought to be bipolar, a condition that used to be known as manic depression. She was prescribed Valium and other antidepressants to help control her anxiety. But that was only part of Ann's problem. She was actually suffering from schizoaffective disorder, a complex mental condition that can affect one in two hundred people. The drugs she was given were ineffective in dealing with her schizophrenia-like symptoms. There were many of these, ranging from delusions and extreme mood swings to seeing and hearing things. Sufferers have strong feelings of sadness, isolation and hopelessness.

So, although there would be long periods when Ann was well, there would still be relapses that were agony for her little daughter although, as she admits, she didn't have experience of anything else. She recalled, 'I was used to watching my mum coming in and out of hospital, get ill, get better, recover, get ill, get better. It was normal for me.'

Tulisa had no idea of the strain that her mother's illness was putting on her parents' marriage. She was basically a happy little girl with a pet snake and a parakeet. She wore glasses and a ponytail, and dreamed of becoming an archaeologist – or a dinosaur expert – after she was inspired by seeing the classic Spielberg film *Jurassic Park* for the first time.

She loved her trips to Ireland to visit Ann's family and to Greece, where her grandparents had built their dream home, a beautiful pink villa in the affluent south Athens suburb of Voula, just two streets away from where the mega-rich Onassis family had a home. This was the height of luxury for Tulisa, and she told her young school friends that she wanted to live in Greece when she grew up. She loved having her own bedroom there and still sleeps in the same room when she visits.

At home in North London, Plato was doing his best to spoil

his daughter. From the age of seven, he would always give her money for her birthday. These presents were not insignificant loose change but as she got older would be as much as £500. Even as a young girl, Tulisa liked money, it seemed, much more than toys.

Mel Vondrau says that Plato was finding it difficult to manage Ann's breakdowns. She claims that the final straw was when he returned home one afternoon and found Ann trying to feed Tulisa raw eggs. The little girl was at the table, saying, 'Please, Mummy, don't. They're raw.'

Eventually, when Tulisa was nine, Plato couldn't stand it any more and moved back into the family house in Asmara Road. He hates any suggestion that he abandoned her. He says simply, 'I would do anything for my daughter.' He does admit, however, that it was a very distressing time. He told the *Sunday Mirror*: 'It was the hardest thing I ever had to tell Tulisa. I could see how sad she looked but I had just had enough. I just needed my own space.'

Mel claims there was a messy custody battle that Plato had expected to win but didn't. Neither Plato nor Tulisa has ever mentioned this. He maintains he remained close to Ann. Whatever the exact circumstances of the split, it did have a distressing effect on a good-natured, happy little girl. From the age of nine, it was just Tulisa and her mum living on the edge. The reality of the situation soon hit home because the split triggered one of Ann's episodes.

Tulisa recalled, 'One minute she'd look all mournful, as if someone had died; the next she'd be angry and aggressive, smashing cupboards and shouting. I wasn't allowed to turn on the TV because she thought it might harm us – the same with the hot water.

'It was impossible to have a conversation with my mum because she'd drift off into her own little world, but at the same time she didn't want me to go out and leave her, so I couldn't even escape to a friend's house. I was like a prisoner in the flat with her.'

Somehow Tulisa managed to keep her problems to herself at the Rosary Primary School on Haverstock Hill, two minutes away from the flat. At least it was on the doorstep and easy enough for her mum to manage the walk to school. The Rosary is a little oasis, protected from the outside world by high blue fencing that lets the children enjoy their day in complete security. One of her classmates observed, 'It was a nice place to be.'

Another classmate, Kyle Forrester, recalls that they were both in Miss Enright's class: 'Tula was very quiet and in a shell when she joined. She would keep herself to herself but she did snap a lot for no apparent reason. From everything we now know from the television, I can understand why. She was quite bright and on the ball in lessons when she had the motivation but there were some days when she would not participate at all.'

The other children had no idea of what Tulisa faced every time she went home. She didn't know what state her mum would be in. She told the BBC, 'When mum is well we have a really loving relationship but when she is ill she becomes completely withdrawn and paranoid, hearing voices and imagining people are out to get her. I will come home one day and she might be crying, really emotional, just needs a hug, just feeling sad. Other times she might be more aggressive and on edge. It's very manic. One minute she's like that. Up down, up down.' Tulisa adds that when she was little she thought she was the only person in the world caring for a 'mad mum'.

Even at this young age, Tulisa was showing battling qualities and becoming feisty. Kyle recalls, 'She wouldn't take any stick at all about her mum. Some of the boys at the school were quite nasty to her but she could handle herself very well indeed.'

She could be quite fierce and Kyle laughingly admits she almost used to make him run away. He says, 'I remember that she nearly made me fall off my bike when she had a strop at the bus stop once.'

The Rosary was a Catholic school and built up a strong sense of faith among its pupils. Its current mission statement explains:

'At all times we aim to centre the teaching in a Christian atmosphere. We welcome the chance to help you give the children a deep faith in God and an understanding of our Christian beliefs and obligations.' The long-serving headteacher Isobel Gaffney observes, 'It's what we're all about. It's a major part of our life.'

The first thing Tulisa, neatly dressed in white blouse, black skirt and striped yellow and black tie, would do every morning was to say prayers with the rest of the children. More prayers would be said before lunch and before going home time. The school was connected by a set of doors in the dining hall to a chapel and a convent beyond. The school chaplain, Father Dermot, was based at St Dominic's, a large imposing church and priory just a few hundred metres further away. He would always conduct a Mass for the children at Christmas and Easter.

Despite her troubled home life, Tulisa was clearly happy at the Rosary. The teachers liked her and she caused them no problems. She had two close friends, Kirsty and Ruth, and the three girls would usually hang out together during breaks.

When she was in year six, there was supposed to be a trip away for a week – a treat before they left and went on to their secondary schools – but it was cancelled because some of the children were so badly behaved. Instead the big school outing was up the road to Hampstead Heath where, on a blazing hot summer's day, the children spent their time eating crisps, playing football and larking about.

Kyle recalls, 'Tulisa spent most of the day just sitting on the grass with her friends Kirsty and Ruth. I remember going over to chat to them with my friends but all they spoke about was the latest music hits. They liked to get up and show off the dance moves from the videos.'

In musical terms, Tulisa had a family background other children could only envy. As a youngster, she was already steeped in music and was used to her dad's keyboards, her uncle's guitars and her mum singing in the kitchen – and that was without the influence of her Irish family, who were all so musical. But, at the age of eleven, she was given the chance to shine in her own right.

She was chosen to play Tallulah, the gangster's moll, in the Rosary's production of the Oscar-winning musical *Bugsy Malone* – a great role for a girl. The actress Jodie Foster was just thirteen when she starred in the original 1976 film. The action takes place in the Prohibition era of Al Capone, and the fun of the original idea was that all the parts were played by children, making it perfect for a school performance.

Tulisa loved performing 'My Name Is Tallulah', the most memorable number from the show. Ms Gaffney recalls that she was 'excellent'. Her mother and father were in the audience in the school hall – it was the first time they had heard her sing properly. Plato recalled, 'It made the hairs on the back of your neck stand up.' Uncle Byron was there as well and he would remember how terrific his little niece was. They filmed her performance as Tallulah and the footage would later feature in N-Dubz live shows when she used it as a backdrop for a grown-up a cappella version. She changed the words of the song to 'My name is Tulisa'.

Tulisa didn't decide there and then that she wanted to be a singer but she never forgot the thrill of singing in public for the first time. She observed, 'People started saying I had a good voice. I was coming out of myself.' From that point onwards, Tulisa has always had the confidence to perform in public.

She would sing in break time or in the street on the way home, pretending to be the Brooklyn-born singer Aaliyah. She liked the R & B star Monica, who had a huge hit with 'The Boy Is Mine', and the rapper Ms Jade, as well as Motown favourites Boyz II Men, but her favourite artist was Aaliyah, who had been a star from the age of ten.

Aaliyah had the sort of solo career that Tulisa saw for herself. She loved the song 'One In A Million', the title track of the second album. It's slow and seductive with the perfect hook for an impressionable, romantic young girl – 'your love is one in a million'. Tulisa, who was just eight when it was released in 1996, was always singing it.

Coincidentally, their backgrounds were similar. Aaliyah's mother was also a singer, she went to a Catholic school and when she was in first grade she had a role in a school play. She was in *Annie* but this experience more than anything ignited her ambition to be in show business, just as it did for Tulisa in *Bugsy Malone*.

When she was nine, Aaliyah had appeared on the American talent show *Star Search*, which just about every young hopeful in the US tried out for, including Justin Timberlake, Britney Spears and Beyoncé. Surprisingly, none of these famous performers reached the final. Tulisa wasn't in any show that big but she did perform in all the talent shows at the Rosary and won a competition one year at Butlin's. Her stepmother, Mel, had helped her learn the song 'Gloria' by Laura Branigan, which became a rock classic after featuring on the soundtrack of *Flashdance*.

Aaliyah's family connections led to her first break, performing on stage with the legendary Motown singer Gladys Knight, who at one time was her 'Aunty Glad', when she was married to her uncle, Barry Hankerson, a prominent entertainment lawyer. Aaliyah signed to the famous Jive Records label when she was only twelve and was just fifteen when her first album, *Age Ain't Nothing But A Number*, sold more than three million copies in the US.

In a blueprint for what Tulisa hoped to achieve ten years later, Aaliyah started acting, appearing on television and in the films *Romeo Must Die*, where she featured on a bestselling soundtrack, and *Queen of the Damned*. Her third album, *Aaliyah*, was released in July 2001, but a month later she was dead. She was one of nine people aboard a light aircraft that crashed shortly after taking off from an airstrip in the Bahamas. She was twenty-two years old. Her achievements were an inspiration to Tulisa, showing that she too could make it as a young girl.

Tulisa

Tulisa has spoken enthusiastically about her love of Aaliyah's music but for some reason she has never mentioned her time at the Rosary – perhaps this happy, Catholic, trauma-free place didn't mesh with the image of a troubled street kid. Or perhaps it reminded her too much of the time after her father had left home and she and her mother were on their own.

3

Jumbo

All Byron wanted was a hit. He used to tell Ray Dorset, 'I just want one hit, just one hit.' He and Plato pooled their resources to rent the attic room at studios in Dollis Hill, two Tube stops away from the family home in Asmara Road. The building was so close to the Tube station that it was practically on the platform and you could hear the trains rattling by. It was run-down, unattractive and far from glamorous but this was the place where the N-Dubz story would take shape.

Jumbo Studios, despite its exterior, had a great atmosphere inside. Ray Dorset recalls, 'It was a cool place.' Fashionable artists, including Tricky and Goldie, could often be found in the 'chilling' room, playing pinball or talking music. Ray remembers relaxing one afternoon when the top nineties band Suede were rehearsing in one of the studios. Byron rushed in excitedly and shouted, 'They're playing "Lady Rose"!' – one of Mungo Jerry's biggest hits. Byron and Plato played it at every gig they did with Ray.

'Cool' and 'chilling' were the right words in more ways than one to describe the attic. It was freezing – a place where you never took your coat off. The most well-known band then using

Jumbo Studios was the enigmatic Future Sound of London (FSOL), who built an enduring fan base with their progressive and futuristic electronic sound. In their attic Plato and Byron were dealing with less cutting-edge sounds, remixing three tracks recorded by former disco queen Kelly Marie, who had a number one in 1980 with 'Feels Like I'm In Love' – a Ray Dorset song. They optimistically decided to call their part of Jumbo Hitt Studios.

They produced a new version of 'In the Summertime', the 'Earth Mix', with Tulisa's mother doing the backing vocals. Plato and Ann were about to get divorced, which confirms his assertion that they always got on well, even after the split.

The work with Mungo Jerry was proving to be too sporadic to provide the brothers with a proper income so they decided to put together another group to get some more regular work. They were still ambitious though, and Byron was quite offended when Ray, trying to help, suggested he could find some work at his sister's beauty salon in Bournemouth. They called their new band Westbound and advertised for a girl singer. A young South African woman called Mel Vondrau replied and was taken on. Mel was twenty-five, some thirteen years younger than Plato, when she met him in 1997. She was working as a legal secretary but wanted to be a singer. They recorded some tracks at the studio, which can be heard today on YouTube.

The new group played mainly functions, especially wedding parties, as well as £100-a-night gigs on the North London pub circuit. They weren't earning enough for Mel to quit her job and much of the cash they earned from music went straight back into Hitt Studios – that was the master plan.

Tulisa didn't seem to mind when Mel and Plato started dating a year later. She never fell out with her father even after he'd left home. Mel told the *Daily Mail* that Tulisa and Plato were very close and she was always happy to see him. Mel observed simply, 'She adored her father.' She recalled that Tulisa was always polite and well mannered, reflecting the importance of respect in the Contostavlos family.

Plato and Mel moved into a rented flat together in Queen's Park, still close to the family home in Asmara Road, and were married at Marylebone Register Office in January 1999 – the venue for illustrious pop weddings, including that of Liam Gallagher and Patsy Kensit and two of Paul McCartney's. Mel, who is far less complimentary about Plato than she is about her stepdaughter Tulisa, says they had no honeymoon because she had to go back to work straight away to pay the bills.

Mel's early impression of Tulisa had been of a 'happy-go-lucky' girl. That apparently carefree attitude would change dramatically when Tulisa left the Rosary Primary School and embarked on her secondary education. It was the start of a miserable few years. Her first senior school was La Sainte Union Catholic School in Highgate Road, less than two miles away; Tulisa used to get the C11 bus from the bottom of her road.

LSU, as it is familiarly known, is an imposing institution with a strong academic reputation and an emphasis on Catholic traditions. Mrs Maureen Williams, the current headteacher, explained, 'Our Catholic identity is at the core of all we do'. The school was founded in 1861 by the Sisters of La Sainte Union and developed into one of the premier schools for girls in North London. The school's mission statement confirms their ideal: 'We believe that a Christian-based education offers a sure hope for the future of religion and society.'

LSU is one of North London's top schools and Tulisa was lucky to be given a place there, ensuring that, academically and socially, she would have a good start in life. But she was bitterly unhappy. She felt lonely and isolated, and she was the victim of some horrid psychological bullying. Her experience at the school would lay the foundation for her compelling need to belong.

Coincidentally, Kate Middleton was also badly bullied when she first went to senior school and was withdrawn by her parents after two terms. Both young women would later support the Beatbullying charity.

Kyle Forrester, who used to live opposite LSU, remembers often seeing Tulisa at the bus stop when she was waiting to catch the C11 home. He recalls that Tulisa used to be quite happy most days but there were other times when she didn't want to talk to anyone. He found out through mutual friends that girls at LSU were 'taking the mick' about her mum's illness and bullying the new girl.

Tulisa wanted desperately to fit in and make friends but it was proving impossible. She was a pretty girl, which didn't help, and although she tried to be popular, she ended up being by herself most of the time. She was well behaved, did her homework on time and got good grades but, as is often the case with a goody two shoes, nobody liked her.

After just three terms her mother and father felt that she had suffered enough. She was unhappy at school and equally miserable at home, where she seemed to be cast more and more in the role of her mum's carer even though she had little idea of how to cope or what to do. She needed a fresh start when her mother had her worst breakdown to date, imagining the devil was climbing the walls of their maisonette.

Mel recalled a disturbing phone call from Ann during which she could hear Tulisa crying in the background. Mel told the *Daily Mail* that soon afterwards they received a call from Social Services saying that Ann had been taken to the Royal Free Hospital but nobody knew what had happened to Tulisa. Eventually they found out from the police that she was with Aunt Louise. Apparently she had walked in the dark to the Haverstock Arms, an old-fashioned boozer two minutes from her home. The landlord there coaxed her into telling him what had happened and luckily knew Louise, whom he called to fetch her niece. Tulisa stayed with her aunt until her mother was well enough to return home.

If Mel's allegations are correct, then Social Services didn't cover themselves in glory on this occasion. Tulisa hasn't confirmed this version of events but she does say that she used to stay at her aunt's whenever her mum became ill. It would become a pattern throughout her childhood. Louise had young children of her own so Tulisa was able to settle into a more stable family environment. She recalls with disarming honesty, 'I used to dread my mum getting better and coming home because it would mean having to leave my aunt's house, where I felt safe and happy and normal, and go back to living with someone whose mood could change as quick as flicking a switch.'

Tulisa felt isolated both at home and at school – a depressing combination for an eleven-year-old. Her concerned family found it difficult to be as supportive as they wanted to be because Ann didn't want them or anyone else interfering in their lives. 'I was eleven and my mum expected me to be her emotional support but I didn't really understand what that was. It was very tough.'

Her stepmother observed that this was the age when Tulisa changed from a happy little girl into a quiet and troubled one. A year later and Tulisa's personal diary is heartbreaking. She reads a section during *Tulisa: My Mum and Me* in which she says that she can't believe it's really her mum she's visiting in hospital and at home she feels that she is the only grown-up although she is only twelve. She writes: 'My mum is a manic depressive and she will shout at me and just go crazy . . . I love her with all my heart.'

By this time arrangements had been made so Tulisa could spend every other weekend with her father and stepmother, which at least gave her a change of environment. They did the usual absent dad things, like going to the zoo, and Mel made sure that she had some home-cooked food. Tulisa has an abiding love of takeaways and fast food because that's what she was used to growing up.

The alternate weekends were a welcome break but they

weren't going to solve Tulisa's problems of loneliness and isolation. Her cousin Dino was enrolled at the Haverstock School so it seemed like a good idea for her to go there too. But things were about to go from bad to worse.

Haverstock secondary has been famous ever since it was revealed to be the school of David and Ed Miliband. The politicians have given it an air of respectability that is not at all endorsed by Tulisa's stories of sex and drugs. The school won't comment on her claims but has a long list of rules aimed at improving the quality of schooling for every child. The rules are a wish list that includes avoiding being aggressive or violent and moving quietly around the corridors and classrooms.

Security was an important feature, as if this were a school in a rougher part of New York rather than in Chalk Farm, North London. Tulisa recalled that there used to be police outside most days to deal with the crimes and misdemeanours of the student population.

Like his cousin, Dino was born in Hampstead's Royal Free Hospital. He was the closest thing to a brother Tulisa would ever have. Even at the age of twelve, he was a charismatic bundle of energy and Ray Dorset recalls, 'He had a great personality and was always dancing around the place.' He was already using the nickname Dappy, short for Dapper, because he was small and neat and liked to dress in the latest designer gear.

Byron used to take him to Mungo Jerry gigs. One memorable occasion was a private party at the Wycombe Wanderers football ground, which ended up getting a bit rowdy. When he returned home, Dappy's mother asked him how it went and he told her there had been women without clothes and it had all ended in a massive fight. 'It was great,' he said. His mother Zoe gave Byron a hard stare before exclaiming, 'What have you been doing with my son!'

Dappy had always been attracted to a fight. At his previous schools, he would start the day with a good scrap – or end it with one. He was expelled from his first secondary school, the

Roman Catholic St Aloysius' College in Islington, for truancy and fighting. It was the same story at the Bishop Douglass School, another Catholic college, in East Finchley.

Dappy always had to contend with other children making fun of him, mainly because of his height. He never grew above 5ft 3in and his younger cousin Tulisa towered above him. If another boy made fun of him, Dappy would invite him to do so again 'after school'. As a result Dappy was at the wrong end of more than a few beatings but he never backed down and was never bullied. He happily confesses that at these two schools he was known for being a 'little shit'.

He was hardly the best role model for his young cousin because he would think nothing of bunking off school. He changed his mind about the value of education when he was older but at the age of twelve, when he ended up at Haverstock School, he thought it a waste of time. He didn't think the teachers gave a damn about him. He was confident, however, and perhaps as a result of that he fitted in well at his new school and had what Tulisa craved – popularity and style.

From the age of twelve he found it easy to talk to girls, so a mixed school like Haverstock was ideal. His routine was always the same: on a first date he'd take them to McDonald's. He knew far more girls than Tulisa did, and they didn't seem to mind his obsession with hats, which made him seem a bit taller. Initially at least, Tulisa found that being Dappy's cousin was a passport to popularity: 'That made me cool. All the girls wanted to know me, because they all fancied Dappy.'

Dappy is a year older than his cousin, which is quite a lot when you're growing up. He decided to take her under his wing, which may or may not have been a good thing for her. Armed with some cash from Plato, he took her shopping the day before term began and made sure she looked the part in her new Nike gear.

Clothes and hair are the really important status symbols for modern girls in urban state schools. Fashion critics might call the 'uniform' of these young girls 'chav outfits' – baseball jackets, hoodies and trackie bums – but they don't have the relentless peer pressure of going through the school gates every day. If you don't have the right label or extensions, then you don't stand a chance: at best you'll be ridiculed, at worst bullied. While it was just manageable for Tulisa to be a geek at LSU, she would have to change if she wanted to fit in at Haverstock.

The problem was that Tulisa was growing up too fast. She was no longer lonely but belonging to a group of girls was like making a pact with the devil for an impressionable teenager. When she'd finished school for the day, she started to hang out on the Camden high-rise estates where her new friends lived rather than return to leafy Belsize Park where her mother would be and where she would again feel alone and isolated.

So, saving up the money her dad gave her, she would buy vodka and hang out getting legless with her new friends until the sun went down and, some nights, until it rose again. She shrugs it off now, claiming she was just a twelve-year-old girl who wanted to have fun, but she was turning into the classic street kid.

In the N-Dubz book *Against All Odds: From Street Life to Chart Life*, Tulisa's story really begins here. This is the street life the title of the book is talking about – not her grandparents' big house in Cricklewood or their lovely villa in Greece where she spent so many memorable holidays. It wasn't the sing-songs at Granddad Tom's, listening to him sing 'Molly Malone', nor the triumph of her school musical at the Rosary Primary School, where she was a happy little girl among friends. Instead, she describes a feral world in which she smoked weed at lunch time and famously claimed that there were twelve-year-old kids 'shagging in the toilets' during break.

4

The Book of Five Rings

Tulisa loved her holidays in Greece, especially when her Uncle Byron was there with his two sons. Dappy was the closest in age and the two of them would join Uncle B, as Tulisa and the family called him, on the roof of her grandparents' villa, where he would teach them some basic karate. He was a martial arts expert and a black belt. When he was on tour he would train before gigs to make sure he was tuned to the height of his capabilities before going on stage.

Uncle B wasn't some sort of Bruce Lee fan, envisaging himself an Asian superhero. Instead, he embraced the culture and philosophy of martial arts and could often be found taking a small, well-thumbed book from his pocket and studying it in his quieter moments. *The Book of Five Rings*, written in 1643 by the undefeated samurai Miyamoto Musashi, is a short text of no more than ninety pages but it encapsulates a life plan that is timeless.

The respected US publication the *Library Journal* observed that it was 'embraced by many contemporary readers as a manual on how to succeed in life.' Uncle B was one of those readers devoted to the 'Japanese Way of the Sword'. It was a philosophy that would underpin his vision for his son's fledgling pop group.

In the preface to his 1993 translation, Thomas Cleary explains the significance of the Japanese word 'shin-ken', which means 'real sword'. To do something with a real sword means to do it with 'utmost earnestness'. The Japanese cultural experience allows devotees to treat virtually anything as a 'life and death situation'. Uncle B treated his musical ambitions with zeal, enthusiasm and single-mindedness.

Musashi killed his first man at the age of thirteen and remained undefeated in combat until he retired at the age of twenty-nine and dedicated his life to the 'science' of martial arts. Uncle B was the Master Carpenter, the role Musashi uses to illustrate his philosophy. He explained the characteristics: 'Efficiency and smooth progress, prudence in all matters, recognizing true courage, recognizing different levels of morale, instilling confidence, and realizing what can and cannot be reasonably expected.'

Uncle B was worried about his younger son. His elder, Spiros, known as Spi, was the sensible one who wanted to be a pilot when he grew up, but Dappy always seemed to be attracting trouble and was in danger of letting his opportunities slip by. Byron would take him fishing along the canal just a street away from where they lived. You could find carp in the Regent's Canal, which threaded its way across North West London, running through Maida Vale, alongside Regent's Park and on to Camden Town and King's Cross. Experienced fishermen like Byron and Plato could always find spots to catch fish on the most unpromising-looking stretches. Fishing helped to promote the inner calm that was so important in *The Book of Five Rings*. Perhaps Byron hoped it would help to calm his son's wild nature.

Dappy's principal passion at a young age was football. He loved the Arsenal and was a useful player for his age. Like many youngsters, he probably would have answered 'professional footballer' if asked what he would like to be when he was older. He also joined his father at karate classes. One evening he started chatting to another boy called Richard Rawson. They got on famously well right from the start and discovered that they both liked sports and music.

Richard was born on 5 February 1987. He was six months older than Dappy and eighteen months older than Tulisa but like them was born in the Royal Free Hospital. His friends called him Steppa or DJ Ricky B – only later did he become Fazer. He was a champion runner in his age group and represented Camden in the 1500 metres. He lived in one of the nicer streets of Swiss Cottage with a white father, Phil, who did some work as a photographer, and his mother, Elaine Barnes, the daughter of a bus driver, who was black and from Swindon in Wiltshire. She was a woman with one of the sunniest of smiles and over the years became a popular fixture in the street. Her son has always doted on her and she has been unfailing in her support of his musical dreams.

In *Against All Odds*, Fazer painted a far from cosy picture of growing up in a black family living in a council flat surrounded by white families who had bought their own homes. As was often the case, racism surfaced, primarily because of the instinctive and unjustified perception that anyone black was a threat to the neighbourhood. Fazer claims the racism spilled over to Haverstock School – even among the teachers.

Life took a turn for the better, however, when Dappy joined the school and the two boys became united against the world. They would hang out together in each other's homes and gradually found themselves becoming more in tune about music. The first time Fazer went to the Contostavloses' home – the 'shoebox', as Dappy called it – Byron and Zoe were shocked that their son was friendly with the young dread-locked black boy. Apparently they'd been warned by the school that he was the pupil Dappy should stay well clear of – so the boys were almost duty-bound to become friends!

Fazer recalled that the first time he met Uncle B he stole his mobile phone and slipped it into the pocket of his jacket. But, in a comedy moment, he was found out when Byron produced another phone and dialled his number. The phone started to ring in Fazer's pocket. In *Against All Odds*, Fazer described what happened next: 'I made some rubbish comment about using it and taking it by accident, but he wasn't having any of it. He said, "Don't lie to me. You wanted my phone. OK, have it. I don't need it. If you can't get your own, then I will give it to you if that's the only way." His dad showed me he wasn't a man to mess about with. I was young and dumb but I learned from him.' Fazer didn't take the phone but from then on he had nothing but respect for Uncle B.

To begin with, Fazer was more focused on music than Dappy. He had a greater interest in the latest trends and, surprisingly, was brought up in a much more musical household than his friend. Byron may have been a professional musician but when he wasn't working he preferred to go fishing and chill out. Fazer's parents, however, used music as their principal pastime, filling their house with their favourite blues tracks. His mum Elaine could play the drums and his dad Phil was brilliant on the harmonica. They favoured classic artists like Billie Holiday and Bessie Smith, instilling a solid appreciation of music in their son.

By the time he was twelve, Fazer was beginning to explore music on his own. In the book *Against All Odds*, he explained that his whole life changed when he heard an album called *Enter the Wu-Tang (36 Chambers)* by the highly influential hip-hop collective Wu-Tang Clan. This group of talented New York City rappers transformed the face of hip-hop music in the early nineties with their powerful combination of spare, stripped-back production and explicit lyrics. *AllMusic* online described it as a 'sonic blueprint that countless other hardcore rappers would follow for years to come.'

The swearing was music to the ears of young Richard Rawson. He admitted that when he first heard it he couldn't believe that they were getting away with such bad language. It was something that N-Dubz wouldn't shy away from in the future.

Coincidentally, the 1993 album had a martial arts connection. The title *36 Chambers* was homage to the film *The 36th Chamber of Shaolin*, which starred Gordon Liu and is regarded as one of the greatest of all kung fu films. More significantly, the album's Grammy-winning producer RZA used heavy, eerie beats and a large number of samples from his favourite martial arts films to create the then unique sound. The final production was a huge influence on the future stars of hip-hop, such as Jay-Z, The Notorious B.I.G., Nas and Mobb Deep.

The artists who made up Wu-Tang had inspired street names that many youngsters in urban areas all around the world would try to emulate. A good name is a good identity. RZA, who was also known as Prince Rakeem, was born Robert Diggs and brought up in the housing projects of Staten Island. There were a million Roberts out there but there was only one RZA. His cousin Gary Grice became The Genius and, later, GZA. Other members of the Clan included Ghostface Killah, Method Man, Inspectah Deck, Raekwon and U-God.

Another cousin, Russell Tyrone Jones, achieved fame and notoriety as Ol' Dirty Bastard. He was the subject of a string of arrests and convictions, was shot witnessing a robbery and convicted of assault before dying from a drug overdose, aged thirty-five, in 2004. He became a hero for a generation of young men when he was filmed for an MTV documentary taking two of his thirteen children for a ride in his limousine to the benefits office to pick up his welfare cheque. At the time he had a solo album in the charts. ODB, as he was often referred to, lived the life that many rappers sing about but few live now that the genre has been taken over by expensively suited executives and multimillion-dollar corporations.

Back in Swiss Cottage, Richard Rawson needed a cooler sounding name than DJ Ricky B. He used to drift over from his home to the local KFC with a bunch of neighbourhood boys, his 'crew', and they would hang out outside. Some of the older teenagers had motorbikes. One of them had a model called a

Yamaha FZS600 Fazer, which was a very rapid sports bike launched in the UK in 1998. It was love at first sight for Richard, who dreamed of owning one himself when he was older. He was forever going over to sit on the bike and checking out the engine and the paintwork, which had the word *Fazer* written in large black letters. Occasionally Richard was allowed to borrow it, even though he was under the legal age to ride a motorbike and looked it. As a joke, some of the kids started calling him Fazer. Richard thought it was a very cool name.

In the beginning he used to call himself MC Fazer. In the old days MC used to mean Master of Ceremonies but in the age of urban music it's essentially a term for a rapper, the person who has control of the microphone. A DJ, by contrast, would be responsible for mixing the tunes. Street names often come and go, and some crew members might have half a dozen and more they answer to, but, for Richard Rawson, Fazer stuck. And, crucially, there was only one MC Fazer – or 'Fazaagh', as Dappy used to pronounce it.

Dappy, meanwhile, was listening to The Police, thinking Sting and Phil Collins were cool, and was still more into playing football than cutting-edge modern music. His father, however, was more aware of contemporary sounds and bought his son a tape deck and a microphone and suggested he try to copy 'Fill Me In', which was a big hit for Craig David. Left to his own devices, the twelve-year-old worked out a rap for his dad and played it for him. Uncle B was delighted with Dappy's efforts, because he was astute enough to recognize that his son had a real talent.

Music now became the focus of Dappy's life. He went over to Greece on holiday to see the family and spent his time writing down lyrics and practising freestyle rapping while sitting in the sun watching the mountains in the village of Platanos, where his mother's family was from. Just like Tulisa, Dappy was inspired by his visits to Greece, where the fantastic climate and his favourite Lykourgos café were a world away from the Camden estate where he lived.

Dappy didn't need another street name. He was the only Dappy, or 'Daps' as Fazer called him. They just needed a name for themselves. They hit upon the Lickle Rinsers Crew. This sounds quite twee but in the world of electronic music rinse is a term commonly applied to a DJ who was doing a brilliant job – his mixes were amazing, he got everyone dancing and the atmosphere was unbeatable – so 'the DJ RINSED it last night!' It can also be slang for oral sex. Dappy and Fazer have always preferred to draw a veil over how they came by the name, presumably because their mothers never knew what it could mean. It was an amusing name when starting out but not for headlining music festivals and appearing on TV.

The new Lickle Rinsers Crew (LRC) would spend hours in each other's home, writing raps, clashin' each other and practising their battles so that they had the rhyme perfect. English was the only subject in school that Dappy liked and he enjoyed playing around with words and rhymes. He was a complete novice whose radio was locked into Heart FM but Fazer was now heavily into garage music and was encouraging his friend to be more current. For someone so young, Dappy had a real sense of injustice and that was beginning to shine through. He was also proving to be a talented keyboard player.

Byron thought it was time to start taking his son to the recording studio. He was back working in a hairdresser's to help make ends meet but when he'd finished for the day he and Dappy would head over to Dollis Hill and Fazer would often join them. Fazer, taking after his mother, was already an accomplished drummer and was proving to be a quick learner in the studio. Byron was pleased his initiative was keeping the boys off the streets.

At this stage Tulisa was not involved. It was just the two boys doing something 'exciting' that was better than school. They had their eye on a pretty girl in class called Rachel, who they were hoping might be their female vocalist.

One afternoon Uncle B was at Jumbo Studios when he

thought of a good idea. It was part of the Master Carpenter ideal: delegate to the best possible person. Just below his studio was another belonging to a young garage producer called Donna Dee, who was one of the innovators of a new sound called 2-step, which was a very fashionable English variation of garage music. Byron put his head round the door and said, 'My son Dappy is thirteen and he can rap and MC. Will you listen to him?'

Donna agreed and the next day Uncle B arrived at her studio with Dappy wearing one of his favourite Peruvian hats and a large silver earring. Dappy's mother used to buy his hats, more accurately known as 'chullos', in Camden Market. She was very proud of her son and would even wear one of the hats herself because it was so warm. She would continue to buy the hats after Dappy became famous. On one occasion the stallholder told her, 'I don't know what's going on. Everyone is asking for this crazy hat.' Zoe answered him, 'I will tell you: it's because of my son.'

Donna preferred his rapping to his hat. She recalled that he was a 'little kid' but he rapped *a cappella* and she was very impressed: 'OK, Dappy, come along some time and we'll build a little tune together and see how it goes.'

A few days later Dappy presented himself at Donna's studio with Fazer by his side. Rachel was supposed to join them but for some reason she never showed. If she had, then Tulisa's life story might have been different. As it was, they had studio time, a song written called 'What Is the World Coming To, Fuck You', but no girl singer.

Uncle B, remembering Tulisa's performance as Tallulah in her primary school musical, suggested they should try her and volunteered to go round to her home and ask her. She wasn't keen. She'd already set her heart on being the next Aaliyah and didn't want to be sidetracked from a solo career. Byron, however, knew the best way to get round her and offered her twenty pounds, which she refused. He had to make it a pinkie – £50 in

N-Dubz world – before she would agree to venture down to Dollis Hill. She was eleven.

Surprisingly, Tulisa was not the first member of her family to embrace urban music. She and her cousin Dappy may be the first of the Contostavlos clan but she is not the first Byrne. Mick Byrne's son Hollis formed a controversial band of the early nineties, called Marxman, who were described as a Marxist hip-hop group, had two MCs and were at the forefront of what became known as the 'Bristol sound', although West Country groups like Portishead and Massive Attack were much more commercially successful. They helped create a sub-genre called trip-hop. Marxman did manage one small hit, 'All About Eve', but were probably too serious for greater success: they wrote songs about domestic violence, the African slave trade and financial injustice.

Hollis went on to sing with another Bristol-based hip-hop group called Offside, with DJ Bungee, and became a well-known graffiti artist in Dublin. His brothers have also carved out musical careers: Goldmund Byrne is a singer–songwriter and DJ; Phelim Byrne is part of hip-hop folk group Day One, another critically acclaimed band from Bristol that has released two albums so far. One critic said their first album, *Ordinary Man*, contained urban campfire songs from the backstreets of any city anywhere. Their younger brother Oisin is a singer and MC with, among others, the Mercury Prize-winning drum 'n' bass star Roni Size. And the family isn't finished yet – there are two more, Jack and Niamh, also involved in the music scene.

The first time the three youngsters who would eventually become N-Dubz got together was in Donna Dee's studio at Jumbo. Their basic way of working never changed: the boys laid down the track they'd been working on, with Fazer in charge of the beats, then both of them would record the rap they'd worked out before telling Tulisa where she needed to come in on the melody. In the future, Tulisa would take more responsibility for her own lyrics.

They finished, recorded and mixed their first track in two days, and that's how it was with the boys. They embraced the spirit of the philosophy of life Uncle B had taken from *The Book of Five Rings*: treat everything with the utmost earnestness and remain positive. Donna Dee observed they had 'tunnel vision' because they knew what they wanted to achieve and they believed in their dreams. Fazer explained, 'If you haven't got enthusiasm, you ain't going to get nowhere.'

Donna was so impressed that she signed a contract with Uncle B in which she would assume some of the management responsibilities for the young wannabes. She took them with her to a gig at the birthday party of DJ Deekline, who was a friend and a key figure in the North London music scene. They performed their song – it was the first time they'd ever performed together in public. She recalled, 'I was blown away by their performance.'

The boys were learning about music all the time. Donna introduced them to 2-step, and Fazer, in particular, liked playing around with the more freestyle rhythms, moving away from the traditional pounding beat of older hip-hop. Donna also took Tulisa to breakdance lessons and thought she picked it up really well – something that would come in handy when she started going to clubs and could show off her moves. Fazer was a good dancer too and was particularly adept at body popping. Dappy, meanwhile, was teaching Fazer how to play keyboards, while Plato was introducing him to the art of engineering.

After 'What Is The World Coming To, Fuck You', the next part of Uncle B's master plan was to create underground interest in his young protégés. He also wanted to make sure that they retained as much control as possible every step of the way. The first job was to get more music together. This never seemed to be a problem for Fazer and Dappy, who were literally at Jumbo Studios every day. They were incredibly dedicated and their enthusiasm gradually rubbed off on Tulisa.

They soon had two more tracks ready: 'Bad Man Riddim' and 'Life Is Getting Sicker By The Day'. The latter was right up to date, referring to 9/11, which had only just happened in 2001. Strangely, Tulisa hardly featured in the second song. Byron decided they would turn these songs into 'white labels', which are CDs specifically designed to send to radio stations to get a band's music played on air. The strategy worked, because some pirate radio stations in the London area did pick them up and play them. The production and engineering on the tracks were of a very high professional standard, overseen by Plato but largely accomplished by Fazer, a young and inexperienced teenager.

Already, one of the trademarks of N-Dubz was in evidence: Dappy singing in that distinctive whiney style, 'Na, Na, Na, Niiiii'. It was a very basic chant but they were the only ones singing it so it became an important part of many of their future records. Every day was an exciting one and it never occurred to the young hopefuls that it might take them another six years to achieve real success.

One of the tracks they recorded at Jumbo but has yet to see the light of day was another version of 'In the Summertime' with Tulisa singing the main vocal instead of Ray Dorset. Ray loved it and would probably make a fortune from songwriting royalties if it were ever released.

5

Jekyll and Hyde

The accepted history of N-Dubz makes much of their struggle to achieve success from nothing. But when Tulisa was twelve and the boys were thirteen, they were living a dream beyond the reach of the rest of the boys and girls hanging around the court-yards of the grim estates of Camden Town or tormenting the counter staff in the Swiss Cottage KFC. They had been granted a free pass to a musical Disneyland, where they were indulged and encouraged, where they were trained and advised and where adults really wanted to help them. That was what Jumbo Studios represented – a safe haven where they could shape their destinies cocooned from the reality of their lives outside.

Their friends and enemies in the real world would have to queue with thousands of others for the chance to sing a few bars of a cheesy hit for Simon Cowell. Dappy would later criticize *The X Factor* for creating manufactured hits – the easy ride to fame for its contestants – but most of them had never been given the chance to polish their craft the way that he was.

Byron and Plato gave their children the opportunity of a life-time. And it was a million times better than school. Having said that, Uncle B still made it clear to them that it would be a hard slog if they wanted to succeed. They didn't have any money at home but 'at work' they had instant access to equipment worth an estimated £100,000.

Tulisa began leading a strange double life. In the studio she was part of something exciting and ever changing. The rest of the time she was struggling with despair and a social life that had seemed so promising for a while but soon became a nightmare.

For the first year at Haverstock School everything went as she'd hoped. She was part of the crowd that drank cheap booze, smoked too much marijuana and had no respect for adults – especially teachers, whose lives they made a misery. Tulisa did no work whatsoever and might just as well have been going to the park every day.

Her attendance record became poor. While the boys would cut school in order to go to the studio, she used to spend the day listening to music and smoking weed. By the time she was fourteen, she was struggling with the effects of too much dope, which included getting heart palpitations. She recalled, 'I used to have panic attacks and get very paranoid.' She also witnessed one of her friends having convulsions while they were sharing a spliff.

Tulisa was already getting the idea that weed was not for her when she saw a fortune teller at a fair on Hampstead Heath, who told her never to mess with drugs because she was the type of person who would always have a bad reaction to them. She stopped indulging and has been completely drug-free since vowing she would never touch them again. Fazer was also anti drugs that could kill you, declaring that he would never do charlie or crack cocaine.

Giving up drugs was just about the only positive achievement in Tulisa's life at this time. She started to lose control of what was going on. She had been on a few dates but nothing special when rumours started flying around the school about her having sex with boys. They were completely untrue, as she is adamant she was still a virgin. She told the *Sunday Times*, 'They'd say I was a slag, that I'd slept with this guy or that guy. It got violent. It got to the stage where I couldn't walk down the street any more.'

Tulisa was always getting into fights and trying to hide the cuts and bruises from her mother and father. Plato revealed, 'It was a very upsetting time. She would come to see me with cuts on her lips and on her eyes.' By 2001, Plato and his second wife Mel had split so Tulisa no longer had the chance to chat to another, older woman about her problems – or to have some home cooking.

Clearly, in light of Mel's later revelations, there was little love lost between the couple. Plato just shrugs when her name comes up, hinting that he only married her because she was South African and needed the certificate to be allowed to stay in the country. They divorced in 2008 and it was only after Tulisa found fame that Mel stepped forward with a hatful of revelations about her life with Tulisa's father.

This wayward, out-of-control girl, who would make up a false ID card to get in to over-21 raves and disappear from home for days at a time, contrasts sharply with the sweet teenager who was filmed for a documentary on the Lickle Rinsers in 2002 when she was fourteen and Dappy and Fazer had just turned fifteen. The film was later released on DVD as *Before They Were Dubz*.

Obviously, the three of them are dressing up for the cameras but they don't look like street kids at all in their immaculate teenage designer gear. They are articulate and fresh faced: Dappy has podgy cheeks, Fazer has shaved all his hair off and Tulisa has a pound or two of puppy fat. When she was thirteen Uncle B apparently told her she was overweight and nobody wanted to see a fat person on stage – a remark that did not meet with the approval of her stepmother Mel, who thought it 'inappropriate'. She was, after all, just a young teenager who spent too much time eating pizza.

They are shown being driven to a gig. Dappy and Fazer are all energy and can't seem to sit still. Tulisa is very pretty with long dark hair in a plait at the front. Tulisa introduces herself to camera: 'My name is Tula Contostavlos and my stage name is Lady T.' She is happy and smiling, perhaps a little self-conscious about being filmed. She clearly has a soft spot for Fazer – she keeps looking over at him while he talks on his mobile phone. Dappy leans over to confide to the camera, 'They got something going on. 'Cos they like each other – I'm telling you.' Much later it was revealed that the two did date as young teenagers.

It was a typical adolescent romance: 'At first he really fancied me and I didn't like him. Then I really fancied him and he didn't like me.' She told *more!* magazine that they went out for about a year until they discovered they didn't really 'like' each other 'in that way.' She added, 'We were like brother and sister. The thought of me and Fazer would be like incest. Yeah, it's like, urgh, don't go there.' Eventually she decided she would 'go there' but that would be eight years in the future. They were kids who, it seemed, had more to think about than dating.

According to Donna Dee, they were the sort of kids for whom 'nothing else mattered in their lives' other than the music. That may have been true for the boys but Tulisa had a very different home life to them. She saw herself as her mother's primary carer but struggled to be taken seriously, especially when she was trying to get help, knowing her mother was about to have an episode.

'She'd be lethargic one minute and then cleaning around the house unable to stop the next. I'd phone the hospital, explain her symptoms and they wouldn't want to know. I was young and they didn't take me seriously. In the end I'd have to take her to A & E to try to get her admitted. But often by the time I got back home from school the next day, the doctors would say they'd done an evaluation of her and she was fine to go home. Sometimes I would spend weeks taking her back and forward to A & E and then finally they would admit her and she'd be in hospital for up to three months.'

Tulisa has revealed with great honesty that she first attempted suicide at the age of fourteen by swallowing a handful of her mother's painkillers. She has admitted that she didn't think she wanted to die but just didn't know of any other way to deal with her problems. Fortunately, she threw up before the pills could do her any damage.

She wrote a lyric about her mother and father and the pain she felt in a song called 'Secrets', which eventually featured on the first N-Dubz album. N-Dubz songs would often be autobiographical. It's the sort of simple, heartfelt message you might write in a diary. She says how much she loves her father, apologizes to her mother for not always caring as much as she should have and declares she can't reveal her secret pain because it would be seen as a weakness. It may seem surprising that under such difficult domestic circumstances Tulisa and her father have always got on so well. Perhaps they understood each other's distress about Ann even though Tulisa was so young.

So while the world of the Lickle Rinsers resembled a modern-day version of one of those early 'puttin' on a show' Judy Garland movies where nothing bad happened, Tulisa's life away from the studio was a much darker and more adult film. She started going out with a very good looking boy and he became her 'first love' when she was still fourteen but she later revealed he treated her badly.

This relationship, in which she was treated like a doormat, was a daunting experience for a young, emotional girl. The boy, who was older and from a tough background, would think nothing of getting off with another girl and then coming back to Tulisa. She would stay over at his house because there was no one to tell her that she shouldn't. Surprisingly, in *Against All Odds* she says she doesn't blame him because he was 'lost' himself at the time. She still barely talks about him. In the memoir she doesn't name him, which is probably lucky for him, as he would forever be known as the guy who was 'violent and abusive' to Tulisa, called her ugly and locked her in the bathroom while he went out with his mates.

Tulisa has never properly explained whether her first suicide attempt was because of unhappiness with her home situation or in this relationship. It was probably a combination of all the things she was bottling up inside and didn't have anyone to talk to about.

If she didn't have enough problems with her rat of a boyfriend, then the trouble with the neighbourhood girls was getting worse. After one nasty spat with a girl looked to be escalating into a full-blown street fight, her father Plato stepped in and withdrew Tulisa from Haverstock. She says she spent nearly a year out.

Tulisa thought the root of her peer problems was jealousy over boys. Plato, however, believed that the trouble she had with other girls was caused by their jealousy of the Lickle Rinsers Crew and the possibility that she might be leaving them and their world behind. More and more young people were hearing about the band. They were doing lots of gigs in local schools, as well as handing out flyers with their pictures. They would loiter outside school gates in order to catch the students as they left to go home.

Tulisa was living the dream of so many young girls who wanted to try for fame and a fortune. Perhaps there was some jealousy over boys because she was a pretty adolescent who had ditched the geeky look she'd had at primary school. But it's also easy to imagine resentment of someone who'd been given a passport out of these grim neighbourhoods.

It wasn't at all glamorous yet. Uncle B bought a second-hand van to drive them to gigs he'd arranged. The early film of Lickle Rinsers appearing live at a school dance is quite an eye-opener because Tulisa in a tight white mini skirt looks about five years older than the boys, who seem like kids. Donna Dee even used to call them 'the kids'.

The boys' enthusiasm for their music was almost childlike. Donna Dee observed it was that passion that enabled them to be so skilful at such a young age: 'They just picked it up like they were born to do it.' She observed that all they cared about was 'work, work, work – writing, writing, writing.'

That may have been true of the boys but Tulisa's private agony was continuing. She started self-harming when she was fourteen. She still has a small scar on her arm where she used to cut herself with a pair of scissors. She also used to pick at her skin incessantly – a classic sign of stress. She didn't want to leave her mum's flat and would spend days literally trapped in her bedroom. When she did go out, she faced running into the girls who had made her life so miserable. In the end she got angry with herself and with them and wouldn't shy away from confrontation, but they were fights in which she would invariably come out of it second best. On one occasion she even had a bottle smashed over her head, although she has never said what damage it caused.

Her mother, who was battling her own problems, must have wondered what was going on when her daughter arrived home at 4 a.m. Sometimes Tulisa would just disappear and then phone her father from all parts of the country asking for him to collect her.

Fortunately, Uncle B wasn't going to let a troubled adolescence get in the way of the bigger picture. His philosophy wouldn't allow negativity. He wanted Tulisa to channel her energy in a positive way and not let the bad people – the 'vampires' as he called them – ruin her life. Most days he would drive over from his home in Camden Town and pick Tulisa up to take her to the studio. He didn't mind doing that every day if it meant keeping her focused. She observed, 'He told me to be strong.'

Plato would also pop in to see how she was and to meet the friends he still had in the area. He bizarrely got his name in the papers when he was enjoying a drink in late 2002 in the Prince of Wales pub in Kentish Town. He was minding his own business when the eighties pop star Adam Ant ran up and threw a car alternator through the window, shattering glass everywhere and injuring Plato. The singer, whose real name is Stuart Goddard, was undergoing psychiatric treatment at the time and was given a twelve-month community rehabilitation order after pleading guilty to affray. He was ordered to pay Tulisa's father £500 compensation.

Tulisa probably didn't want to but she had to go back to school. She was fast running out of suitable options in the area. Eventually a place was found for her at Quintin Kynaston (QK), a comprehensive secondary school in St John's Wood that already had a musical connection, as former pupils included Suggs, the lead singer with Madness, and the R & B star Shola Ama, whose biggest hit was the mellow 'You Might Need Somebody' in 1997. After attending two Catholic schools earlier in her school career, QK was different again because about eighty per cent of the pupils were Muslim. More than a hundred different languages were spoken at the school.

Under the guidance of headteacher Jo Shuter, QK has been a huge success story. It became a poster school when Tony Blair launched New Labour's Extended Schools programme at QK in 2003, the year that Tulisa caught the bus down the Finchley Road to the St John's Wood Tube station which, according to one contemporary, was where pupils would gather to chat, hang out and smoke weed.

Ms Shuter herself has been awarded the CBE and her school has been the subject of glowing Ofsted reports. She has an enlightened view of education, believing that some children need extra support to 'liberate' them from the constraints the outside world puts on them. She believes schools have a duty to 'drive up self-esteem, aspiration and expectation' – a way of thinking that helped her become Secondary Headteacher of the Year in 2007.

Writing in the *Guardian*, Ms Shuter illustrated the type of pupil QK was trying to help, a boy she described as 'a troubled adolescent with an extremely challenging life outside school; emotionally and physically abused, from a single-parent household and a drug-using mother, he is the primary carer for his three younger siblings.' Tulisa was not exactly in that boat but she was from a single-parent home and was the primary carer for her mentally ill mother. Her emotional and physical abuse came from bullying outside the home.

Ms Shuter's initiatives came too late to make much of a difference to Tulisa, although she did receive some positive guidance from student counsellor Miss Shield, who is the only teacher she has ever given a warm reference. Miss Shield had her hands full with Tulisa, who was going through a stage when she was showing two fingers to the world.

She was never much of a morning person even as a schoolgirl and not many of her contemporaries fancied getting to school in time for morning assembly, which was 'so boring'. QK was like many schools, with the children sneaking off in large groups at break time to have a cigarette behind a wall at the back of the buildings.

Tulisa wasn't too bothered about making any real friends at her new school because it was quite a way from her home patch. Bullying at QK wasn't the problem it had been for her at Haverstock. One of the teachers explained, 'I don't know of any serious issues. In my opinion bullying is a word overused when teenagers are being immature and unkind.'

That might have been true when Tulisa had previously faced jibes about her mother's condition. Her current predicament was a different story. She was toughening up and was now the proud owner of a small baseball bat that she tucked into her shoulder bag when she set off to visit friends in Kentish Town. She said she was frightened that she would meet a girl gang coming in the opposite direction. Fortunately, she never did.

Her immediate problems were solved, however, when she fell in with a group of older girls who were the toughest in the neighbourhood. 'They were the hardest of the hard in the area.' It's easy to see why there are so many gangs of young people in deprived areas – there's safety in numbers. Tulisa has confessed that at this difficult stage of her teenage years she did some 'naughty things', like nicking a few handbags and getting involved in fights, but mostly she was relieved to feel protected within the group.

Her description of her life then in *Against All Odds* makes for uncomfortable reading in the light of future controversies she would face. She describes getting a real buzz out of people being scared of her and her 'associates'. Apparently there were 'about twenty of us' and they enjoyed a reputation that people were afraid of – a 'gang of chicks' out to cause trouble who you wouldn't want to meet on a dark night. She declares *she* was the bully then.

A year after publication, just before she started as a judge on *The X Factor*, she was playing down the whole thing to the *Sunday Times*: 'I wasn't part of a girl gang. We were just a group of troublesome chicks.' She doesn't mention being a bully at all.

Tulisa's underachieving school life was about to come to an end. She decided not to take her GCSEs, so she left QK with nothing. She would have to ensure the Lickle Rinsers Crew made it. During the *Tulisa: My Mum and Me* programme she asks her friend DJ Maze what he thought would have happened to her if she hadn't had music. He replies, 'Probably in a council flat, twins, signing on . . .'

Music would eventually take her out of this world but not before a more serious suicide attempt.

6

Blood on the Page

One of the many problems for Tulisa as a wayward teenager was that nobody seemed to notice her private agony. They didn't know that when she went out her mother would leave her sixty messages on her mobile, send her thirty texts a day, phone up everyone she knew to ask where Tulisa was and even ring the police to say her daughter had gone missing. Tulisa was invariably in a club with her mates or at a rave. She was a teenage girl who no longer made any effort at school.

It was a time in her life when she started to lose respect for her mum. While it's undoubtedly true that Tulisa saw herself as her mum's carer, she clearly went through a stage of resenting her situation, which she described as a 'living hell'. Neither parent nor child seemed capable of looking after themselves, let alone each other.

At Quintin Kynaston, as with many forward-thinking schools, there has been a big push to recognize some of the symptoms that young carers show to help teachers understand the problems and alert experts that a child is struggling. These days a defensive and angry girl like Tulisa, who couldn't be bothered to learn anything, is much more likely to set off an alarm that she needs help.

In November 2005, when she was just seventeen, she writes in her diary that her mother has had a panic attack and a seizure. Tulisa had spent the whole day with her in hospital but was finding the conflict between the stress she was feeling and her desire to help her mum becoming too difficult to cope with. She self-harms and wipes the blood on the page of her open diary and writes, 'This is my blood. This is what life has done to me.'

Nearly five years would pass before Tulisa felt strong enough to share this desperately sad passage of her life with the world in the BBC documentary *Tulisa: My Mum and Me* that was both moving and dispassionate at the same time. The programme in some ways revealed a young woman coming to terms with her problems – her 'suicidal stage' as she called it.

The very worst of it was when she was by herself one night and slit her wrists. There was blood everywhere and she had to grab a towel to try to stem the flow. She told the *Daily Mail*, 'I panicked because I realized what I was actually doing to myself.' Fortunately, she had missed slicing a vein and a friend came over to comfort her. It was a classic cry for help but also a wake-up call that something needed to change or she might end up dead.

The solution in the short term was to move in with her father. It gave her more stability and routine in her life. Plato's soon-to-be second ex-wife Mel Vondrau recalls running into his daughter at the house in Asmara Road before it was sold. She was upset to see that Tulisa was 'pale and withdrawn'.

Tulisa's miserable relationship with her first love had finally ended when he went off with another girl yet again and she was left single. That was not the signal for her to put out the flags and celebrate. Instead she was too upset to eat and her weight started to plummet. She has estimated that she lost one and a half stone and weighed just seven stone, which was far from ideal for a young woman of 5ft 6in.

Tulisa, however, gets really annoyed at the suggestion she

was ever anorexic, a word used far too often these days. Anorexia nervosa is a serious illness. Tulisa told Dan Wootten of *Now* magazine that she had never had an eating disorder and was a 'proper piglet'. She got skinny after a break-up – a common emotional reaction – but that's all. The dilemma for Tulisa is that she has put so much sensational material about herself into the public domain that everything seems dramatic. Occasionally she has to take a step back and put things in perspective for us.

Another side effect of the break-up was a short period of promiscuity, which left her feeling completely dissatisfied. She tried to get on with her life by starting a job as a receptionist at a record company, which didn't last long when it became apparent that Tulisa wasn't cut out for 9 to 5 work.

There were some fun times, however. She enjoyed going dancing with her mates, although one night did involve one of the most embarrassing incidents of her life. She was showing off some of her best dancing moves on the stage of a West End club when she slipped and 'fell on my arse right in the middle of the dance floor.' The whole crowd went 'ooh!'

The need for Lickle Rinsers to succeed was becoming increasingly obvious to everyone. Uncle B was refusing to be negative, though even his positive outlook must have been challenged by the age it was taking to get any sort of recognition. He could put his head round the door of record companies but was never invited in. They would hear the white label discs and were interested but nobody seemed to get what they were trying to do or want to take it further.

Their strategy clearly wasn't working. They were getting coverage in magazines and snippets here and there in local papers but the record companies remained unimpressed. They also seemed unable to break through into mainstream radio. Uncle B had even entered them in one or two local talent contests, which weren't exactly *Britain's Got Talent* but they did well. They were still getting bookings, although sometimes they were playing to

Tulisa's early years in North London were happy and normal – as a bonny baby, celebrating her fourth birthday, playing with the kittens and sharing a cuddle with her beloved mum Ann.

A Christmas picture with her dad, Plato. They remained close even after he left home when she was nine.

Tulisa's grandfather, Spyros, who worked for the United Nations in London, was worried about his sons pursuing a musical career. He still joined Plato to watch the occasional gig, however.

Tulisa's love of floral designs began when she was a youngster. Here she poses in a favourite dress at home in Belsize Park.

The cheeky look is unmistakably Tulisa.

Tulisa's Uncle Byron (Uncle B) was the key figure in her early musical career and she was devastated by his sudden death in 2007. Here he is pictured with Plato's second wife, Mel, during a gig in the Haverstock Arms.

Tulisa said they were thinking of giving it all up before N-Dubz won the 2007 MOBO for Best Newcomer. She dedicated the award to Uncle B.

Tulisa harbours ambitions to be an actress. Her first TV role was in 2007, playing Laurissa, a budding pop star with an abusive boyfriend, in Channel 4's *Dubplate Drama*. This scene is from the 2009 series.

On stage at T4 on the Beach in Weston-super-Mare . . . Tulisa was making a name for herself as a girl with a belting voice.

N-Dubz were one of the most popular live bands in the country by the time they performed for BBC Switch Live at the Hammersmith Apollo, London, in November 2009.

One of the last times N-Dubz performed together, at the V Festival in Chelmsford in August 2011.

Tulisa was in love with Justin Edwards *aka* MC Ultra when she posed with him at the MOBO after-show party at the Corinthian, Glasgow, in September 2009.

After Tulisa split with Justin in 2010, she enjoyed a holiday fling in Ibiza with handsome Stockport County footballer Luca Havern.

Tulisa has a competitive streak, which she showed when struggling to tackle actress Kaya Scodelario during the Celebrity Soccer Six tournament at Charlton Athletic's Valley Stadium in May 2010. Her team won.

Prince Charles said he thought Tulisa looked amazing in her evening gown at the Royal Variety Performance in November 2010. The boys looked smooth in their Vivienne Westwood suits.

Calling all *X Factor* contestants – this is how you do it! Tulisa on fire in her trademark unitard at the Manchester Arena during the *Love.Live.Life* tour in April 2011.

just a handful of kids. Something bolder and more original was needed.

Eventually they all realized it wasn't going to happen and they had to do something else. Perhaps they needed to change their name. They weren't getting anywhere as Lickle Rinsers so they decided to call themselves NW1 after their Camden roots. The trouble with this choice was that only Dappy was actually raised in NW1; Tulisa and Fazer were brought up in NW3, which is also the famous postcode for Hampstead and one of the most prestigious in the country. Still, all three had killed plenty of time in Camden so perhaps nobody would notice the flaw in their new name.

A better strategy was to make a video. It could open up many more avenues, especially the key one of television, so important for getting the band out there. They had to find the money, for starters, which wasn't easy as there were occasions when they were looking around for something to pawn just to put petrol in the van. Uncle B scraped together £500 from cutting hair in order to make it happen.

They invited a young film student at the Arts Institute at Bournemouth called George Burt to shoot a video for a new track they had written called 'Every Day of My Life'. The result may have been little more than a home movie but it was to kick-start their momentum again. It was also the beginning of a very fruitful association with George, whom Fazer called 'uni-boy'.

The song showed how the band had developed musically over the past four years. Dappy and Fazer may have indulged in some 'naughtiness', as the former likes to describe it, but throughout that time they remained focused on improving their music. Fazer, in particular, had become very skilled on the sound equipment and had improved both his drumming and keyboards. Dappy was always walking around with a thesaurus to polish up his lyrics. He had left Haverstock School at fifteen but returned to education a year later to secure an A grade in his English GCSE and a B in Music at the WAC Performing Arts and Media College on Haverstock Hill, two minutes from where Tulisa lived.

WAC, which stands for Weekend Arts College, began as a Saturday drama class for a handful of kids some thirty years ago but had grown over time into a leading charity-funded college for young people who have difficulties within the mainstream educational system. WAC moved from Kentish Town into new premises at Hampstead Town Hall in 2000 and could boast state-of-the-art facilities for all age groups, from the under-fives to the under-25s. It's a pity Tulisa didn't enrol there, as the college would have been perfect for her too.

Dappy was lucky to go there but, more importantly, he also knows how fortunate he was that Uncle B was always around to take him to Jumbo Studios and keep him away from the large group of young men who used to hang around the estate where they lived. Surprisingly, considering how little it meant to them while they were there, N-Dubz are very pro-education and have always advised their fans to stick with their schoolwork. The boys have never been too specific about their teenage 'naughtiness'. Dappy prefers to refer to it as going out on the streets and causing madness. He is certain that without music his life would have gone down a bad path: 'We could have went: bam! Prison, stabbed, jail, shot, finished!'

They started off being obsessed with garage, 2-step and grime, a mix of UK garage and hip-hop, but as time went on they were bringing a pop element into the sound. Mostly that was Tulisa's job. Her voice, which was maturing all the time, gave NW1 melody. They might just as easily have styled themselves 'NW1 featuring Tulisa' because sometimes she seemed more like a guest vocalist than part of the band.

Unsurprisingly, 'Every Day of My Life' begins with Dappy saying hello to the world by singing 'Na Na Niiiii, Oohh Na Na Naow' – a clever move because such a distinctive introduction could only come from him and soon fans would expect it, as if it were the theme music to a favourite TV show. You can hum this before the real business of the song begins. The track itself is a snapshot of elements of the street life of young people today and the lack of hope they have – thirteen-year-old boys snorting coke, others becoming the victims of violence or trying to sell drugs themselves. And every day it's the same. You can't trust anyone and the police are always circling.

The video may have been shot on a 'crap' camera but George Burt managed to convey the pace of life around some of the grimmer areas of Camden – a good choice, as the action begins and ends with the name NW1 filling the screen. Despite not eating, Tulisa looks shapely in white jeans and a low top with perhaps a touch too much make-up, more in keeping with a junior edition of *The Only Way Is Essex*. She is seen hanging out with some of her friends and then with Dappy and Fazer, racing around an estate and in front of the Tube station and dodging the traffic in Camden High Street.

For £500 it's a remarkable piece and it really worked. Uncle B set about trying to use the video to promote the band. He sent it to, among others, Channel U (now Channel AKA), the British digital satellite music channel that was extremely influential in the contemporary music scene. Channel U accepted the video for broadcast. This brightened the mood at Jumbo Studios, although the airtime was limited to some plays late at night, which wasn't quite the exposure Uncle B was hoping for.

The next break, however, came unexpectedly with the sale of the family house in Asmara Road. With his share of some of the profit, Uncle B was able to bankroll the NW1 project properly. They were working hard, of course, but here was another example of how they were more fortunate than the average street kid.

Byron set aside £50,000 to bankroll future projects. The first things he did was to buy George some proper equipment, investing in high-definition cameras and Apple Macs, which resulted in N-Dubz declaring they were the first group in the country to shoot a promo on HD video.

George recruited two other students from his college, Justin

Brown as cameraman and Tommy Holman as cinematographer, to help with the next shoot. Together they formed the LRC production team, which could have stood for Lickle Rinsers Crew but was actually short for London Record Connections.

Byron wanted to release a self-funded single on LRC Records for download at the same time as a video that would be of much higher quality than the first. They chose the track 'You Better Not Waste My Time', a very catchy song. It begins with Dappy's usual 'Na Na Niiiii, Ooh Na Na, Ooh Na Na Naaaaa'. But this time Tulisa, too, introduces what would become her trademark. The boys suggested she try a little opera thing, which she didn't appreciate. She told Michelle Adabra at britishhiphop.co.uk, 'I was like come on I ain't Charlotte Church and then we ended up using it on every track. I was doing some messed up things with my hands, going "Ha Ha, Ha Ha", waving my hands around like an idiot'. Tulisa would know it had caught on when girls started to come up to her in the street, wave their arms about and begin wailing 'Ha Ha' in their highest voice.

At the end of the new track, they sign off with 'N-Dubz, N-Dubz, N-Dubz' to alert everyone that this was now the name of the group. Dubz was a corruption of the letter W, so the new name embraced every postcode associated with the group. The word, which can also be spelled 'dubs', is common in hip-hop and can mean anything you want it to mean – a sort of fill-in word. Sometimes it can mean double and be used as a quantity of drugs in urban slang. This was much better than NW1, which was the sort of name Simon Cowell would have given one of the boy bands on his show.

The other big change was that Lady T was no more and Tula Contostavlos had become 'Tulisa', adopting her childhood nickname. She too is given a name check on the track. For a while she toyed with different, trendy, text-friendly spellings like 2lisa before settling on the version that would become famous. Her friends still called her 'T' but professionally there was only one Tulisa, just as there was only one Dappy and one Fazer.

They all had unique names. This would be crucial later on as their brand developed.

For the moment the most important thing was getting 'You Better Not Waste My Time' noticed. Dappy explained, 'It's about people who weren't around at the start of our careers. But as soon as they see us having a bit of a success they come out of the woodwork, sniffing around.'

Two aspects of the track stood out: first, the line that they are addicted to money, which certainly seemed true. According to the lyrics, they were into 'Gucci and Prada'. And, secondly, Tulisa's verse, which was an early reflection of what happened when she was thirteen and jealous rumours left her isolated. N-Dubz would continue to build the story of their lives through the lyrics to their songs.

They filmed the video on some very cold days on location in Camden (naturally), Elephant and Castle and Bournemouth. An indication of how smart N-Dubz were at gathering as much publicity as possible was an invitation to a young journalism student to join them for a day's shoot. The young reporter, Krystle Osafo-Jones, observed that there was a 'youthful, fun element' to the footage. They had young children dancing and droves of boys running after N-Dubz, as well as close-ups of Dappy and Fazer with their mates: 'They were clearly feeling the track and enjoying being on camera. They seemed so excited that poor Tulisa was pushed out of shot a couple of times.'

Once again Uncle B managed to interest Channel U in the video. This was a much classier production than the first home movie and showed that Dappy for one had a flair for acting. It also had a sense of humour, beginning with a picture of an old-fashioned pram. As the camera moves closer, we see that instead of a baby, Dappy is tucked up inside. He also appears in a hot tub surrounded by some very attractive girls not wearing much. The outfits for the others were looking just a little more expensive. Tulisa is super-slim in an all-white trouser suit with a bare midriff. Alison Jane Reid, the former *Times* fashion writer, described the outfit as a 'chav uniform' emphasized by permed hair, oversized hoop earrings and trashy jewellery: 'It plays down her femininity.'

The overall effect was money well spent, because in the years since it was first made in early 2006, it has attracted more than one and a half million hits on YouTube. This time Channel U promoted the song to their daytime list. The station had a system whereby you could vote for a video you liked. 'You Better Not Waste My Time' received so many votes – not just from Uncle B on speed dial – that it was being played every hour and went to number one in the Channel U chart.

The track was made available through LRC Records as a digital download on 19 August 2006. Having some money behind them meant that N-Dubz could 'self-fund' them-selves in the direction they wanted to go. They were one of the first UK bands to exploit the power of online marketing completely. The next time Uncle B went to the record labels, he would have a much stronger product to sell. Tulisa explained, 'It's very important to build up your own underground fan base because they will be the ones who buy your records.' The fans were only able to carry the song to a chart position of number 147, however.

The progress in her musical life was helping Tulisa put her troubled teenage years behind her. She was still only seventeen but now had more of a reason to get out of bed and not spend the day hanging out on the street: 'I decided to focus my mind on music, stay positive and not get involved in that lifestyle at all.' She also suggested that when she was moving on with her life she rediscovered a connection with her faith, a throwback to the happier times she'd had at the Rosary Primary School.

She barely had time to dwell on the past because in September 2006, a month after their first single release, they had another – a result of having written so much material together during the previous five years. 'I Swear' was an up-tempo song about infidelity, once again combining melodic and repetitive hooks with a very personal lyric.

Tulisa has spoken about her first serious boyfriend's habit of cheating on her but on this record she is the one saying sorry and it is Fazer who sings about coming home from tour and finding his girl in bed with someone else. One can only speculate about how autobiographical he is being here because Fazer has always been the least outspoken of the trio when it comes to laying his personal life open for public scrutiny. Tulisa's 'character' in the song admits to cheating on her man but offers the excuse that he wasn't offering her enough love and reminds him that she forgave him when he did the same thing.

This time the track did a little better than their first self-funded release, reaching number ninety-one in the charts and selling an estimated 1,000 copies, which may not seem a great deal but was outstanding in the context of an unsigned band relying on word of mouth. The sales may or may not have been boosted by Uncle B buying up copies to try to generate interest from the large mainstream outlets.

The lyrics from these first three important N-Dubz tracks reveal a band that was in tune with the lives and problems of the audience they were trying to reach – kids of their own age, as well as those younger than themselves, who were facing up to a life in which drugs, lack of money, bullying and the lingering threat of violence were part of their daily lives.

'I Swear' was favourably reviewed online. These unofficial music and review sites were becoming more influential in modern culture and suited the N-Dubz game plan of grabbing an underground swell of support. Almost anyone can review a track these days so it's important to have as much positive feedback as possible. On *Ciao!*, for instance, a reviewer wrote: 'Their slightly crazy voices work so well on the chorus. A perfect mix of rap and vocals means you don't get bored of it and it tells a great story of infidelity.'

The download included the previous release, 'You Better Not My Waste My Time', and a new song called 'Manufactured Bands', a Dappy rant against the world of reality TV and artists such as Will Young and Gareth Gates, who were early stars of *Pop Idol*, and Blazin' Squad, a UK rap group who are labelled 'fake' in the lyric. Dappy says that if only N-Dubz were given a chance with a million-pound advance, then they would be a chart act with a string of hits. They want everyone to get used to their names – Tulisa, Dappy and Fazer – because they're going to sell records worldwide.

That was unlikely to be for a while but suddenly it seemed that N-Dubz were an overnight success. 'I Swear' was the number one track on Channel U for eleven weeks, which led to Dappy jokingly describing it as Channel Us. That exposure led to other stations, such as MTV Base, giving it some airtime.

The popularity of the track on Channel U was vital because more influential people in the music business were taking notice – in particular, Jez Welham, one of the popular DJs on Kiss 100 FM. Jez had been at Kiss for twelve years, since he'd been a wet-behind-the-ears teenager trying to get a break in the business, so he understood the effort N-Dubz were putting into making it. Tulisa has never forgotten his importance in their story: 'Jez Welham just took it and it's almost like he took the record and shoved it down other DJs' throats because now they are all playing it.'

At last, probably as a result of this wider exposure, a record company was taking them seriously. Uncle B, acting on Ray Dorset's advice, involved a lawyer to work out a deal with Polydor Records. While that was going on, N-Dubz continued to press on with the policy that would serve them well in the future: be as open and available as possible for press and publicity. And they proved to be brilliant at it, always confident in their own identities. Jez Welham was in no doubt: 'N-Dubz give the best interviews, every time. They're a real volatile mix, so raw and refreshing.'

Nothing ever seemed too small or too big for N-Dubz. Uncle B had recognized that little fish were sweet when it came to publicity. They gave interviews to anyone who was interested in them, whether it was their local paper, the *Camden New Journal*, or an online site such as britishhiphop.co.uk.

Every mention mattered to them. Every glimmer of interest needed to be addressed, as they continued to treat each day with the 'utmost earnestness' *The Book of Five Rings* demanded. They even piled into the van to appear in Gosport High Street for the Hampshire town's annual turning-on of the Christmas lights. They didn't have the job of actually flicking the switch: that honour went to the top of the bill for the evening – Orville the Duck.

7

Drama

When the television serial *Dubplate Drama* got in touch, Tulisa grabbed the chance of furthering her acting ambitions. Dappy was already signed up to play a rapper called Sleazy, which would involve a couple of months filming at the start of 2007. The producers asked Tulisa if she would like to play Laurissa, the girlfriend of one of the main characters, another rapper called Bones, played by Adam Deacon, who later starred in the film *Adulthood*. Fazer too was on board for a brief cameo as Flames, a DJ. A dubplate was a track sent to an influential DJ to play on an exclusive basis.

Dubplate Drama was an innovative idea for a television programme. It was billed as the world's first interactive drama series: viewers could decide what happened. The series invited viewers to vote on how its plot unfolded through a cliffhanger, an alternative-choice dilemma at the end of every episode. They could either text or vote online for plotline a or b. The concept was a clever one, tapping in to the audience's desire to be involved. Part of the success of the big reality shows like *The X Factor* and *I'm A Celebrity Get Me Out Of Here* is the involvement of the public. We can decide which celebrity has to undergo the

Bushtucker Trial, as well as choosing which ones stay or go, thereby shaping the destiny of the programme. *Dubplate* was similar except it was fiction.

The concept was devised by a youth marketing group called Livity. Co-founder Michelle Clothier said, 'We made it interactive because we want young people to talk about the various issues raised by the weekly dilemmas.' The idea was to use as much new media as possible, so the show was broadcast on Channel 4, MTV and E4 as well as being made available for download on the 3 mobile phone network and the Sony PlayStation Portable.

The first series was broadcast on Channel 4 in November 2005 and starred MC Shystie, a Hackney-born rapper and aspiring actress whose real name was Chanelle Scott Calica. Her manager, Justin Stennett, had the idea that she should front her own interactive show. She had been making a name for herself touring with Basement Jaxx and The Streets and he was now looking to broaden her appeal.

Shystie, who is six years older than Tulisa, was at the forefront of new British urban scene. Some of what she had been doing was similar to N-Dubz – sending out her music to pirate DJs, learning about sound engineering, MCing with the boys at her sixth-form college and practising non-stop. Finally she signed to Locked On Records, who helped fix up a recording with the Wu-Tang Clan in New York. She was already on the path that N-Dubz were seeking to follow.

In *Dubplate*, as it was commonly known, she played 'Dionne', a girl trying to make it in the music business and facing a different set of challenges each week. It was set in the urban world all too familiar to Tulisa, Dappy and Fazer – a world of white label discs, rapping and clashin', music rivalries and street gangs and drugs and violence. The audience lapped it up. More than three million viewers watched it on all the various media outlets available. When the series finished, MTV and Channel 4 broadcast the six fifteen-minute episodes together as a film, which was shown twenty times in a two-month period.

Two of the big draws of the show were the soundtrack and cameo performances from established artists, including Ms Dynamite and So Solid Crew. For a while Ms Dynamite was one of the biggest urban acts in the UK, winning two BRITs in 2003 and the Mercury Music Prize for her album *A Little Deeper*. *Dubplate* was part of her return to the limelight after the birth of her son Shavaar. But her time as one of the queens of British R & B was short-lived. She was about to be overtaken by newer and brighter acts.

The producers of *Dubplate* were keen to replicate the winning formula when the series returned in 2007 by resuming the story of Dionne. Once again they wanted to get real stars involved and thought of N-Dubz because they'd noticed how much the camera loved the group in their Channel U videos. They could see that Dappy was a natural on screen. While he revelled in his role as Sleazy, he was essentially just being Dappy. One reviewer, Jeremy Clay of the *Leicester Mercury*, pointed out: 'Quite a few of the rest of the cast appear to have modelled themselves on Dappy from N-Dubz. Hang on: one of them *is* Dappy from N-Dubz.'

Before she was required for her two weeks of filming, Tulisa joined the boys to film the video for their next self-funded release on LRC Records. The track was called 'Feva Las Vegas', which had absolutely nothing to do with the famous Elvis Presley film *Viva Las Vegas*, although the title was a neat parody of that 1964 romantic comedy. Presley also sang the title song, which became a classic party record. N-Dubz weren't singing about partying in the Nevada desert but were hitting out at people who wanted a piece of their fame – a favourite Dappy subject that he had already explored in 'You Better Not Waste My Time'.

The video was shot exclusively in a studio and had a more expensive, smoother look than their previous ones. Both Fazer and Dappy wore white chullos but the headgear never suited Fazer that well. Tulisa looked seductive in a selection of outfits that included a figure-hugging dress and cut-off shorts. She had moved a million miles away from the pale, unhappy girl of two years before. In one scene, a record industry executive tries to offer them a briefcase full of money, which in effect is what actually happened: they were offered £80,000 for all their publishing rights by someone seeking to take advantage of cash-hungry teenagers. Fortunately, they turned the instant money down, believing they would be worth much more in the long term.

A photographer captured some of the moments from the shoot, including Tulisa wearing a black and white Union Jack T-shirt. Uncle B was there and he featured alone in one picture, wearing jeans, a big waterproof coat and a woollen hat (not a chullo). He looked tired and drawn, and not at all well.

Shooting videos like this one was teaching Tulisa to relax in front of a camera. When she moved on to *Dubplate Drama*, she immediately showed talent as an actress. The first time we saw her on screen was in episode six, when she is in a brief scene, sitting on a sofa with Bones after he has been hit by a car.

The next episode provided her first big scene and was the one in which she had to prove her acting ability. She needed to cry copiously – not a little weep but a great wailing. She has just discovered that Bones has killed himself by jumping off a roof and she is grief-stricken. Tulisa took a large onion with her to work. The director, Luke Hyams, was impressed with her dedication. Before the big scene she hacked the onion in two and held it right up to her eyes to make them run.

Luke gave her some advice on how to handle the scene: 'A lot of people I work with are not old enough to have experienced this kind of emotion. Hopefully you have something inside you that will act as a trigger and you've just got to work with that.' Luke couldn't know all the heartache Tulisa had suffered in her life with her mother and the bullying she'd received.

In the end the tears flowed easily and she gave a powerful performance. Afterwards she explained that she forgot the cameras were there and just tried to focus on the worst thing that had happened to her in her life, the one that made her want to scream out loud. She didn't reveal what it was she was thinking of but did say that she'd been listening on her iPod to an a cappella version of a classic anthem to loss, 'One Sweet Day' by Mariah Carey and Boyz II Men, to help put her in a sad mood. That song alone is more likely to bring a tear to your eye than any onion.

Tulisa was happy it had gone well and laughed, 'I enjoyed it. I needed a good cry.' Later that day she would have something very real to cry over.

The lights were on inside the 'shoebox' but Dappy couldn't get a reply. Annoyingly, he didn't have his keys because he'd expected his father to let him in. His mother was away visiting family in Greece so he knew she wasn't home. He banged on the door and tried to ring Uncle B on the phone but couldn't get a reply. He was tired after a day filming his role as Sleazy in *Dubplate Drama* and just wanted his bed for the night. In the end he rang up a friend who lived on the estate so he would have somewhere to stay.

The next morning Dappy strolled round to discover his mother waiting outside because she couldn't get in. Again they tried ringing Uncle B but without success. This didn't feel right so they called Fazer to come round and help. He had been with Uncle B the previous night, looking at a new studio space they were thinking of moving to from Jumbo. It was an exciting time because Polydor had finally come up with a firm offer for one single with an option for an album. The signing fee of £25,000 would enable them to upgrade, so Fazer and Uncle B had made plans to meet up to discuss the equipment they might buy for the new studio.

DJ Maze, whom they had brought in to help mix the N-Dubz tracks, came along with Fazer, as it looked like they would have to break the door down. Fazer told *Bliss* magazine how the dramatic events unfolded. He was the first to walk into the lounge, where the television was still blaring, tuned into Channel U. Byron was sitting very still on the sofa with the remote control in his hand. Fazer recalled, 'He didn't look right. As I got closer, I froze with shock and horror. He felt cold and my head spun as I realized he was dead.' It seemed he had died while waiting for their new video to appear on television.

For an instant, Fazer didn't know what to do. Should he call the police or an ambulance? But then Dappy followed him into the lounge and could see straight away that his father was dead. He immediately went out of control and, before Fazer had a chance to calm him down, he was charging around the house, smashing everything as he went. They called an ambulance but Uncle B had been dead for many hours. He was fifty-three.

He seemed to have suffered a heart attack but it transpired that he had been ill for some time with a worsening lung disease, which was dripping poison into his body and led to a blocked artery. Nobody knows if he knew he was dying but he'd been making plans for N-Dubz's future, including the possibility of new management. He'd chain-smoked roll-up cigarettes all his adult life but it's impossible to speculate on how much effect that had on his health.

Tulisa, meanwhile, was filming her big onion scene. Afterwards, when she switched her phone back on she was alarmed to see so many texts from Dappy and Fazer saying they needed to speak to her urgently. Then the phone rang and it was them but they wouldn't tell her what was wrong. Instead, they insisted that they were coming over to the set. She collapsed with grief when they told her.

The dramatic and tragic story of Uncle B's death when his protégés were on the brink of success has been told and retold since it happened on 12 April 2007. It doesn't make it any less sad.

Dappy understandably was the most affected of the three but they were all so young and had lost the rock on which they depended. Fazer was strong on the day but later admitted he broke down in tears when he had some quiet time to himself. Tulisa couldn't stop crying but tried to be brave for her cousin's sake. And Tulisa's father, Plato, was overwhelmed by his elder brother's death and has never played a gig since. She explained, 'My dad felt he'd lost the other half of himself.'

While Dappy was happy to talk about his father in interviews and acknowledge the group's debt to him, he was extremely brittle if anybody mentioned Byron casually. A club-goer who used to see him out and about with Tulisa recalled that she was given one piece of advice, 'Whatever you do, don't mention his dad.'

Soon afterwards Dappy had a large tattoo drawn on the right side of his neck that read 'RIP Dad'. He rarely called his father 'Dad' though, preferring to refer to him as Uncle B or simply as B. He also set about writing a song in his honour. 'Papa Can You Hear Me?' would become one of the group's best-loved tracks. It's a moving tribute to a father, asking for forgiveness for the things he, the son, has done, for the bad things that have been said, and declaring that he never knew how much he loved him until he was gone.

Tulisa wrote a heartfelt and poignant letter to Uncle B, the 'greatest uncle in the world', which would later be published in the sleeve notes of their first album. In it she wonders whether he would still be alive if it hadn't been for the stress of N-Dubz. She acknowledges that he was always the one who never gave up, always offering a chink of light when everyone else was lost in the dark. She promises to tell her children one day what a great man he was, and to save him a seat at the BRITs – winning one of those coveted awards remains an unfulfilled ambition.

Uncle B's death may have had a traumatic effect on Tulisa, Dappy and Fazer but they still had important commitments. The very next day they had to go to a gig without Uncle B driving them in the old blue van. The easy thing would have been to cancel and stay at home with the blinds closed, but that would have gone against everything that Byron Contostavlos stood for. Fazer explained, 'We decided we had to do it because that's what he would have wanted.'

Coincidentally, Uncle B, perhaps knowing he was ill, had signed a contract that would give N-Dubz a new tour manager, Mark Sutton, who stepped up to the plate when the band needed him and became their friend and protector, making sure their day-to-day lives ran smoothly. They were playing a series of gigs that reflected Uncle B's interest in helping to keep underprivileged or troubled children off the streets.

Two weeks after the death of Uncle B, Tulisa was back on the set of *Dubplate Drama* and between takes was interviewed on film about his importance as the man who had taught them it was OK to have dreams. Puffing discreetly on a cigarette, she says, 'It was all down to that man. He gave us the faith, the studio, the money, the time. He drove us everywhere. He put everything he had into us.'

PART TWO
TULISA

8

Big Strings

N-Dubz needed new management. They couldn't do it themselves and even if Uncle B had been alive, he would have had to
pass over the reins sooner rather than later. His protégés were
already far too big for one man to handle. They chose to go with
Jonathan Shalit's organization. Shalit had achieved notoriety as
the man who'd guided the career of the young Charlotte
Church before it all ended in tears. He was an excellent choice
if you wanted to build a brand – more of an old-fashioned
impresario than an über-trendy shaper of modern culture. He
is, moreover, very shrewd. The former editor of the *Sun*, Kelvin
MacKenzie, a man not normally lavish with his praise, observed
that Shalit was 'a very clever agent and an engaging personality.'

They could make a film about Shalit's life and if they did
much of it would be set at the famous West End restaurant The
Ivy, where he holds court several times a week. His big breakthrough happened there in the early nineties. He had always
loved the world of entertainment, a passion inherited from his
grandmother, Henny Gestetner, who was a great patron of the
arts and a founder of the Chichester Festival Theatre. Shalit grew
up watching shows from the wings. As the son of a prominent

banker, he had a very wealthy, privileged childhood in rural Sussex but, as children do, he rebelled and, rather like Tulisa and Dappy, went from school to school as his parents despaired of him ever completing his education.

He'd always wanted to work in show business but to please his parents he was working as a broker at Lloyds when he decided to take desperate measures to set himself on a new path. He persuaded a window cleaner to take a note up to the office of the chairman of advertising giant Saatchi & Saatchi. The window cleaner tapped on the window and showed the note. It read 'Look Down', which everyone did – to see Jonathan wearing a sandwich board. It read: 'Young, creative and able. Please interview me.' He was interviewed and got a job.

Shalit heard through contacts that the legendary harmonica player Larry Adler wanted to make an album to mark his eightieth birthday. Jonathan thought he should record a series of duets, so he cold-called The Beatles' producer, George Martin, and managed to persuade him to come to lunch at The Ivy. For the first time he was granted a table in the main restaurant and knew he'd arrived.

Jonathan tells the story with relish of how, at the end of a meal of salmon fishcakes and sautéd spinach, George agreed to produce the album and picked up the bill: 'That was a great relief as I probably couldn't have afforded it.' The subsequent release, in which Larry played with, among others, Elton John, Sting and Cher, sold more than two million copies and enabled Jonathan to set up his own business as an agent. A picture of him with Adler, Martin and Sting had pride of place in his new office.

His next breakthrough happened in 1997 when he travelled to Cardiff to meet Charlotte Church, then aged eleven, her mother Maria and her singing teacher Louise Ryan, who accompanied Charlotte on the piano while she sang 'Pie Jesu'. Jonathan was immediately smitten: 'It was like an adult's voice but when you opened your eyes there was this amazing child.'

Under Shalit's energetic management, Charlotte Church became one of the most famous singers in the world. She was signed by Sony Records after Jonathan obtained a meeting with the head of the label and she sang for him in his office. Within a year she had released a debut album, *Voice of an Angel*, which went double platinum in both the UK and the US. This was just the sort of success that N-Dubz were hoping for.

Charlotte famously sang for President Bill Clinton, as well as performed for the Queen and Pope John Paul II. She also became one of the richest teenagers, with a fortune estimated at anything between £10 and £20 million. It came as a considerable shock in the world of show business when Jonathan was fired, apparently in a letter from Charlotte's mother, Maria, a former housing officer. It proved to be the making of his career.

The matter, rather bitterly, ended up in the High Court in November 2000. He claimed damages for breach of his exclusive management contract. On the first day of the hearing, his counsel Ian Mill, QC, said, 'He had a vision for Charlotte and believed in her. Initially his dream was not shared by others and his early approaches were rebuffed with derision by record companies.

'But he put his money where his mouth was and offered her management and recording contracts. He paid for demonstration recordings and wrote directly to the chairmen of the five largest record companies.' If the barrister had been talking about Uncle B and N-Dubz, he might easily have made the same remarks.

On the second day of the case, they came to an out-of-court settlement just before Jonathan was due to give evidence, which might not have been too complimentary about Charlotte Church's family. The deal was apparently brokered by Paul Burger, the head of Sony Music UK, who had decided that the negative publicity might affect the success of her third album, *Dream a Dream*, which had been released that week.

Jonathan received £2.3 million, which almost instantly moved him up a division. With the cheque in his back pocket, he was gracious about his former client: 'Charlotte Church is a remarkable talent. She has presence, beauty and intelligence. She's Julie Andrews meets Audrey Hepburn.'

He invested some of his windfall in a plush apartment in Kensington and the rest in expanding his business. He began to sign a roster of television-friendly clients with commercial potential. His intention was to find talent he could promote with a 'multi-platform approach' and it was this method of working that first attracted him to N-Dubz.

Crucially for the future career of Tulisa, Shalit recognized the value of reality television and set about exploiting its possibilities for his clients. He signed up Christopher Biggins, a panto favourite and the only man who dined at The Ivy as much as he did. Gradually he built a list of celebrity names that included Lorraine Kelly, Russell Watson, Kelly Brook, newsreader Kate Silverton and Claire Sweeney. Sweeney was an early example of how to link television success with commercial opportunity, with diet books, jewellery and fitness videos adding to her value as an actor.

Jonathan used a similar approach with even greater success when he took on the former pop singer turned classical artist Myleene Klass. He approached her at the Classic BRIT Awards and with a flourish told her, 'You should be hosting this'; two years later she was. Myleene stated simply, 'He knows absolutely everyone', which is just about the highest praise you can give your agent. Her career reached a new level after she too appeared in a popular reality show. In her case, she was runner-up to Matt Willis in the 2006 *I'm A Celebrity . . . Get Me Out Of Here!*, and provided the most famous incident in the history of the programme when she took a shower wearing a skimpy white bikini.

From this platform Jonathan has helped her to build one of the widest-ranging show business careers. She is, according to Shalit's website, a musician, a TV presenter, author, business-woman, model, interviewer, columnist, pop star, designer, DJ and mother. At this stage Tulisa was none of these things but in a relatively short space of time with Shalit she could begin to tick them off the list.

The business model for Myleene Klass wasn't something that was troubling Tulisa at this stage. Of more significance to Dappy, Fazer and Tulisa in the short term was Shalit's surprising move into urban music. He revealed, 'I have had a passion for this music for a long time now.'

He proved the point by signing up the group Big Brovaz. He took himself away from The Ivy to a council block in Camberwell, where he told the astonished band members, 'It's not cool to be poor.' Their debut album, *Nu Flow*, went platinum in the UK, which was quite an achievement for a hip-hop band in 2002. Some bad publicity when one of the band was caught smuggling cannabis into LAX (Los Angeles International Airport) may have contributed to their second album doing less well and they split in 2007. Interestingly, they hadn't branched into other things so they had no fallback position when their popularity waned.

Shalit realized that a man now well into his forties wasn't going to be able to connect indefinitely with the teenage buying market for urban acts. Fortunately, he received a letter from an ambitious young A & R man called Rich Castillo, who had moved to London from his native Nottingham at the age of twenty to seek a career in music. He asked for a meeting to explain to Jonathan how he would make him a lot of money. It was just the sort of bold course of action the impresario would have tried himself. Rich explained, 'I borrowed my mate's suit and my other mate's shoes for the interview.' Needless to say, he got the job.

The first act he helped Jonathan with was the multiple MOBO Award-winning singer Jamelia, who also won Best R & B Act at the 2005 Urban Music Awards. In the middle 2000s, when she was in her early twenties, Shalit moved her more into the mainstream with endorsements, including Pretty Polly and

Reebok, charity initiatives and television appearances. She has made documentaries and hosted the National Lottery. If her musical career ended tomorrow, she would still be successful.

When Uncle B died so suddenly, Polydor wanted to help and Colin Barlow, then boss of their British division, fixed up a meeting with Jonathan, Rich and the group. It was a delicate time because their emotions were still raw after their bereavement.

Rich wanted to see if he could make a connection with them: 'I stalked them for a month and a half. I went to every show and I got to know Fazer very well. I was the face that kept turning up and we just got on. I was a big fan of what they do because they had this incredible energy.'

Eventually N-Dubz signed with Jonathan Shalit's agency, tapping into his contacts book and Rich Castillo's patience and enthusiasm. Jonathan said, 'N-Dubz have put their trust and faith in me. I have a massive obligation to make sure they are as successful as possible.'

Dappy said of his new manager, 'Mr Shalit pulls big strings. He can get us on GMTV and *The Paul O'Grady Show*.' He was also an admirer of Castillo's philosophy, which mirrored that of his late father, namely, a belief in perseverance and the longer game. Dappy once offered Rich a view of ambition that would stay with him: 'He said you should never give up on something that you can't go a day without thinking of.'

Perhaps surprisingly, there's much similarity between Charlotte Church, Myleene Klass and N-Dubz in that the urban act from North London needed to cross over into the mainstream. Charlotte and Myleene originally switched between classical music and pop; N-Dubz needed to cross over from grime. The dilemma facing urban acts was summed up by one of its new stars, Chipmunk: 'Why does it always have to say "urban artist gets to number one"? Everyone else can just be an artist. Why do we have to have urban in front?'

Despite Shalit's mainstream connections, the problem for N-Dubz remained that major record companies were slow to back urban acts. Rich explained, 'As far as the labels were concerned, all the kids that were into this kind of music stole music. They didn't pay for it so the labels couldn't see a way of making money – because there just wasn't any.'

That dilemma would need to be addressed in the future, however. Rich's first job was to keep them moving forward on the path set by Uncle B. Their single 'Feva Las Vegas' was released on LRC Records as a digital download and as a CD single six weeks after Uncle B's death and reached number fifty-seven in the charts. The B side of 'Feva Las Vegas' was a song called 'N-Dubz vs NAA' (New Age Army), a group whose nickname was 'N-Dubz' because dubz can mean double, as in the double A of NAA. This 'clash' was a clever and light-hearted way of defusing a potentially embarrassing situation. The video again showed the acting talents of Dappy and Tulisa. Dappy is hilarious as he pretends to box the opposing crew and collapses to the ground when he is bopped on the head. Tulisa does her operatic notes as if she is warming up to sing an aria at Covent Garden. It was good fun and fortunately nobody was confused about the names.

Both videos were played constantly on Channel U and N-Dubz were becoming one of the most talked-about groups in the country despite not having released an album. They started a school tour as part of a campaign to keep kids on the right track. As well as the music, they included motivational talks for the children organized by a community intitative called Diverzion, which sought to spell out the dangers of drug and alcohol abuse and crime. Diverzion wanted to inspire youngsters to make something of themselves and saw N-Dubz as positive role models for that.

N-Dubz weren't turning into a goody-two-shoes band, however. Their next record was their most controversial yet. In July 2007, they released 'Love For My Slum', the last single on LRC Records. The video featured Dappy standing next to a rich kid, who is trying to look like a gangster, in front of an expensive-looking block of flats. He tells the kid that he wouldn't last a minute where he (Dappy) comes from, then grabs him by the coat and punches him in the face. The rich kid collapses to the ground. If you blinked, you missed the action.

The instant violence of the video, even though it was pretty tame, caught the attention of senior police. They were concerned that the rising levels of crime outside clubs featuring grime music were associated with videos showcasing violence and thuggery. One article in the *Independent* pointed out that a grime performer called Crazy Titch was jailed for life for murdering a rival producer over a row about lyrics. It was a bit of a stretch, however, to link that criminal act, as the newspaper did, with Dappy racing around the greyer areas of Camden singing about his love for his slum.

The founder of Channel U, Darren Platt, was moved to explain that his station did vet the videos they were sent and the latest N-Dubz one was heavily censored. 'I get maybe twenty-five a week, of which six or seven make it in. We already censor over and above the guidelines. If kids want to see violent videos, there are plenty of other places on the Internet where they can do that.' Dappy, while acknowledging that all publicity was good publicity, told *Time Out* that the *Independent* journalist was 'obviously an idiot that didn't know anything about hip-hop and took the easy way out, to stereotype it.'

'Love For My Slum' featured another rap artist, Baker Trouble, and is really a Dappy record – Fazer and Tulisa don't appear until near the end, when she chips in with some of her trademark operatic notes. Dappy shrugged off criticism of the song's violent associations by suggesting that if you listened to the lyrics properly, the song was about appreciating what you have. He was raging against middle-class kids who already had money and prospects but were embracing the grime scene because it was fashionable. Ironically, the young people living the street life for real were desperate to make money and become rich kids. He said simply, 'It's not ghetto and it's not fabulous. Don't sit there and think it's great.'

He was right, of course, and in interviews he made it clear that N-Dubz were against the sort of rapping that seemed to glorify violence gratuitously. They were interviewed by Charlotte Chambers for their local paper, the *Camden New Journal.* She recalled that her interview with them topped their website search poll every week and said, 'They were bright, animated and primed for success.' They told her that they wanted 'mums, window cleaners and granddads' to go and buy their album.

The only problem with that was there looked to be little prospect of an actual album on the immediate horizon. They were achieving more exposure, however. *Dubplate Drama* gave them a connection to Tim Westwood, a former pirate DJ, when he appeared in a cameo role. Westwood, the son of a bishop, had been presenting the Radio 1 Rap Show since 1994 and was one of the biggest names in the genre. He achieved notoriety in 1999 when he was shot in what appeared to be a Yardie-style assassination attempt in Kennington. A motorbike pulled up beside his Range Rover and the pillion rider opened fire, hitting Westwood in the arm.

Appearing on Westwood's radio show was big news for N-Dubz. He gave them a plug for the new series of *Dubplate* and the album they were recording. Tulisa admitted that she and Dappy had arguments when they were in the studio, usually over some 'inappropriate' lyrics Dappy had written. She also said that she enjoyed being recognized in the street, although Fazer seemed less pleased that he couldn't even go to buy eggs for his 'mumsy' without being mobbed. They managed to reinforce the emerging N-Dubz brand at every opportunity, with Dappy demonstrating how to sing 'Na Na Niiiii' from the belly and Tulisa singing 'Ha Ha, Ha Ha'. The interview finished with Dappy showing his remarkable talent for freestyle rapping. Tulisa, who can't rap, was just a bystander as her cousin hogged the microphone.

Tulisa

The year 2007 was proving to be a rollercoaster with the most dismal news about Uncle B mixed with many high spots in their career. There was also some better news for Tulisa privately, after her mother Ann was finally properly diagnosed with schizoaffective disorder. At last Ann was on the correct medication and both she and her daughter could look forward to many episode-free years in the future.

9

Crying Under Shades

N-Dubz might have given up if it hadn't been for the MOBOs of 2007. The Music of Black Origin Awards are big news in the music industry. When N-Dubz were nominated in the Best Newcomer category in August, it was just the boost they needed after the death of Uncle B. The MOBOs are probably ranked second only to the BRIT Awards. They were founded in 1996 by Kanya King, an inspirational woman who turned a dream into a commercial phenomenon with passion and acumen – just the sort of success story that Tulisa aspired to emulate.

Kanya grew up in North West London, the youngest of nine children with a Ghanaian father and an Irish mother. She was thirteen when her father died, making things financially difficult for her family. After a stint working in a bakery, she got a job in television as a lowly researcher and made her way up the ladder to become a senior researcher with Carlton Television and a founding member of the production team on *The Chrystal Rose Show*, an early nineties talk show.

In 1996 she started developing an idea for awards that would showcase the talent of black performers. She felt there wasn't a platform for them to be heard in a music world still dominated by *Top of the Pops*. She started the MOBO Organisation from the bedroom of her home, which she remortgaged without telling her mother. She couldn't afford an office so she would try to raise sponsorship through phone calls she made while lying on her bed in her pyjamas. Her secret, she explained, was 'passion' and an ability to 'fake it till you make it'.

A few months later she had generated enough funding to hold the first ceremony at the Connaught Rooms in London. The original awards were exclusively for black musicians. The Fugees were the big winners on the night, although Lionel Richie was given a Lifetime Achievement Award. In retrospect, the biggest name in black music to win an award then was the late hip-hop artist Tupac, who won Best Video.

Critics of the awards were disappointed that commercial interests seemed to take over quite rapidly, with white artists being squeezed into the categories, sometimes for no better reason than they sounded a bit black. Joss Stone, for instance, was nominated in 2005 as Best UK Act. David Lister, the Arts Editor of the *Independent*, asked, 'What on earth was the white Devonian Joss Stone nominated for – toughing it out on the mean streets of Paignton?' He called the awards a 'patronising piece of ghettoisation.'

Despite critical misgivings, the MOBOs were big business. They were the first music awards ceremony to be broadcast live on the BBC, with an estimated worldwide audience of 250 million. Kanya observed that they brought 'urban music to the masses'.

Just the nomination was a big step forward for N-Dubz. Jonathan Shalit had the added bonus of another nomination that year for Jamelia, who had also been chosen to host the awards at the O2 Arena in East London. Their competition for the award, which was voted for by viewers of *London Tonight*, the regional evening news programme, was Mutya Buena, who had been a member of the Sugababes and was probably the favourite, Tinchy Stryder, UnkleJam and Sadie Ama.

The show, which went out on BBC Three, would prove to be a huge showcase for Dappy, Tulisa and Fazer. The awards are slightly bonkers. The Best International Act, won by Rihanna, was presented by Sinitta and boxer Frank Bruno, who received the biggest cheer of the night. The Best Song, Ne-Yo's 'Because of You', was presented by Quentin Tarantino. The honours for Best UK Newcomer were performed by Wil Johnson, a black actor best known for his role in the crime series *Waking the Dead.*

Johnson introduced brief clips of the artists, which ended with a few seconds from a new video version of N-Dubz performing 'You Better Not Waste My Time'. Their segment was greeted with the biggest cheer, which continued when the result was announced and they'd won. Dappy led the victorious 'Dynamite Trio', as he called them, at almost a run on to the stage. Tulisa, wearing a floaty gypsy dress and violent blonde hair, hid her face as she followed. She couldn't believe they'd won. Dappy, despite his emotion, had removed his shades and again proved himself to be the master showman by telling the audience that he wanted 'all the males to say Na Na Niiiii' and then inviting all the females to sing 'Ha Ha' in Tulisa's operatic sigh. It was a clever touch to remind everyone that these were the two N-Dubz trademarks. Dappy began by thanking Jonathan Shalit, Rich and his mum before moving on to two important members of the N-Dubz crew – DJ Maze and Face Killa. He finished with an RIP for his dad.

Tulisa, who had expected Mutya to win, was teetering on the brink of tears as well as her heels. She thanked the fans, her mum and dad and Uncle B, as well as tour manager Mark Sutton, whom she'd relied on so much since Uncle B's death. While, quite understandably, Uncle B was very much in everyone's thoughts, it's a pity nobody gave a bigger acknowledgement to Plato, whose technical expertise in the studio had been so vital to their musical progress. Before Byron died, they had given an interview in which they declared that Tulisa's dad had been the man who taught them. His natural modesty meant he never took any credit.

When Fazer took the microphone he was articulate and low key, praising all the great talent in the arena that night and reminding his audience that the new N-Dubz record 'You Better Not Waste My Time' would be out on 22 October.

He didn't say so on stage but Fazer later admitted: 'If we hadn't won, we might not have carried on really. Winning was for Uncle B and if we'd failed him, then we would have thought "we're crap, it's not worth doing any more and that's it."'

Tulisa confirmed that they were on the verge of giving up, unable to see the point of it all after Uncle B died: 'But when we won, it literally made sense to us – it meant the world to us. We were crying underneath our sunglasses that day. We never thought in a million years that we were going to win but we did.'

They were so overwhelmed that in the excitement of their big night the happy trio took their trophy home, which was a surprise to the organizers, who expected it to stay with all the others to be engraved. They thought it had been stolen but it turned out the award had pride of place on top of Dappy's mum's fridge.

Award ceremonies are sometimes amusing to look back on because some of the winners and nominees make it and some don't. From the class of 2007 Tinchy Stryder would become one of the big stars of hip-hop. UnkleJam released three singles in 2007 and were never heard of again. Sadie Ama, the younger sister of Shola Ama, managed only one single release and is still seeking her first big break. Mutya Buena was dropped by Universal Records in 2008.

What was in store for N-Dubz? At least they could say that they won the only award voted for by members of the public and, although it wasn't announced at the time, they did so by a record margin. The popularity they'd gained through building an underground fan base was huge.

Polydor decided to strike while the momentum from the MOBOs was at its strongest and put out the single 'You Better Not Waste My Time'. Everybody was expecting great things. Tulisa announced, 'We're taking over the world.' And Dappy, even more optimistically, said, 'We're going to the moon and back.'

Disappointingly, despite a barrage of publicity that included an interview in the *Guardian* newpaper, the single flopped, only making it to number twenty-six in the charts, which is pretty much nowhere in modern music terms. The *Guardian* article did, however, confirm that N-Dubz made good copy, endorsing the opinion of their old supporter Jez Welham that they were the best interview in the business.

We learned that Tulisa – or 2lisa as the paper called her – did not 'shit gold'. Fazer told the story of dropping his mic on stage and being groped by some girls when he bent down to pick it up. The newspaper described them as 'hoodies with harmonies' and thought that David Cameron would definitely want to hug them.

It was good fun except, worryingly, the newspaper tried to pigeon-hole them as the British Black Eyed Peas. This is what the media likes to do – everybody has to be a new something or other. Tulisa would later have to suffer being the 'new Cheryl Cole'. The only connection between N-Dubz and the Black Eyed Peas seemed to be that both groups contained two guys who could rap and one girl who could sing. They sounded completely different.

With hindsight, the label made a huge mistake releasing a track that most N-Dubz fans already had. An estimated 40,000 owned the track from legal downloads and then there were all the fans who had secured a copy illegally. A new video, which trimmed more than a minute off the original, was uploaded onto YouTube the same day as the MOBOs but failed to improve sales despite being number one in the Channel U chart for seven weeks.

Dappy blamed the disappointment on Polydor for their lack

of vision and not listening to them. Tulisa thought the problem was not targeting their main fan base: 'It did gain us new fans but, at the same time, we missed out on how many thousands of fans we already had because we didn't bring out a fresh track.'

While Dappy was unquestionably the front man of the band, all verve and personality, Tulisa was gaining the confidence to speak out in an articulate and blunt manner. She summed up the state of the music industry for Eddy Lawrence of *Time Out*: 'the problem is that there's a lot of good UK acts out there, and there's a lot of crap as well ... there's these individual UK acts that actually have the potential to go mainstream and be something that everyone wants to listen to. That's too much of a risk for the music industry. I think they feel very safe with their pop acts; they can say: "Well, I'm not gonna lose any money. Oh look, there's three girls that can sing and dance and shake their arse, I'll put my money into that." Rather than taking a risk that will make you either loads of money, or very little – which is what the music industry used to be about – they're too scared to do it.'

Tulisa was growing up and was no longer the shy girl filmed for the documentary at Jumbo Studios. She had opinions and she was not afraid to voice them. The death of Uncle B had been a jolt of reality that had shown her that they were no longer children messing about in their parents' studio. It helped that part of the strategy to gain popularity was actually to get out and meet potential fans. In one week plugging the single, they breezed into sixty schools. You weren't going to get anywhere if you couldn't engage with the public.

Tulisa wasn't much of a morning person but this was different from being at school herself. Now she jumped out of bed at 6 a.m. and rushed around all day, sometimes just visiting schools or at other times giving interviews and chatting on radio programmes. Then in the evening N-Dubz would have one or maybe two gigs so it was always a late night. And the following day they would have to do it all again.

N-Dubz were in their element in the school environment. They probably spent more time in the classrooms and school halls on this tour than they did during the whole of their own education. When they arrived they would be greeted by mass screaming. They weren't stars coming among young fans to look cool; they made a genuine connection and the kids loved them. Tulisa would give a little speech in which she said she almost gave up her musical ambitions when she was thirteen or fourteen. 'I stuck with it because sometimes it's like you are here for a reason – that you are doing something with yourself. It's an amazing feeling.' They were trying to encourage the children to believe in their dreams as they had done.

After giving the audience a pep talk, Dappy and Tulisa sang a cappella with Fazer beatboxing. They would invite kids on stage to help sing 'I Swear' and 'Feva Las Vegas' – even the teachers were encouraged to join in with 'Na Na Niiiii'. The young fans knew all the words to all the songs. Then N-Dubz drove off in their 4 × 4 to the next school, leaving behind happy faces taking pictures on phones and cameras. It was brilliant marketing and provided the schoolchildren with a welcome change from double maths.

Trying to reach a wider audience was the strategy behind Dappy's much-talked-of appearance as a guest panellist on the long-running television pop quiz *Never Mind the Buzzcocks* in November 2007. Dappy was apparently a stand-in for Lee Ryan from boy band Blue, who withdrew at the last minute. He looked very out of place sitting next to team captain Phill Jupitus, who looked almost old enough to be his granddad, and opposing a team that included Keith Chegwin, a popular figure of TV and panto but hardly cutting edge. The host Simon Amstell found Dappy an easy target for put-downs, although he took it all pretty well.

At least he had made the effort and produced a 'Dappy hat' for Amstell to wear. The other team captain, Noel Fielding from *The Mighty Boosh*, observed that he looked like a knitted poodle in the headgear. At one stage Dappy took off the chullo to reveal that he did have hair. Dappy had the last laugh, however, because nobody remembers the names of the other panellists on the show – they just remember him.

Tulisa sprang to her cousin's defence: 'People are scared of what they don't understand and they find it a lot easier to knock it. The first thing they do is look at this dude in a hat and say, "What an idiot."' Dappy wore hats to get noticed and maintained, 'It's an image for the kids which is very important. And, anyway, it's working. The hats ain't going nowhere.'

Coincidentally, the night after that notorious episode of *Buzzcocks* was broadcast, Dappy and his chullo were back on stage at the Islington Academy, where they were supporting the Walthamstow-born rapper Lethal Bizzle. The audience obviously didn't care one bit about *Buzzcocks* and cheered from start to finish.

Rachel Wade, writing for *wiredradio* online, observed, 'a delighted audience . . . ended up singing practically every word through the act's set-list. Two rappers and a truly talented female vocalist, N-Dubz was obviously either more than familiar with such admiration, or they were just true naturals at performing on stage.'

Dappy was clearly right when he said the image was working. In the immediate future, however, they had more to worry about than Simon Amstell and Dappy's hats. They were about to leave Polydor.

As is often the case when artists and record labels part company, the question of who dropped whom is a grey area. Polydor had given them a deal for one single with the option for an album. It was an option that they showed little sign of taking up and the lack of positive activity after 'You Better Not Waste My Time' was potentially terminal for N-Dubz. The year 2007 should have ended in triumph for them but their frustrating situation was neatly summed up when they were stuck on the M25 when they should have been turning on the Christmas lights in Crawley. They decided to ask Polydor to release them from any future obligations. They weren't exactly back at square one but they needed a boost.

Instead of releasing another single straight away, they decided to make a video to revisit what had worked so well before – round-the-clock coverage on Channel U. They already had a track in mind called 'Ouch', which they'd been hoping Polydor would release before they chose 'You Better Not Waste My Time'. 'Ouch' was 'I Swear' part two and would have dovetailed nicely with that single. Tulisa explained the song to *Female First*: 'It's basically the other way round to "I Swear"; it's me being a girl, coming home, finding my boyfriend cheating on me. And then Dappy and Fazer come from a boy's point of view and they're sort of asking for me back, "it's not my fault", that kind of business. It's all about a whole debate between a woman and man after finding out the man's cheated.'

George Burt was brought in to shoot the video, on which they spent £7,000 of their own money – not a huge amount but considerably more than their first collaboration. Tulisa, looking softer, more glamorous and no longer a teenager, arrives home to discover her boyfriend in bed with another girl. She has never said if this actually happened to her with her first boyfriend but she does convey the agony in a way that revealed a sharpening of her acting skills since her spell in *Dubplate Drama*.

Fraser McAlpine, writing on his BBC Chart Blog, observed, 'There's more passion, fire and proper acting going on here than in ten episodes of *EastEnders* ... It's really impressive to hear a song which manages to get across both sides of a row without flinching or trying to resolve it all at the end.'

The video seemed to touch a nerve with young people and millions went online to watch it. Within a year of its official release on YouTube in May 2008, 'Ouch' had received an unprecedented ten million hits. Luckily, Channel U, which was also playing the track – and other N-Dubz videos practically in rotation – had a financial relationship with a go-ahead independent record label called All Around the World, which was distributed by Universal. Darren Platt, the boss of the television channel, mentioned N-Dubz to Cris Nuttall, his opposite number at AATW.

Rich Castillo observed, 'There was such a buzz about N-Dubz in the urban world but not in the mainstream because the dots hadn't been connected yet. The mainstream TV and press had yet to acknowledge the impact of the urban world.'

All Around the World offered a one-single deal, which N-Dubz accepted; if the first record did well, then they would pick up another one. This time N-Dubz achieved what they wanted and 'Ouch' was released first as a digital download on 20 September and then as a CD single the following week. At last you could buy an N-Dubz record in a store. The track peaked at number twenty-two, perhaps once again suffering from overfamiliarity. The song itself was the most melodious track from N-Dubz to date and, for the first time, showcased Tulisa more than the boys. John Dingwall in the *Daily Record* called it a 'dramatic infidelity anthem'.

The *Urban Review* online highlighted the 'hot instrumentals, wicked beats & story-telling lyrics that make this a potential grime smash.' The *Review* also pointed out, 'Although they are household names among the urban audience, they still don't have an album out, but with the arrival of a new record deal, let's hope that changes soon.'

It *was* about to change soon because All Around the World were prepared to commit real cash to making N-Dubz a success. Rich Castillo explained, 'The label took a massive risk and spent a load of money on television and decided that they would put an album out.' That was the signal for Rich to join the 'Dynamite Trio' in searching for the material they had recorded at Jumbo over the years to make sure they had enough for the first album. They were literally looking in cupboards for the old hard drives.

The album was ready for release in October 2008. Uncle B had already chosen the title of their first album a couple of years before. He wanted it to be called *Against All Odds* because he used to say that it would be against all odds if they got there in the end. His protégés, however, had other ideas. They chose *Uncle B* as the title in a personal and long-lasting tribute to their mentor.

The album had been talked of so much and so many singles had been released, videos made and played that it seemed like their debut album was also a greatest hits compilation. Six songs had already been made available and a seventh, 'Papa Can You Hear Me?', was ready to be released to coincide with the album. The idea was that the song, written as a tribute to Uncle B right after his death, should come out at the same time as the album named in his memory.

10

Building the Brand

Uncle B's ambition was to have one hit and, when he achieved it, to retire to the side of a lake where he could spend his days fishing. Plato had the same dream except he wasn't so bothered about the hit. Their children wanted fame but, more than that, they were motivated by money. Just as Dappy had said in 'Love For My Slum': they wanted to earn enough to be able to move out of the world they lived in.

When they were filmed as teenage hopefuls for Jessie Grace Mellor's documentary on the Lickle Rinsers, they were asked what their ambitions were by the time they were twenty. Dappy, being Dappy, said, 'I want to be driving a car and I want to say, "Hey girls, come inside my car."' Tulisa wanted to be famous: 'I want to get some money and get myself a nice house.' Throughout her life she has basically had that one ambition.

Her desire for money was one reason why Tulisa was so outraged by the suggestion that N-Dubz promoted violence. She told britishhiphop.co.uk, 'Basically we're not here to be all about the hood and that – we're here to make music and that's it. When you mix the two together – they don't mix and you don't make any money.'

By the time she had left her teenage years behind, Tulisa's ambition had moved on from simply being rich. Now she wanted a £2 million house and a Lamborghini sports car with a Range Rover on the side. Presumably the 4 × 4 was to ferry her children around. She has never been too specific about when she wants to start her family but it definitely seems to be part of her plan for the natural progression of her life.

On the set of *Dubplate* she was once asked what made her happy. She replied simply, 'Money makes me happy. I want to build up a bank account for my future and for my children and that makes me happy.'

Her desire for wealth moved a step further when the first N-Dubz album, *Uncle B*, was finally released on 17 November 2008. Tulisa was twenty. They seemed to have been working on it forever but when it eventually reached the record stores, it was immediately worth the long wait. In the first midweek chart it reached number four, ahead even of the acclaimed *I Am ... Sasha Fierce*, the third album from Beyoncé, which nobody could have predicted no matter how positive they were trying to be. Rich Castillo recalled, 'As soon as that happened, it just went nuts. Everyone was calling us!'

The highest official chart position was eleven but the public response was so good that the album went platinum by Christmas, signifying sales of more than 300,000. Since then sales have climbed to over 600,000. The reviews were a little mixed. Alex Macpherson of the *Guardian* noted the hard graft they had put in: 'Their talent is raw, to say the least, and you feel they are not yet sure how to use their strengths. Still, at a time when so many teenage pop stars seem to be old before their time, it is refreshing to hear an act with such messy youthfulness.'

Sam Wolfson, his counterpart on the *Observer*, was less impressed: 'N-Dubz are like So Solid Juniors – three youngsters with lyrics so tame they've been allowed to play UK secondary schools.' He did concede that it was a 'slickly produced party album rammed with massive choruses destined to be ringtones'.

More encouragingly, Michelle Adabra, who has written many articles about N-Dubz, observed for *New Nation*, '*Uncle B* is a multi-layered album filled with epic strings and harmonies, as well as grime-influenced beats ... there is something for everyone on this album.' The most interesting comments, however, were reserved for Tulisa, who was edging more and more into the spotlight. Michelle noted her 'brilliant, angelic vocals'.

Even more fulsome praise came from Joe Ward, writing on the *Subba-Cultcha* site. It was also the most prophetic: 'In female member "Tulisa" they have a genuine talent and a voice that cuts through the rest of the group lines where needed and when unleashed in "Secrets" it's easy to envisage that a career can be forged for her if things here don't take off in current guise.' 'Secrets', the first lyric Tulisa had written many years before, was her most personal song on the album and she sang it with great conviction.

The new single, however, was 'Papa Can You Hear Me?', which reached number nineteen in the charts. Not everyone liked it, with some critics complaining that the lyric was crass even if heartfelt. *Flavour* online said, 'It might give you goosebumps to listen to, but the message is clear – don't leave it too late to tell the people who love you that you feel the same.'

Usually the first single is released either at the same time as the album or a little before to maximize its promotional effect. N-Dubz had already released four singles over a two-year period before 'Papa Can You Hear Me?' became the fifth. Again the video seemed more important for the band and was released first so that it was almost an advertisement for the album. The strategy worked when it received two million hits on YouTube in three weeks. For a while it ranked just below the acceptance speech of President Obama as the most viewed.

The video is not the liveliest N-Dubz offering because of the sombre nature of the lyrics, although Tulisa does sport a pair of hoop earrings so large that even Pat Butcher from *EastEnders* would have thought twice about wearing them. She also wears a low-cut dress in her favourite shade of pink. All three are seen clutching a T-shirt with Uncle B's face on it and Dappy is filmed with his arm around his mother Zoe as he promises always to look after her.

When *Uncle B* was released, the man himself had been dead for eighteen months and his demise was not as big a story as it might have been if the album had come out a year earlier. The three young members of N-Dubz were more the focus of attention. Everyone knew Dappy from his hats and his appearance on *Never Mind the Buzzcocks* but the media were also beginning to notice Tulisa, a girl one reviewer said offered 'something for the dads' appeal.

She was, it was becoming clear, cut from a different cloth from the boys, who liked to listen to Phil Collins and Magic FM while she preferred old school garage and R & B. She dreamed of working with the great American producers like Timbaland. He was associated with much of the vibrant talent in modern American music, including Aaliyah, Jay-Z and Justin Timberlake.

Tulisa was at the heart of the next N-Dubz video, 'Strong Again', the sixth track released from *Uncle B* and the first to make it on to a *Now!* album, featuring on *Now That's What I Call Music! 72*. The song was arguably more pop than grime, with a strikingly catchy chorus and an anthemic rallying call that life can only get better. The message is unashamedly positive: Tulisa can hold her head up high because she is strong again. For the first time an N-Dubz song was upgraded from the Radio 1 B list to the A list, although a chart position high of number twenty-four did not reflect their growing popularity. Perhaps it should have been released as a single before the album came out.

The critical reaction was positive, with David Balls of *Digital Spy* observing that it 'sounds like the Black Eyed Peas just bumped into Dizzee Rascal and got on like a house on fire ... this manages to sound accessible and radio-friendly without sacrificing its all-important street cred. Expect to hear it blasted at full volume from the back of the bus very soon.'

The line about the bus was a good one because the sound of N-Dubz was everywhere in 2007, as their catchphrases and choruses became the sound of teenage ringtones up and down the country. Dappy observed, 'You've heard of us, even if you don't know it yet. Remember that boy driving you mad every morning on the No. 42 – the one playing music on his mobile at full volume? He's listening to us. So is his sister, his best mate, his best mate's older brother and his teacher.'

They filmed the video for 'Strong Again' in a big North London warehouse with a huge number of film crew and Tulisa shivering in a little black bodice top and tight black leather jeans with chains hanging from a hipster belt. Alison Jane Reid commented, 'She looks really good. It's less chavtastic and more rock chic. And she's got a fabulous cleavage and looks sexy. Her tattoos emphasize that she is a strong female character and not a pushover.'

While there is the obligatory beginning 'N-Dubz, N-Dubz, Na Na Niiiii, Ha Ha', Tulisa, with flowing blonde hair, a discreet diamond nose stud and heavy black eye make-up, commands the stage. It's her song. Having said that, it was Fazer who had the best line in the song when he raps that even his mum is famous now. It may be looking back with perfect hindsight but for the first time you could imagine Tulisa leaving the boys behind in the mainstream world where a hot, charismatic girl singer has more currency than two engaging and talented male rappers. The video, which was released on YouTube at the start of December 2008, has had six million views, which sounds impressive until you check the hits for 'Papa Can You Hear Me?', which eventually grew to more than 14 million.

While they were filming the videos and preparing for their first proper nationwide tour, they were also being followed around by their friend Zee (ZeeTVD), who filmed the day for *Behind the Scenes*.

Tulisa, Dappy and Fazer happily talk to the camera, as do the ever-swelling members of their entourage, including their newly appointed product manager, Naz. They had just one album out but already had a product manager. She was clearly doing a good job too, as the name Adidas seemed to loom large around the set. N-Dubz had already secured a deal with Adidas and they would be wearing logos on their tour in the same way that famous sportsmen do.

The film is one long promotion for N-Dubz. The entire cast of characters continually plug their name, the upcoming tour and the fact that the *Uncle B* album has gone platinum. Tulisa is the undoubted star – but not quite a diva – rehearsing in a pink hoodie and a baseball cap with her hair pulled back into a pony-tail, although she does spend a lot of time with stylists getting ready for the video shoot. The best moment is when she sings freestyle to the camera, 'My name is Tulizza and I love pizza', which of course she does.

Behind the Scenes is an early demonstration of how N-Dubz were building a business. The strategy was to let fans into their world. Tulisa explained, 'We see ourselves as a brand. When people like N-Dubz, it tends to be not just because they like the music, they tend to buy into the brand as well.'

The example they were trying to follow was the Spice Girls, who in the mid-nineties had taken building a brand to an art form with 'girl power'. The music was important but so were the lyrical content, the clothes and the controversies, as well as the individual characters of the five girls. They had their own iden-tities but everything they did separately benefited the group business as a whole. The Spice Girls had what Tulisa called an 'image and vibe and a lot of character.' She observed, 'That's what it's like with N-Dubz. We are one big brand, and everyone buys into every aspect of us.'

Intriguingly, with an eye to how Tulisa's solo future might develop, Victoria Beckham has been by far the most successful Spice Girl since the group's demise. She still has a brand – the Beckhams have moved forward as a global business embracing fashion, cosmetics, lifestyle, charity, family values and football. It's a bandwagon that shows no sign of slowing down.

Tulisa wasn't a one-woman corporation yet but it is what she dreamed of becoming. The theme of female empowerment would loom larger in her strategy as her solo career beckoned, in particular with her adoption of the slogan 'The Female Boss'.

'Strong Again' is an important song not just because it was a showcase for Tulisa but also because, unusually, it was not produced exclusively by Fazer and Dappy but by Fraser T. Smith and Kane Robinson. Now best known for his work with Adele, Smith had graduated from being a pub musician to become one of the top producers in the country. He was earning a living as a session guitarist when he was introduced to the then unknown Craig David in the late nineties and became his right-hand man during the singer's most successful years. He won the Urban Music Award for Best Producer in 2008.

Crucially for N-Dubz, Smith forged a link with some of the leading names in R & B and hip-hop, including the young, charismatic rapper Tinchy Stryder, as well as Plan B and Taio Cruz. He had produced Tinchy's first solo record, 'Stryderman', and a collaboration between him and Taio called 'Take Me Back', which almost reached the top of the charts. His next record with Tinchy did reach the pinnacle and, by a stroke of good fortune, Dappy was involved.

Fraser recalled, 'It wasn't necessarily going to be Dappy on the hook. I'd worked with him on "Strong Again" and I wanted to work with him again because he's an amazing talent. "Number 1" came about from a co-writing session and it sounded so good that we thought it had to stay.'

Dappy insisted that when the record was released it was credited as Tinchy Stryder featuring N-Dubz, even though at this stage Tulisa and Fazer had nothing to do with it. It wouldn't do the band any harm at all to have a hit record while they were touring. 'Number 1' was more than a just a hit – it became the first song with that title actually to become number one, selling more than 87,000 copies in its first week and spending three weeks at the top of the charts. The track was in the top forty for eighteen weeks, which was publicity gold for N-Dubz. One of the curious aspects of the Tinchy–N-Dubz connection is that Tinchy has always been a bigger chart act but N-Dubz are arguably more popular and are headline performers wherever they appear.

Tinchy Stryder presents a superb business model on how to succeed as an urban artist, and is on his way to becoming the British equivalent of Jay-Z, the most successful rapper business-man in the world. Tinchy's nickname came from his small stature. At 5ft 1in, he is one of the very few people in music who has to look up to Dappy, who is 5ft 3in. He chose his surname after his favourite arcade game, Strider, which he used to play for hours when he was younger. His real name is Kwasi Danquah III and he was born in 1986 in Accra, the capital of Ghana. He was brought up in Bow in the East End of London and, like Dappy, initially harboured ambitions to become a professional foot-baller. He was well on his way when he joined the academy of Wimbledon FC as a fourteen-year-old. While Dappy is a lifelong supporter of Arsenal, Tinchy is a devoted Manchester United fan, a friend of former England captain Rio Ferdinand and has a private box at Old Trafford. He had to choose between foot-ball and music and chose the latter.

Tinchy was part of the Roll Deep collective formed in the early 2000s by the influential producer Wiley. The collective, which also featured Dizzee Rascal, was largely responsible for bringing the new sound of grime to a wider audience. Wiley is often referred to as the 'godfather of grime'. Like Dizzee, Tinchy found greater fame as a solo artist.

His breakthrough coincided with meeting two young entre-preneurs, a local MP's son called Archie Lamb and his friend Jack Foster, in a Norwich nightclub in 2006. Together they started to market Tinchy's T-shirts under his other street name, Star in the Hood. Tinchy's first album was also called *Star in the Hood*, which was a neat way of advertising the business. From small beginnings, making £6,000 a month, they have expanded into a multi-layered business. They formed Takeover Entertainment Ltd, which is now allied to one of Jay-Z's companies, Roc Nation. Takeover also joined EMI Music Publishing to form a joint publishing company just in time for the release of 'Number 1'.

Tinchy Stryder is a business, just as N-Dubz is a business. They represent a new breed of pop stars who are looking to safeguard their financial future. They prefer investments and commercial opportunities to living a rock and roll lifestyle. In his spare time Tinchy plays a good game of golf and has even given Jay-Z and Beyoncé a lesson. Dappy and Fazer loved to go fishing. Tulisa, who has never been a sporty type, likes to laze on the beach sunbathing.

Tulisa could bask in the glow of N-Dubz's first number one even if she wasn't really featured in it. She did show up to film a video in which she played a gangster's chick who was after Tinchy but, in the end, a more straightforward film shot in the studio was released. Tulisa was glimpsed only twice during the whole song and you missed her if you blinked.

The next N-Dubz video was more interesting because, for the first time, they had a proper storyline and were filmed on location at a grand country house in Hertfordshire. The track 'Wouldn't You' is about a girl asking her boyfriend if he would like to have her all to himself – an exclusive relationship with neither party straying.

In the video Dappy, unconvincingly and for no apparent reason, plays a mechanic. Clutching a large wrench and smeared with grease, he is exchanging meaningful glances with a beautiful girl dressed as if she were on her way to a cocktail party on the French Riviera. Tulisa, with big blonde hair and a short dress, is in the bedroom of the house with a handsome young man. He has to leave when her real boyfriend arrives at the house. The track only reached number sixty-four in the chart, proving that seven singles from one album were too many.

Despite that poor showing, the N-Dubz business model was clearly working. The strategy was simple: do everything yourself, including most of the writing and producing, and watch the money come in. Their first royalty cheque for publishing was £250,000.

11

More Drama

Tulisa, wearing large hoop earrings with her hair pulled back from her face, leaned forward to explain what mattered to her. She wanted 'to be all that I can be.' Her short, conspiratorial piece to camera was part of an advertisement for a project called 'Spit It Out' that *Dubplate Drama* was running in conjunction with the children's charity ChildLine. The idea was to encourage young people to film themselves 'spitting' original thoughts and lyrics on issues that mattered to them and upload their efforts onto *Dubplate*'s MySpace page.

The serious purpose was to promote the message that whatever matters to young people also matters to ChildLine and that talking about your problems is the best way to solve them. Tulisa was very supportive of ChildLine and its association with *Dubplate Drama* and urged young people to call the number if they faced any of the issues and problems raised in the programme.

ChildLine is a service launched by the television personality Esther Rantzen in 1986 to provide 24-hour counselling for children and young people to discuss their problems. As part of the NSPCC, it has advised and helped more than 2.6 million children since it began, with more than 400,000 ringing because of bullying.

In her contribution to 'Spit it Out', Tulisa said, 'It's good for me to take time out and look in the mirror and find out the little things I could do to change, for the better, for myself and for the people around me.' She could have been more forthcoming about some of the relevant things that had affected her in the past and still mattered so much – the problems faced by youngsters acting as primary carers for a parent or the agony of being the victim of bullying at school.

Dappy's promotional advertisement was also a little bland – he just wanted to go into the studio every day and make hits. Fazer spoke of his need to be creative at all times so that he could make positive music.

The winning entry in the competition was an inspiring piece written and spoken by a young black teenager calling himself 'mph' entitled 'Life Matters to Me' in which he urged people to give respect so that they would get it back. His piece was firmly against gang culture and gun talk.

Uncle B, for one, would have been pleased that N-Dubz were involved in good causes. He wanted young people to be off the streets and finding something worthwhile to do with their lives. It wasn't the first time his protégés had become involved in important issues. The previous year they had all popped back to Haverstock School to perform at a free concert to raise awareness about gun crime. Tinchy Stryder's old collective, the Roll Deep Crew, were also on the bill, which sought to inspire and educate young people in Camden.

The organizer, Folora Duang, who founded a local initiative called True Colours, said, 'It was amazing to get the support from the guest speakers and music artists like N-Dubz. In Camden we haven't quite reached an epidemic with gun crime yet so we want to tackle it before it becomes a massive issue. I believe that prevention is better than a cure and putting on positive events for youngsters in the local community is something that I've always wanted to do. It's nice to work with these teenagers and show them crime can destroy families.'

The real-ife problems encountered by Tulisa were as serious as those faced by the characters in the next series of *Dubplate Drama*. She had been promoted from a minor player to a starring role. Her part was a grim one. Her character Laurissa, who has a serious coke problem, was now the main competition for Dionne, still played by MC Shystie. Laurissa is the lead singer of a group called The Fam and puts on a brave, smiling face for their fans but behind that charade she is trapped in an abusive relationship with Prangers, the former manager of her dead lover, Bones.

At the end of series two, it seemed that Prangers was intent on making a move on Laurissa and two years down the line, in series three, they are a couple. Tulisa explained, 'It's pretty sticky for Laurissa.' He beats her and threatens her and Tulisa's character clearly doesn't have the strength to leave him. She accepts, it seems, that this is her life and there is nothing she can do about it.

Ricci Harnett, who played her horrible boyfriend, had the difficult task of making Prangers a believable character rather than a cardboard villain. He had the menace of one of the thuggish Mitchell brothers from *EastEnders*. He explained his role: 'Half the challenge is to try and make him endearing to the public, which is not all that easy when you're beating women up.'

On screen there was real chemistry between them. Tulisa observed that Ricci was really easy to work with but that 'when he goes for me he's scary.' Ricci, however, put things in perspective: 'Then I go and put the kettle on and we have a nice cup of tea.'

Tulisa's acting had matured and improved since her first tentative steps with an onion. She was much more confident – not just as an actress but as a person. The scenes in which she threatens to jump from a multi-storey car park are arguably the most memorable in the whole of *Dubplate*.

The series got under way with a proper premiere at the Prince Charles Cinema in Leicester Square. It was not as well received as its earlier, less polished predecessors, however. Perhaps the new 50-minute episode length didn't suit the original concept as well as the more immediate and rapid, shorter segments of the first two series.

Tulisa confided that the times filming *Dubplate* were among the happiest she'd had so far that year. The show afforded her good training in the art of acting. It could not, however, help her with the drama involving her boyfriend in real life.

At the age of nineteen Tulisa became engaged to a North London fitness instructor and club DJ called Adam Bailey. His daytime profession was somewhat ironic, considering Tulisa's aversion to working out. Like Fazer, he had been a brilliant runner as a boy, winning lots of cups for the family mantelpiece. Tulisa had dated Adam briefly when she was younger and they got back together in a two-year relationship that she did her best to keep out of the public eye. Their engagement was a whim one wine-fuelled evening but Tulisa did wear his diamond ring, which won many admiring glances.

In the sleeve notes to *Uncle B* she gives him a glowing name check, clearly expecting a long-term relationship, and says, 'I love you baby. I'm always here for you.' She would soon need to make good her promise in circumstances she could never have predicted.

Caught up as they were in their glamorous and exciting new world, you could be forgiven for thinking that Tulisa, Dappy and Fazer had left the street behind. But the truth was that they had yet to move on completely. A night of high drama on the Finchley Road ended up with Tulisa getting arrested and Adam facing very serious charges in court.

Tulisa feared for her life. She would later claim that she

thought she would be shot when violence flared between Bailey and a gang of hoodies outside a convenience store near the Finchley Road Tube station. It was like something out of *Dubplate Drama* but this was all too real. The trouble in the early hours of a September morning in 2008 couldn't have come at a worse time, with the debut album finally ready for release a couple of months later.

All the advertising and marketing for N-Dubz was about to kick in, timed to coincide with the video release of 'Papa Can You Hear Me?' in October. Publicity about guns, knives and baseball bats was the last thing the group needed after they had been so careful to promote a non-violent image since the controversy created by 'Love For My Slum'. They said they wanted granddads and nans to listen to their music, but what would they make of Tulisa, a beautiful young woman of twenty, being caught up in a fracas that ended with a man found stabbed in the abdomen? The injured man, Mark Nagle, spent two weeks in hospital after emergency surgery.

Fortunately, on the night itself Tulisa had the presence of mind to call Jonathan Shalit and any fallout was well managed. Incredibly, the arrests of Tulisa and Bailey never even made the papers at the time. That would certainly not happen today when she is a far bigger star.

Tulisa has never talked about what happened except when she was called to give evidence at the trial at Blackfriars Crown Court in December 2009. There she said she was celebrating her boyfriend's twenty-fourth birthday with a few friends, including Dappy and FeFe, also known as the rapper Fearless. They stopped off at the store, when apparently words were exchanged between the men and several youths. The jury were told that Bailey returned to the shop later in his silver VW Polo to stock up with more alcohol. Tulisa and the others were following behind in another car.

When she arrived, there seemed to be a commotion involving as many as twenty young men, so Tulisa jumped out of her car to see if Adam was all right. The next thing she knew, some of the boys had started walking towards her in a menacing way. She told the jury how the drama unfolded: 'All I heard was "Where's the 'ting? Buss it", which I know from 50 Cents' songs means, "Where's the gun? Shoot it." When I heard that I thought, "Oh my God, he's got a gun." I turned my attention back to the car and ran back.

'There was one of them in particular. His body movement was almost like an animal, swaying from side to side. He picked up a dark object and put it down his trousers and he moved towards me.'

At that moment she spotted Bailey driving towards them in his car and they turned their attention on him. She continued, 'I saw one of them take an object and throw something at the vehicle. I saw his car flip out of control. It did a full tumble and ended up on its side. I thought, "Oh my God, he's dead." I was screaming hysterically. I screamed at Dappy and FeFe, "Somebody help him." They were just staring. I thought, "If he's not dead, they are going to jump on him and they are going to kill him."

'Adam had got out of his car and he's got a bat in his hand and another hand on his head, looking around disorientated, swinging the bat. He was just swinging at anyone, trying to get a metre space away from everybody to protect himself. I shouted at Dappy to wind down the windows and I screamed, "Get in the car! Get in the car!"' When Bailey jumped in, she sped off, leaving his Polo upturned by the kerb.

The scary events were just the start of an ordeal that cast a shadow over Tulisa's life for almost all of 2009 until the case came to court. Some time after she had driven off, Mark Nagle was found slumped in the central reservation by people living nearby.

The court heard that the following day Tulisa accompanied Adam, who lived in Cricklewood, when he handed himself in to Holborn Police Station, where they were both arrested. No further action was taken against Tulisa but her boyfriend was charged with wounding with intent and dangerous driving. He was not accused of using the knife himself but was charged under 'joint enterprise' laws, which would view him as guilty for being involved in the incident that led to the stabbing. He pleaded not guilty.

The prosecution's version of the evening differed wildly from that of the defence. Prosecuting counsel Mark Ward explained their account of what happened to Mr Nagle: 'He says he was in a shop in the Finchley Road. He hears a bang outside. He steps outside and sees the car overturned. He sees two men emerge from that car and he sees one of them holding a baseball bat.

'He sees another car pull up and two men emerge from that car – one of them has a knife. The four men started running towards him. He heard someone shouting, "He was with them." He is hit on the ankle with the baseball bat and a moment later, while he is running away, he is stabbed in the abdomen.'

The prosecution noted that Bailey had told police he had a baseball bat in his car – something that Tulisa's evidence confirmed. Mr Ward maintained that the defence were trying to 'conjure up' a second man with a baseball bat when the only person who had one was Bailey. He added that to suggest another group 'entirely unconcerned' with the events involving Bailey was responsible for the attack on Mr Nagle was 'just an extraordinary coincidence'.

The defence maintained that it was a clear case of mistaken identity. The victim, Mr Nagle, hadn't been involved in any altercation involving Bailey. Richard Horwell, QC, explained, 'The men involved in the first incident, namely Dappy and Bailey, were not involved in the attack on Mr Nagle. And why Mr Nagle? No one suggests he had anything to do with the first or second incident, so why should Adam Bailey become involved in an attack against him? There is no motive at all.'

It was a nerve-racking time while the jury retired to consider their verdict. The charges, involving a knife crime, were extremely serious. Just four hours later they were back with a not guilty verdict on both charges, which had been reached unanimously. Tulisa was not in court to hear the outcome, although one can imagine her chewing her fingernails until she heard the news.

Her evidence had been the most dramatic thing about the whole affair. The slightly tricky question for her to answer had been why she had called her manager rather than the police. She explained to the court, 'My life is run by other people. Every move I make is controlled by somebody else. Everything gets done for me and my job is just to work.' She has never mentioned the matter again.

She had kept her promise and stood by Bailey even though by the time of the court case they weren't together any more. They had split in the summer, though not because of the impending trial. The online rumours were that she had dumped Adam because she was too famous for him. She strongly denied this. She also had to deny more gossip that it was because she had cheated on him. Much more likely was that they had drifted apart.

She was still wearing his ring in June 2009 and he was spotted at her twenty-first birthday party in July at a West End restaurant. Tulisa was pictured, all smiles, with a number of star guests, including the handsome rapper Mr Hudson and various members of the Sugababes. Many photographs of the evening were posted online but there was no sign of a happy snap of her and Adam together, which prompted online discussion as to whether he even existed. By the end of the month, however, they had definitely gone their separate ways. The newspapers suggested she wanted to concentrate on work. The *Sun* quoted a 'source' that claimed she wasn't talking to him and wanted no contact until she had made up her mind about everything.

In the end, she did make up her mind – Adam was history. Intriguingly, she wrote a song called 'Comfortable', which would feature on the second N-Dubz album. The speculation was that it was about Adam, although Tulisa hasn't confirmed this. She observed, 'It's about growing apart and realizing you've become different people.'

'Comfortable' is one of the softer N-Dubz tracks. It showcases Tulisa's maturing vocal style; it's a chance to hear her properly without the boys butting in. She harks back to the time when she was sixteen, waiting every Saturday to be picked up by her boyfriend, who was always late. Jump five years and she is still waiting for him. The timeline certainly fits Adam, although the lyric that notes his heart is full of hate is not the most flattering if it is meant to be him. As Tulisa said, it's about realizing as you grow up that nobody and nothing stays the same forever but, at the same time, not wanting to lose your best friend. If it was Adam, then she did lose him. In fact, when Tulisa came to talk of her love life in the book *Against All Odds*, she doesn't even name him.

Tulisa wasn't the only member of N-Dubz with a cloud over her head in 2009. Dappy was keeping his fingers crossed that news of his conviction for assault wouldn't leak out. Just before the turn of the year he was up before magistrates in Chelmsford, where he pleaded guilty to two counts of assault.

He had picked up a female fan during a night out in Chelmsford and gone back with her to the hostel where she was staying. Dappy reportedly got into an argument with another woman who was also living there. Things apparently escalated, resulting in the first woman slapping him and spitting at him. In retaliation he showered the girl and her friend with a hail of spit. The two women called the police, which resulted in the court appearance.

Dappy pleaded guilty under his real name, Costadinos Contostavlos. For each count he received four weeks in jail, suspended for twelve months, to run concurrently, and one hundred hours' community service. He was also ordered to pay £50 compensation and £300 costs. All in all, he was far from let off and the conviction would prove troublesome in the future when he applied for a visa to enter the US. He somehow managed to keep his crime a secret for nine months – perhaps because he was charged under his real name and took off his Dappy hat in court.

This was not the sort of publicity N-Dubz needed before embarking on their *Uncle B* tour, which would take them all over the country. The last thing they wanted was worried parents banning their children from going to the concert.

Perhaps it was just as well then that Dappy returned for a second round of *Never Mind the Buzzcocks*, and it went much better than the first. He told Simon Amstell, 'Everything you say to me is very sarcastic', which it was. He must have been highly relieved that Amstell knew nothing about his court appearance. He was sitting next to Dermot O'Leary, the host of *The X Factor*, but unusually Dappy wasn't rude or outspoken about the talent show; instead they discovered they shared a love of fishing.

The signs were there, however, that without the steadying hand of Uncle B, Dappy might be reverting to the bad old days of 'naughtiness'. Along with Fazer and DJ Maze, he had to be escorted off a plane from Edinburgh when it landed in London in February 2009. They had apparently been far too boisterous on board, reportedly swearing at kids, being foul and threatening passengers. A 'source' told the *Sun* that cabin crew called ahead so that police were waiting for the flight. Tulisa wasn't involved but the three boys were held for more than an hour after they landed. A statement from the band said, 'Fazer apologized on the plane at the end of the flight. They're sorry if their high spirits offended anyone.'

Perhaps becoming a dad would calm Dappy down. He was a father for the first time in January 2009 when his eighteen-year-old girlfriend Kaye Vassell gave birth to a son called Gino. They'd met in the summer of 2007 after she'd obtained his phone number from a mutual friend. Dappy himself was only twenty-one and showed no sign of settling down, although he has always spoken very fondly of his son and, despite his wayward image, likes nothing better than spending an evening with Gino and his 'babymum'.

Tulisa was at the birth, an experience that didn't make her feel broody. While Dappy was trying to take pictures on his mobile phone, she was watching the head coming out and recalled, 'I nearly had a heart attack.' Afterwards she made it clear: 'I officially don't want kids till I'm about thirty-five and I have no use for what's down below whatsoever.'

The newspapers finally put Dappy under the spotlight in September 2009, a couple of weeks before the prestigious MOBO Awards. The first controversy didn't concern his conviction. Instead he had to apologize for making a video the previous year with Face Killa for the track 'Babylon Fi Get Shot'. This was much more serious than the overblown criticism of 'Love For My Slum' because the track was clearly promoting extreme violence and anti-police views.

Dappy explained: 'I was young and dumb, and I've grown up a lot since then. I'm an adult now and turned my back on those views a long time ago as they are wrong. Doing the job I do now has made me realize you don't have to hate the police and be negative about them. N-Dubz are all about positivity and neither myself nor the band would ever air views like these lyrics in our music today.'

The new, responsible Dappy tried to put this rash of bad publicity behind him by joining Fazer and Tulisa to back a new scheme launched by the Schools Secretary Ed Balls. The idea was to urge schools to make a major effort to keep music on the curriculum. Mr Balls said, 'I want to create a generation of talented performers who can sing, dance, play instruments and fly the flag for Great Britain.'

Ironically, none of the members of N-Dubz relied on their schooling for their musical education. Fazer and Dappy 'trained' at Jumbo Studios, while Tulisa listened to her mum sing in the kitchen and joined in. That didn't stop them from endorsing the campaign. Dappy explained, 'We wrote a song today. In four months' time thousands of people are going to be listening to it and singing along to it. How about that? If you put your mind to it you can do anything you want ... Put your mind to it brother, sister.'

Mr Balls was proving to be an unlikely ally to N-Dubz. Their relationship was further enhanced when they supported Anti-Bullying Week, which was due to begin on 16 November 2009. The slogan that year was 'Stay Safe in Cyberspace'. This was a cause that was already close to Tulisa's heart.

Tulisa had appeared earlier in the year on *Newsbeat* to draw attention to this unwelcome by-product of online social networking. She was promoting a scheme to stop cyberbullying called CyberMentors. Young people who found it difficult to talk to their parents and teachers about bullying were being encouraged to talk to a CyberMentor through a new social networking site, www.cybermentors.org.uk.

Tulisa said she still suffered from cyberbullying herself because she was a celebrity, but the problems she'd faced as a young girl both at home and at school had toughened her up: 'Luckily for me, considering my character, I don't take too much notice of it and it doesn't bother me at all, but there are people out there that, you know, are a lot more sensitive than me and take these things to heart.'

When she first heard the term 'cyberbullying' she thought it was all a 'bit silly' until she attended a launch by the Beatbullying charity at which the names of twenty young people who had been affected were read out. They had all killed themselves. 'I was like "wow". I really did not realize how serious this situation is, so I think it's a very deep issue that needs to be taken notice of.'

One of the problems of bullying in general and cyberbullying in particular is that it affects people in different ways – something minor to one child may be major to the next. When she was still a virgin Tulisa had to face untrue rumours at school about her sleeping with boys. She explained, 'You get kids going to school and people messaging rumours about them and everyone in the school finding out, and to them it's a joke but when that person goes into school the next day their whole life could be falling apart at the age of thirteen.'

Tulisa had harsh words for the 'sad people' who are bullies: 'They've got a lot of hate and anger within themselves and rather than taking it out on a punch bag, they're taking it out on other innocent people.'

A government-backed survey had revealed that the problem was even worse than they thought. The study by the National Centre for Social Research revealed that half of all fourteen-year-olds are the victims of bullying. Cyberbullying in particular was spiralling out of control and was as common as name-calling among teenagers. Tulisa would have nodded in agreement at the research conclusion that girls were more likely to be excluded from friendship groups and become the victims of bullying – just the things that made the adolescent Tula feel so isolated.

Bullying has become a bit of a cause célèbre in the celebrity world, especially after Kate Middleton was revealed to have been a victim at school. The suspicion that bullying is just a fashionable bandwagon is challenged by the figures that shocked Tulisa: more than a million children are bullied every week and up to twenty young people commit suicide each year as a result.

N-Dubz released an anti-bullying single to back the campaign entitled 'R U Cyber Safe?'. Ed Balls was delighted: 'N-Dubz are great ambassadors for CyberMentors ... This shows once again that if all young people come together and show their solidarity against bullies, we can make bullying a thing of the past.'

The catchphrase for the 'Stay Safe in Cyberspace' campaign was 'laugh at it and you're part of it'. Nobody was laughing at the behaviour of Dappy after he made a guest appearance on the Chris Moyles breakfast show on Radio 1. Chris has always enjoyed a good relationship with N-Dubz, and with Dappy in particular, but even he was shocked by what happened.

As usual, listeners were invited to text in comments or

questions for the guests. One young woman, Chloe Moody, a single mum aged twenty-two, was on her way to work with her mother when she texted some unflattering opinions of N-Dubz, suggesting they were 'losers'. She singled out Dappy as being 'vile' and 'a little boy with a silly hat'.

Chloe was taken aback the next day when she missed two calls from a number she didn't recognize and sent a text asking who it was. It was Dappy, who replied, 'Your gonna die. U sent a very bad msg towards Ndubz on The Chris Moyles Show yesterday Morning and for that reason u will never be left alone!!If u say sorry I will leave u alone u ****.'

To begin with, Chloe didn't really think it was Dappy: 'I didn't think it would be him because I seriously didn't think he'd be bothered.'

She continued to receive texts: 'U dum f****** ***head u can call me names over the radio but when I call u direct u chicken out u punk!nana f****** niii, Dappy.'

Eventually Chloe answered his call but refused to apologize. She recalled, 'He was just ranting, saying, "Why are you saying this about me?" If I had had a number one single and got a message from a nobody to a radio station I would not be too concerned. It obviously hit a nerve.'

Dappy's behaviour definitely hit a nerve with N-Dubz's new best friend Mr Balls who said, 'The text message was completely unacceptable ... I know that many artists work with Beatbullying because they genuinely want to use their influence with young people to campaign against bullying. But that starts with ensuring their own behaviour sets the right example.' Beatbullying was equally quick to condemn Dappy's threatening message and announced they had no further plans to work with the band.

In a statement Dappy said, 'I called her in the heat of the moment when I was angry, but that is no excuse for my behaviour. I'm genuinely sorry. I'd also like to send my sincerest apologies to Radio 1.'

Just how Dappy got hold of Chloe's number has never been

properly explained. A BBC spokeswoman suggested that he had taken down the number from the production team's text console in the studio. Chris Moyles admitted that he felt let down by the incident. He told the *Sun*, 'I've supported him and said, "Do you know what, N-Dubz aren't just a bunch of dippy chavs, they're really good." So for him to go and do something like that is a bit rubbish.'

Not everyone joined in the condemnation of Dappy. In the *Independent on Sunday*, Sophie Heawood wondered why celebrities are supposed to have a thick skin: 'Although Dappy's response went too far and was creepy and disturbing, there is something touching in a man who has sold a million records and has legions of adoring fans actually caring about one woman not liking him. Part of me wants to applaud him for giving a toss.'

Tulisa made no comment about Dappy's behaviour.

12

Feeling Crap

Tulisa couldn't stand the sight of the boys any more. It seemed that they had lived in each other's pockets for nine long years and their first nationwide tour was proving to be a step too far. When they'd begun at the Wulfrun Hall in Wolverhampton on 27 March 2009, it had all seemed so exciting. They opened the show with three hits in a row – 'I Swear', 'You Better Not Waste My Time' and 'Feva Las Vegas'. Tulisa wore figure-hugging pink leopard-print leggings and a sheer top before changing into a blue mini dress. Dappy wore a selection of chullos. The highlight for her fans was a solo spot halfway through the show when the boys left the stage while she sang a soulful version of the 1997 Natalie Imbruglia hit 'Torn', which she found 'nerve-racking'. The rest of the show was like one big school party with the audience singing every word of each song.

The set ended with 'Ouch', 'Papa Can Your Hear Me?' and the number one, 'Number 1', with Tinchy Stryder himself joining them. Tinchy was at most of the twenty-three dates all over the country and also sang with them on 'Defeat You'. When he wasn't there, Chipmunk, another rising star of hip-hop, stepped in. Ipswich was a lucky venue because the audience there had both young stars joining N-Dubz on stage for the finale of 'Number 1'.

But afterwards there was the bleak prospect of the tour bus. Tulisa hated it. Dappy and Fazer always seemed to be travelling with a gang of mates, while Tulisa would be the only girl and trying to ignore their high spirits. She sat right at the front with her headphones firmly in place, listening to her favourite Kate Nash album or reading the latest Martina Cole novel. Dappy confessed, 'We try to stay as far away from her as possible. We read that The Killers had to travel separately to their shows, but we are probably a lot worse than them.' The problem was that Tulisa was growing up and the boys, it seemed, were not. When they were much younger, Tulisa was a girl who could be one of the boys. Now that she was nearly twenty-one, she was a young woman who found their boisterous antics tiresome.

She explained, 'We hate each other in the way you would hate your little brother if he went into your room, read your diary and broadcast it around school. We say some terrible things to each other, but I guess we can get away with it because we are family ... People find it funny but we do literally go home and rip each other's heads off'.

The solution in the short term was that Tulisa was driven to gigs separately. She much preferred it. She could relax, listening to her iPod, snuggle into her pink car pillow for one of her daily power naps or just enjoy a chat session with her friends on her BlackBerry, the one thing she would feel lost without.

Tulisa's growing reputation for being a feisty girl was enhanced during the tour. She was also not above throwing the odd tantrum. It didn't help that she felt tired and rundown most of the time. The boys would fill up the tour bus with junk food and she did her best to avoid it because her diet had been so poor in the past.

She once described what she ate: 'Anything I want, that is my diet.' Her favourite breakfast for a while was spaghetti on toast, although if she didn't have time for that she would grab a sausage roll or a slice of cold pizza. Dinner would be pizza or an Indian, although, if she was staying in, she quite enjoyed cooking. And she would wash it all down with Lucozade or Ribena. Even Dappy, who could just about manage making beans on toast, was moved to say, 'You love your junk food, Tulisa.'

For the first time, however, she ate less pizza and fried chicken, choosing instead to travel with Tupperware containers filled with salad and some of her mother's home cooking. She recognized that she needed to do something about her health by drinking more herbal tea and less Red Bull. She also needed to start taking vitamins. If she didn't look after herself more, she was in danger of suffering from burn-out, an all too common condition among pop stars living out of a suitcase.

While the constant bickering with the boys, in particular with her cousin Dappy, might seem amusing to some, it did have its serious side. She revealed to the Scottish *Daily Record* that one of their selling points as a band was that they were different people but it was those differences that made them argue: 'You could say the thing that makes us a good band is the same thing that might break us up.'

This was April 2009 and the first time that anyone had mentioned that N-Dubz might not survive. So far it had been all about succeeding, pushing on to get a hit record. *Uncle B* was a huge success and the tour was a sell-out even if they weren't headlining at the O2 in London just yet. While Dappy declared that N-Dubz would never split up, the band also let slip that they would make at least another three albums. That turned out to be the exact number before solo projects took over. It was all strangely prophetic.

Already Tulisa only had to scan the magazine racks to see how she might prosper as a solo artist. If it wasn't the perfect white smile of Beyoncé shining on the front covers, then it was the similarly glossy and elegant Cheryl Cole. That same April, Cheryl was voted the world's sexiest woman by *FHM* magazine. She had just won a BRIT Award and mentored Alexandra Burke to win the latest series of *The X Factor*. Tulisa's first chance of a big solo cheque came in August 2009 when *Playboy* offered her £250,000 to pose nude. She turned them down, although the mere fact that she was asked was good publicity.

The *Uncle B* tour had other dramas besides the constant arguing. They had to postpone three shows in Norwich, Ipswich and Sheffield when Dappy went temporarily deaf. He was found to be suffering from 'acute noise trauma'. Later, when he was asked what the one essential item he liked to take on tour was, he replied, 'Earplugs.' The situation is quite serious for Dappy because he now suffers from ongoing tinnitus, almost certainly a result of having his headphones turned up too loudly for too long. Kaye Vassell revealed, 'He was in huge amounts of pain and was told to be really careful if he doesn't want to go deaf.'

Kaye also said that Dappy had trouble sleeping because of the constant ringing in his ears and would always make sure there was some background noise to distract him. Sometimes he would leave the shower on all night in the en suite, as the sound of running water helped, or he would place an old fan with a noisy motor next to the bed and keep that on all night. Such measures may have helped Dappy sleep but they didn't help Kaye.

Some controversy helped keep the publicity bubbling away. Dappy apparently fell out with Tinchy and they 'almost' came to blows. Reports suggested that they had a series of rows about who deserved the credit for 'Number 1'. Dappy apparently thought that Tinchy was unfairly grabbing all the plaudits for himself, which may or may not have been true.

Any supposed animosity was missing during the highlight of the tour – a two-night stint at the Shepherd's Bush Empire in London. It was their home town show and even attracted the attention of *The Times*, which also noticed the party atmosphere: 'Every song is greeted with the sort of hysterical screams once reserved for boy bands and now usually aimed at American R & B stars.' The reviewer, Lisa Verrico, compared Tuilisa's 'interludes' with Lauryn Hill, the lead singer of The Fugees, who won a hatful of Grammies as a solo artist in the late 1990s. Overall she praised N-Dubz for a mix of pop, hip-hop, grime and R & B that was 'unusually melodic'.

The lowlight of the tour was when they got together for a cup of tea in one of their hotel rooms the morning after a gig. Dappy looked inside the kettle to see if there was enough water in it for a cuppa and saw a used condom lying there. Tulisa laughed, 'If he hadn't lifted the lid up, these two would have been having sperm tea for breakfast!'

The tour ended at the O2 in Sheffield on 29 April, and Tulisa flew out the next day to rest and recharge her batteries at her grandparents' villa. She was planning to enjoy some sun and indulge in Yaya's famous home cooking, which she adored so much, but she was unable to do either from her hospital bed in Penteli on the outskirts of Athens.

She had fainted on the flight out and needed some medical attention. As a precaution when she landed, she was transferred to hospital to undergo tests. Jonathan Shalit confirmed that she had been taken ill on the flight. He said, 'Her bandmates are all very worried about her. They've just completed a massive nationwide tour. We've no idea how she got ill but the nature of being a singer is that you meet and shake hands with a huge amount of people.'

Swine flu was so much in the news at the time that anyone feeling poorly with flu-like symptoms was suspected of having the disease. The *Sun* carried a dramatic picture of Tulisa lying in her hospital bed, wearing a green mask to prevent her breathing on anyone. A source told the paper that she was 'very poorly indeed ... It is a terrifying time.' An official spokesman was less dramatic: 'We are hopeful Tulisa will be given the all-clear and will be well enough to leave hospital in the next couple of days.'

Fazer's mum, Elaine, saw the story and rang her son to tell him that Tulisa had swine flu while he was sunning himself on a beach in Malaga. He couldn't believe his ears and had to call Tulisa in Greece to find out what was happening.

If Tulisa had been unlucky enough to contract the disease, then it was very serious and potentially fatal. Fortunately, the tests proved negative, although she was kept in isolation at the hospital for five days, which wasn't much of a holiday.

Afterwards Tulisa suspected that she had normal flu coupled with exhaustion after the tiring schedule of the tour – twenty-one official dates in thirty-three days. She explained, 'As soon as I got on the plane ... I passed out and had difficulty breathing. Because I was on a plane, and there was a swine flu scare, people obviously started panicking and they straight away thought I'd got it.'

The panic frightened her. She told the *Daily Record*, 'I didn't really know much about the disease, just that people had died from it, and I literally flipped out. I didn't even think there was a cure so I was actually thinking I could die. Being in hospital was very scary. Everyone had masks on and I had to wear one myself. I literally shit my pants!'

After she was finally discharged, she had only four days to relax before she had to fly back for Radio 1's Big Weekend in Swindon.

13

The Rap Sheet

Tulisa wore a shocking pink dress on the red carpet outside the SECC in Glasgow, where the MOBO Awards were being held. It may have seemed a good idea at the time but she failed to check what the boys were wearing and they appeared to have raided the tartan shop for the night. Dappy, in particular, was a vision of Scottishness. They all clashed horribly, which was not the best start for what promised to be the biggest night of their career so far.

Just two years after their breakthrough at the 2007 awards, they were nominated in three of the biggest categories: Best Album for *Uncle B*, up against Tinchy Stryder, Kanye West and Beyoncé; Best UK Act, with Mr Hudson, Chipmunk and Dizzee Rascal among the opposition; and Best Song, in which they had two nominations for 'Strong Again' and 'Number 1' with Tinchy Stryder.

Dappy was in great form on the red carpet, telling the crowd how 'we'd be nuffin' without you lot. I remember the day when I never had nuffin' in my fridge.' It was his theme for the night. When they won the award for Best Album, he told the crowd, 'I remember the day we never had a pot to piddle in, you get me, and now we're here among all these great artists.' Tulisa, less dramatically, said, 'I really want to say a massive thank you to Uncle B, the man who the album is named after. Rest in peace, Uncle B.'

When they picked up their second award for Best UK Act, she remembered to thank the fans. Fazer thanked his mum, dad and two younger brothers, Lewis and Dean. He shouted he was 'over the moon' as he came off stage. In comparison with the other two, it was unusual to see Fazer so thrilled. He had always been the least extrovert of the trio, happiest in the studio developing the sound of N-Dubz rather than in public promoting the band's image.

One of the give-aways at these awards ceremonies that a particular act is going to win is that they perform at the show. N-Dubz did three numbers, beginning with 'Papa Can You Hear Me?' before moving on to their new single 'I Need You', and finishing with 'Strong Again'. Tulisa admits to being nervous before she goes on stage, worried that she is going to forget the words. Sometimes she has a small glass of wine or champagne to help calm her down.

She couldn't finish the bottle after their performance because she had to perform again as part of the big last number at the ceremony. She was leading a Band Aid-style collective called the Young Soul Rebels in performing a version of The Killers' most famous track, 'All These Things That I've Done', which they had renamed 'I Got Soul' after the chorus. The song had been one of the hits of the Live Aid concert in Hyde Park in the summer of 2005. Young Soul Rebels was an unlikely mix of some of the most popular chart acts, including N-Dubz, Pixie Lott, Tinchy Stryder and Chipmunk, who had been brought together under the umbrella of the War Child charity.

The idea for the project had taken shape at an after party honouring War Child at the BRIT Awards in February. Coldplay, U2 and Take That joined The Killers on stage for a celebratory sing-along in which they chanted the chorus for the benefit of 2,000 guests. The next day, Bono told Radio 1, 'That chant, "I've got soul, but I'm not a soldier", has a whole new meaning when there is a War Child banner behind your head.'

War Child, founded in 1993, is a children's charity working in some of the most dangerous war zones in the world, including Afghanistan and Iraq and the strife-torn countries of Africa, such as Uganda and the Democratic Republic of Congo. The aim is to help children caught up, exploited and injured in these international conflicts, especially with the inevitable problems of poverty and lack of food that wars bring. The charity had already received much mainstream publicity from the support of long-established stars like Sir Paul McCartney and Sir Elton John, so this was an opportunity to raise awareness among a younger generation.

Tulisa had heard little of the charity before N-Dubz were asked to become involved. She soon appreciated the important nature of its work and gave a promotional interview in which she urged people, 'Just for one day take time out and really put yourself in the shoes of those young children and realize, as well, how privileged you are to have what you have and, you know, you should really be giving back since you've been so lucky.'

The collective spent the day recording the song at the Metropolis Studios in Chiswick with Fraser T. Smith in charge of production, renewing his link with Tinchy and N-Dubz. The video was simply a film of the recording, so there were lots of shots of pop stars wearing headphones, mixed with some more thought-provoking film of the children they were seeking to help.

Pixie Lott sang the opening verse but she couldn't attend the MOBOs, so Tulisa took over her part on the big night when the song reached a worldwide audience. Everyone took it seriously, turning up to a special rehearsal day at the Shepherd's Bush Empire. Tulisa enthused, 'It sounded bangin'.'

The charity was given a special BeMOBO award for its worldwide contribution to broadening the understanding of such a significant problem, before Tulisa led out the other 'rebels' for a good-natured and rousing rendition of the song, which closed the show. She wore a silver mini skirt and a black top that, combined with her blonde ringlets and bright red lipstick, made her stand out centre stage. Dappy and Fazer were there, dancing around, as was Chipmunk, who had become a close friend of Tulisa and had been working with N-Dubz on the new album.

At the time Chipmunk was the boy wonder of British grime, winning the MOBO for Best Newcomer and Best Hip-Hop in 2008, the year after N-Dubz, when he was just eighteen. He was Jahmaal Fyffe, a fourteen-year-old schoolboy in Tottenham, when he started to MC. He came to the attention of Wiley, who championed his music, which led to an impressive debut on Tim Westwood's radio show. He joined up with N-Dubz to write and perform on a track on the *Uncle B* album called 'Defeat You'. He featured in the third series of *Dubplate Drama* and Dappy appeared in the video of his first single, 'Chip Diddy Chip'. Tulisa, in particular, hit it off with 'Chippy', as she called him.

There was time for N-Dubz to cause the only controversy at the event earlier in the day when they were waiting with *The X Factor* runners-up JLS for rehearsals to begin. One of them, probably Dappy, leaned in and told them, 'No miming, guys. This is the real deal.' The remark was captured by the Tannoy and overheard by at least two hundred people. Whether it was a joke or not did not concern the media, who were determined to turn it into a feud between the two groups – never a bad thing for publicity.

The alleged bad blood between the bands was missing when N-Dubz crashed Radio 1Xtra's post-award interview with JLS and there was much hugging and laughing, so perhaps there was much less to the 'feud' than met the eye. Dappy hadn't finished with them, however, and told the BBC, 'At the end of the day, they're a manufactured band. They just sing other people's songs. And they were miming.'

JLS refused to rise to the bait and had the last laugh on the night when their 'Beat Again' won Best Single ahead of both 'Strong Again' and 'Number 1'. It was the only setback for N-Dubz on a night of triumph. Tulisa thought taking the MOBOs to Scotland had been such a success that next year they should bring the Highland Games to Brixton. She did complain afterwards that she had a sore throat because she had done so much singing that day and had only drunk one glass of champagne.

Some of the gloss was taken off the MOBO victory by the news that Breakbeat had been arrested. Breakbeat was the street name of the original N-Dubz drummer, Aaron Fagan, whose energetic and skilful beats had helped turn N-Dubz into such a dynamic live band. He had featured in ZeeTVD's *Behind the Scenes* film, in which he is seen practising hard before the *Uncle B* tour.

His actual status within the band was a grey area at the time of his arrest. Jonathan Shalit said in the aftermath of the police involvement that he had personally fired Fagan three months before the MOBOs. It appears, however, that he was still with the band on the big night. Jonathan stated, 'He is not involved in the band professionally but obviously it is up to the band what they do on a personal level.'

Breakbeat was still acknowledged by both Fazer and Tulisa in the sleeve notes to *Against All Odds,* which was released in November 2009. Fazer thanks him for his 'bad boy drumz on da stage and in da stoodz.' Nobody thanks him on the 2010 album *Love.Live.Life.*

Breakbeat's arrest followed an allegation of sexual assault by two female university students at an N-Dubz gig immediately after the MOBOs. At the time it was reported that he was released without charge. Afterwards the drummer told reporters, 'When you're in the limelight people want to bring you down but the truth always comes out in the end. The truth is this whole thing is over now and it was all lies.'

Nine months later he stood trial at Glasgow Sheriff Court for sexually assaulting two girls at the John Street Union. One of the girls told the court that he had approached her after the concert and asked if she wanted to go to an after party. She was walking with her friend up a flight of stairs when he grabbed her bottom and slapped her friend's: 'He then moved round behind me and, with both arms reaching round from behind, started to grab my breasts ... he was saying that he was going to take us back to his hotel and also said that he was having me tonight. He said I was a very dirty girl and asked if I knew what he meant by that.'

The girls left after they told him they wouldn't be going to the party. On their way out they alerted a bouncer as to what had happened and the police were called. In his evidence, Breakbeat claimed the girls made up their allegation after being knocked back from the band's party. He said he was like 'honey to a swarm of bees' when it came to female fans.

He was found guilty by the judge, Sheriff Johanna Johnston, who told him, 'I do not accept your account of events and I consider that you said what you did to try to avoid responsibility for your actions.' He was placed on the sex offenders' register for six months. As he left the dock, Breakbeat shouted, 'This wasn't justice today.'

Afterwards he claimed he had been the victim of racial prejudice: 'I'm a black man and I have been tried by a white jury. It's pretty clear what happened in that court and it's the opposite of justice.' In fact, he had been convicted solely by the Sheriff as, in the Scottish legal system, no jury was required for his case.

His solicitor, Paul McBride, said he had made his comments in the heat of the moment and now 'fully withdrew those statements' when it came to sentencing three months later. He also explained, 'As a result of the conviction he's no longer with the band that he'd been with for a long period of time. He was earning up to £3,000 a week but that has now come to an abrupt end and he's now applying for state benefits.' He was given six months' probation by Sheriff Johnston, who told him that he had 'shocked' and 'upset' the young women.

While the downfall of Breakbeat was embarrassing for N-Dubz, it was just one of a growing list of crimes and misdemeanours – some real and some not. Dappy had started the ball rolling with his conviction for assault. Tulisa's boyfriend, Adam Bailey, had been charged and acquitted of assault. A month after the MOBOs, DJ Maze was arrested on suspicion of rape and common assault after an N-Dubz gig at Butlin's in Skegness.

The arrest was deeply shocking as DJ Maze, or Mazer as he was often referred to, was practically joined at the hip to N-Dubz, and had been an important member of their entourage and part of their musical set-up for years. He was even introduced properly to the world in the notes to the *Uncle B* album, where they referred to him as their 'right-hand man' and a 'tight friend' to them all. He was co-producer under his real name, Junior Edwards, on the tracks 'I Swear', 'Ouch', 'Defeat You' and 'Sex'. Unofficially he was almost the fourth member of N-Dubz and acted as DJ for their gigs. Tulisa said he was like a brother to her.

Mazer was questioned at Skegness Police Station and bailed without charge. The police later said they wanted to speak to Dappy and Fazer to see if they had witnessed any of the alleged events.

Yet again Jonathan Shalit was called into action as a spokesman for the band, strongly emphasizing that they were not suspects: 'The three members of N-Dubz were one hundred per cent not involved. The police have confirmed that no one else is being treated as suspects. N-Dubz are very responsible to their young fans and have naturally told Junior Edwards that he is to be kept well away until the charges are dropped.'

He wasn't behind the decks when they began their next tour at the Cliffs Pavilion, Southend, in late November 2009, where Twin B from BBC Radio 1Xtra took over. The *Sun* reported that N-Dubz had given Mazer the boot and added that they were finally 'binning bad news hangers-on', which was not very fair on a man who had been such an integral part of their story. Mazer had production and writing credits on four of the tracks on the second album, *Against All Odds*, but only one, 'Skit featuring Fearless', on the third, *Love.Live.Life*, which came out in November 2010. He was never charged with any offence and has continued a thriving musical career.

After Dappy, Mazer, Breakbeat and Adam Bailey had encountered problems with the police with varying outcomes, it seemed inevitable that Fazer would join the growing list, although by comparison his brush with the law was small beer. November was proving to be a bad month all round for the band when he was banned from driving for six months after being caught driving without insurance in St Albans.

Potentially more serious was a raid by the feds – as Dappy liked to call the police – on Fazer's new flat in Chelsea. Acting on a tip-off, officers from the Operation Trident team were looking for a gun that had been used in a shooting. They also searched Sensible Studios in Brewery Road, Camden, where N-Dubz had recorded a great deal of material after leaving Jumbo Studios, including the final production of 'I Swear', 'Papa Can You Hear Me?' and 'Feva Las Vegas'. Nothing was found at either location and no charges were brought against anyone. A spokesperson for N-Dubz said, 'Fazer is helping the police with their inquiries and is one hundred per cent not involved in the police investigation. The second search was nothing to do with N-Dubz, it just happened to be in the studios where they have been recording.'

The new tour had originally been planned as a series of promotional gigs for the second album but instead became the *NDubz Christmas Party* tour. A sign that they were at last reaching a more mainstream audience came when their performance at the Shepherd's Bush Empire on 10 December was reviewed in the *Independent*, which said, 'It's hard not to be impressed by N-Dubz's superstardom.' Their various controversies had kept the band's name in the paper and their more senior MOBO Awards had given them mass market credibility. The serious press were waking up to N-Dubz and the fact that their fans would sing along word for word throughout a concert, including to the new songs from *Against All Odds*.

The reviewer, Matilda Egere-Cooper, was impressed by Tulisa's 'strong' vocals and the way she played up to her 'street diva status'. Her performances on tour were feisty and sexy in equal measure: she introduced the infidelity anthem 'Ouch' with the observation that it was dedicated to 'the twat in your life'.

14

Tulisa in Love

It was time for Tulisa to go out and buy her first dream car – a white Audi A5 convertible. She could easily afford it, even though her Coutts bank account dropped by more than £31,000. She couldn't wait to show it off to her dad, who was a little concerned by how fast she was driving. She might have to wait a little longer for a Lamborghini but this was a stylish set of wheels in keeping with the image of an independent young woman who was going places. And she had paid for it entirely from her own earnings, not with the credit card of a rich boyfriend.

The year 2009 was one in which she seemed to have suffered just as many downs as ups, especially where her health was concerned, but it was ending well. She couldn't help but tell the world how happy she was in a new relationship.

Justin Edwards was a handsome young black R & B singer better known as 'Ultra'. By the time the album *Against All Odds* was released in November 2009, he was a fixture in Tulisa's life. In both the record and later the book of the same name, she acknowledges his importance with the sort of deeply personal message that sweethearts write when they exchange cards at

Christmas or on Valentine's Day. It read: 'Thanks to Justin for simply makin' me happy, ha ha love you puffin … I'm your thumper for life!' Sharing something so personal with the public is not a typical Tulisa thing to do. For a young woman who talks about her life so much online and in the media, she is extremely reticent regarding her men.

Justin seemed to change that for a while. Tulisa admits to a chronic mistrust of men. She is very insecure where they are concerned. Amateur psychologists could point to her father leaving home when she was nine or her bad experience with her first teenage love, who didn't seem to think there was a problem with him seeing other girls. It didn't help being around Dappy and his mates, whose attitudes towards women were cavalier to say the very least. Tulisa observed, 'I don't think I could ever date one of Dappy's friends.'

Justin, however, seemed able to deal with her anxieties. He would send her affectionate little texts to surprise her during the day and, most importantly, tell her he loved her. She told *more!* magazine, 'He's romantic every day. We'll wake up in the morning and he'll be like, "I love you so much". When he goes out, he knows I am quite insecure so he'll ring me up every ten minutes. I'm so cool with it now I'm like, "Babe, you don't have to ring me up, it's fine, I trust you!"'

By a strange coincidence, Justin, like Adam, was a previous boyfriend. They had first met as teenagers in a club when he unsettled her by staring at her for twenty minutes with a blank expression on his face. She recalled, 'I was like "Are you all right there, mate?"' Justin's chat-up tactic of being completely silent worked. It was like the old game of who was going to blink first. Tulisa blinked first because, as she said, 'He drew me in. I love a challenge.' They got on famously and laughed at each other's jokes. He made her feel comfortable and relaxed.

That teenage relationship didn't last but they got back in touch online after she'd split up with Adam Bailey for the second time. The older Tulisa was in a much better place in her life thanks to her professional success and she was more confident as a young woman. Having money for the first time empowered her. She and Justin arranged to meet up and this time it was a proper grown-up romance.

Within three weeks they went on holiday together to Greece – not to the family villa but by themselves to the island of Kos in the Aegean, not far from the Turkish coast. It was the perfect setting for two young people falling in love and Tulisa called it her 'best holiday ever'.

Justin was the son of a musician and had grown up in North West London on the same streets as N-Dubz. He had also been around music and studios most of his life, which meant he had plenty in common with Tulisa and, like her, his dream collaboration would be with Timbaland. He too had progressed through hard work, beginning as an MC, then as a rapper before becoming a fully-fledged vocalist. He was much in demand at clubs and festivals both in the UK and internationally. He once performed in front of 30,000 people in Lagos, the capital of Nigeria.

Within a short time of going out, he and Tulisa no longer just liked each other; they were in love, and Tulisa was happy to go public with her new romance. Justin made one of the ultimate sacrifices in Tulisa's world: he gave her his 'chick chip'.

Like many other young men in her circle, he had two mobile phone chips, one was for the number that everyone used day to day and another secret one that was the 'chick chip', reserved exclusively for speaking to potential conquests. Justin told Tulisa he didn't need his 'chick chip' because she was the only one he wanted to be with. This was a declaration that it was serious between them.

As a couple they didn't need to go out all the time. Instead Tulisa enjoyed the evenings when they relaxed at home playing Nintendo or on her PlayStation. She loved curling up on the sofa with Justin and a pizza to watch *Pretty Woman* or *My Best Friend's Wedding* – she is a big fan of Julia Roberts. Most of all she loved the cult David Bowie film *Labyrinth* and could watch it over and over. These were the times when she shut the door on Tulisa and became Tula Contostavlos again – an ordinary girl wanting a bit of privacy. 'Tulisa' was a public image she and her management team were building – a strong and independent young woman who would become 'The Female Boss'.

Now that she had the car and the good-looking boyfriend, Tulisa was thinking about finding her own home. She was dividing her time between her mum's flat, Justin's place and her dad's new house in Neasden. She was also spending so long away on tour that her suitcases were her wardrobes. Fazer and Dappy had already left North London and moved into places of their own. Fazer had found an apartment in an exclusive area of Chelsea, while Dappy and Kaye had moved into a big loft-style space in Docklands. Tulisa was the only one left at home.

She didn't much care for walking around the local area, especially in Camden Town, because she was worried that she might get attacked by some of the jealous local girls she had left behind. She faced a negative mentality – they wouldn't want to congratulate her for doing so well. She observed, 'If I step into any hood, it feels like the whole world wants to kill me.' She wanted a house well away from such menace and decided to look in rural Hertfordshire. The problem was finding the time to hunt for the right property.

Being a member of N-Dubz was not something that could be picked up whenever she felt like it. The commitment was 24/7 – literally so, because Tulisa 'came alive' after midnight and recording sessions often lasted through the night, with a bleary-eyed trio stumbling home at 5 a.m.

N-Dubz toured twice in 2009 – the *Uncle B* gigs in the spring and the *N-Dubz Christmas Party* in November and December tours. Between tours they recorded their second album, *Against All Odds*, and did a selection of summer dates to please their fans and keep their name in the public eye.

The *Independent on Sunday* described N-Dubz on the road as

'urban panto', especially when Dappy whipped up the crowd to chant 'Fazer is a plonker'. But their brand of infectious energy and enthusiasm worked its magic around the country, from the Opera House in Bournemouth to St Helens Live Music Festival in the Lancashire town's Victoria Square. They attracted a vast crowd to the main stage at Wireless 2009 in Hyde Park in July. Tulisa was playing in front of tens of thousands of people long before her 'breakthrough' on *The X Factor*.

But where N-Dubz scored most highly was still connecting with children despite their success – they found time to perform at the Crompton House School in Manchester, where six year nine pupils had won an unusual radio contest in which an appearance by N-Dubz was the prize. Once again the group were promoting an anti-bullying message as well as singing for the excited children.

Tulisa was still feeling rubbish during the four months they spent recording the second album at Fisher Lane Studios near Guildford, Surrey, which were renowned as the recording home of Genesis. Fazer and Dappy loved it because they could while away their spare time fishing at a nearby lake. The country air seemed to agree with the boys far more than Tulisa. Even though the studios are residential, Tulisa liked to whizz back to London whenever she could.

She told the *Daily Mirror*, 'I was all over the place ... living out the boot of my car, not eating properly or getting enough water or vitamins. I got the flu plus a really bad kidney infection. It was a lot to do with not being settled.'

She also discovered that she had huge tonsils: 'Every time my doctor sees me she has a look down my throat just for the fun of it. I say "aaah" and she goes, "Jesus, I cannot believe the size of those tonsils. You must be getting ill 24/7."'

The last-minute finishing touches to the album were done at The Chairworks in Castleford, West Yorkshire, which was not the peaceful, rural retreat everyone had hoped. The recording complex was near the Castleford Park Junior School and there was pandemonium before and after school as the children hung around hoping to meet their idols. It was Fazer's fault. He popped out on a break to sign some autographs, so then everyone at the school started gathering to see if Tulisa or Dappy would emerge.

They had settled into a regular writing routine – Fazer would provide the beats and the backing track, Dappy would do his verses and the hook and then Tulisa would come in and write her verses and help with the bridge. It worked well, although she was more than a little miffed if the boys tried to take all the credit.

'I Need You', which they had showcased at the MOBOs, was chosen as the first single from the album and was released on 9 November 2009, just a week before the album. The new song was well received. Sarah-Louise James in the *Daily Star* observed, 'Imagine shaking a bottle of Coke for five minutes then taking the top off – this is the aural equivalent.'

Fraser McAlpine in his Radio 1Xtra blog identified the lyrics that enabled N-Dubz to connect with their young audience: Dappy included searching all over Facebook, while Tulisa sang about popping to the ladies' and coming out to discover the guy she was talking to has left. Fraser asked, 'Can anyone else remember the last time a pop song mentioned going to the toilet? EVER? I mean people talk about keeping it real, but there's pop song real and then there's actual real.' He was impressed that their songs never played it safe: 'N-Dubz seem to wander over the lines of acceptable behaviour almost as if they don't realize they are there.'

Tulisa in her sections was proving to be a master of pathos in a way that anyone could understand and relate to. She *was* that girl in the club. You could believe that she was left looking foolish in her LBD (little black dress) and 'bang bang' shoes, all dressed up and embarrassed. She also managed to slip in the line that she was one in a million, a small bow to one of her favourite childhood songs, 'One In A Million' by Aaliyah.

It was a deceptively simple situation but one young people the world over were facing – going out to a club, finding someone you like, not getting their number and spending hours on Facebook trying to find them.

'I Need You' was a warning shot that *Against All Odds* would see N-Dubz progressing from *Uncle B*, which had mostly been written when they were barely teenagers. They were certainly going up in the world with a video that cost £50,000 and was made by the acclaimed American director Rage (Dale Resteghini).

He went for a very glossy, expansive canvas with the three of them arriving stylishly – Dappy in a helicopter with the N-Dubz logo on the side, Fazer on a Yamaha motorcycle and Tulisa at the wheel of a white Lamborghini Gallardo. She may not have owned it yet but this was the next best thing.

It's not absolutely clear why the three of them were posing at Battersea Heliport with such fashionable transport. You could be forgiven for thinking they were about to pour some drinks and advertise Bacardi. On the surface it might seem that such showy displays of wealth didn't fit with their image of struggle – against all odds – but to desire and achieve material wealth is perfectly acceptable in the urban culture of today. The biggest American stars in the genre were dripping in diamonds.

Tulisa, who was squeezed into a little black dress, showed off her acting skills as the girl left bemused in the club, although why anyone in their right mind would want to bail on her touched a nerve with the users of YouTube. Fashion expert Alison Jane Reid noted, 'She looks incredibly pretty, dressed as the perfect blonde. It was quite fun.'

The video was put up two weeks before the MOBOs and had two million hits in its first four days. That ensured everyone knew the words by the time N-Dubz performed it live in Glasgow. For once they saw the benefit of a video's popularity, because the song attained the highest placing in the singles chart that N-Dubz have had without collaborators, reaching number five on debut and selling nearly 50,000 copies in the first week. The track was also number one in the UK dance chart.

Dappy was reportedly peeved that they didn't make number one in the regular chart because they were outsold by four *X Factor* records. Two of them, Leona Lewis and JLS, were former contestants, while Cheryl Cole was the darling of the country since she'd become a judge on the show. Top of the charts were the Black Eyed Peas, who had performed the track 'Meet Me Halfway' on the show the previous week. Dappy certainly felt that *X Factor* acts 'don't deserve it like we do.' But at least they outsold Britney Spears, whose latest, '3', was two places lower. Overall, 'I Need You' sold a more than respectable 145,000 copies.

The great excitement of recording the new album was meeting and working with Gary Barlow who, since the re-forming of Take That, had risen phoenix-like to the top of the pop tree. How could N-Dubz, very much a current band promoting an urban image, combine with the bordering on middle-aged fig-urehead of the nation's favourite boy band? It seemed so unlikely but it worked.

Gary was delighted when Jonathan Shalit got in touch at N-Dubz's request to ask him if he would be interested in working together. Jonathan had promised him he'd be really impressed by how talented the band were – and he was. Until then Gary had only heard the track 'Number 1' and so kept an open mind about what to expect.

He arrived at Fisher Lane in his Aston Martin and spent two days with N-Dubz. While he had nothing to contribute where the raps were concerned, he did help them find 'a big hook for the track'. He also enjoyed watching Fazer and Dappy pro-duce the tracks themselves, describing it as 'making music their way'. His most fascinating comments, however, were reserved for Tulisa: 'It was great to discover Tulisa's voice as I think she's a great singer.' This was close to two years before they started judging *The X Factor* together and evidence of the very small world of pop music. As Tulisa was discovering, it's all about connections.

Gary Barlow did have more in common with N-Dubz than might have been apparent at first. He started performing in public at the age of eleven and had done more gigs in his teens than the average artist would do in a lifetime. He had also written two of Take That's best-loved songs, 'Why Can't I Wake Up With You?' and 'A Million Love Songs', before his sixteenth birthday. He'd discovered early on that the more you do yourself in the music business, the greater share of the money you get to keep.

The result of their collaboration, during which they spent most of the time chatting and eating curry, was possibly the most melodic track on the album, 'No One Knows'. *IndieLondon* online called it 'synth-charged, pretty urgent and a mix of rap and sung chorus. But there's a keener sense of melody that owes much to Barlow's presence.' The rousing chorus was very much latter-day Barlow. *The Music Magazine* described it as a 'dreary, windswept council estate ballad ... and hauntingly beautiful.' Gary was modest about his contribution, observing on his website that they didn't really need him at all on the record but adding, 'God I'm cool with my kids because of it!!'

The presence of Gary Barlow on an N-Dubz record guaranteed some useful attention. Another tried and tested publicity device was the celebrity 'feud', in which the media were always willing partners. The alleged spat with JLS was an example of an ongoing story that could be dusted off whenever the two groups came within touching distance of one another.

Robbie Williams was the king of the feud, for many years seemingly starting an argument with everyone he met. Cheryl Cole, of all people, had an ongoing animosity with Lily Allen. Tulisa started one of her own with Elly Jackson, one half of the eighties-inspired electropop duo La Roux. Tulisa had apparently taken exception to some remarks that Elly had made about R & B, which she'd called 'lyrically really, really bad'. She had also taken a pop at the way women in hip-hop dressed and suggested Tinchy Stryder didn't deserve the praise he was receiving.

Tulisa observed, 'She is obviously one of those girls at school who got no love.' She was quoted in the press: 'She basically said all women that do urban music and UK R & B dress too sexily, so when I heard that I was insulted … You don't talk about other people's jobs like that. It's just wrong. I think she's a twat.' She also said that she would win a fight between the two. Tulisa later told *Sugar* magazine that she did say it but she was only joking.

N-Dubz were on a roll and when *Against All Odds* was released the media were falling over themselves to review it on the back of the success of *Uncle B* and their takeover of the 2009 MOBOs. The negative publicity they had been getting had done them no harm and Dappy was still seen as a rascal by the press. The *Daily Telegraph* thought the album was 'absolutely not intended for anyone over twenty.' That remark could have been made at the first incarnation of Take That in the nineties. Twenty years later the band were performing to the same fans who were now middle-aged but had never lost the love for the sounds of their youth.

BBC Music online treated the new album very seriously. Mike Diver wrote, 'This is an honest, authentic audio document of contemporary teenage Britain, and all should be thankful it's almost exclusively positive of message – if you can dream it, you could well achieve it.' The review had focused exactly on what Dappy, Fazer and Tulisa had been stressing for years: their music was positive. The *Mail on Sunday* said *Against All Odds* was 'the perfect album to lift the winter blues.'

'No One Knows' wasn't chosen as the follow-up single to 'I Need You'. Instead 'Playing With Fire', a collaboration with urban star Mr Hudson, was chosen. It proved to be an inspired choice because it would become one of N-Dubz's biggest hits.

A nice warm fire was exactly what Tulisa had wished for while filming the video on a wooden pier in the middle of the Thames near Tower Bridge at four o'clock on a cold autumn morning with no jacket. 'It was not fun,' she said. She was wearing a black sequined dress with very blonde hair. Alison Jane Reid observed, 'Men in her culture expect her to look overtly sexy and the dresses have to be short and skin-tight. Her image is the urban ideal of a hot babe.'

The theme was yet again lying and cheating, which was clearly a key issue of modern life for N-Dubz. In the video, Dappy is a cheater who gets caught. Tulisa is a girl who checks her boyfriend's texts and realizes what he's been up to, then storms out of the hotel room into a waiting limo, where she bursts into tears.

The chorus was very catchy in the N-Dubz ringtone manner and helped to propel the song to number fourteen in the chart. Mr Hudson is a handsome ash blond R & B singer from Birmingham whose real name is Benjamin McIldowie. He gained mainstream popularity quite late, winning the *Q* Award for Best Breakthrough Artist in 2009, when he was thirty. For a while he was the collaborator of choice, featuring on tracks by superstars Jay-Z and Kanye West as well as N-Dubz. He was also an Oxford graduate in English literature, which made him an unlikely ally of N-Dubz. But he became very friendly with them, particularly with Tulisa, which prompted some online gossip that they were dating.

'Playing With Fire' remains one of the most popular of all N-Dubz tracks. But, despite its success, two platinum-selling albums and the huge popularity of the group's concerts, they have failed to receive any sort of recognition from the BRIT Awards. 'Number 1' was nominated for Best Single but N-Dubz have had nothing for themselves. Nick Levine, writing about 'Playing With Fire' for *Digital Spy*, asked: 'Would it have killed the BRIT's panel to give N-Dubz a proper nod?

15

Empowered

After spending New Year with Justin on a beach in Bali – where she rode elephants in a safari park – Tulisa was ready for change in 2010. She was talking more about bringing out her own solo album, produced by Fazer and co-written by Dappy. She was invigorated with new ideas and ambitions, keen to put behind her the months of feeling rubbish and the nagging worry about court cases and the negative effect they might have. She also wanted to move ahead with her acting career and started going to auditions: 'I really, really want to get into acting . . . I want to get into Brit films. That would be amazing.'

In the music world, Tulisa might have been a coming force but directors weren't beating down her door to cast her. If she wanted to get anywhere as an actress, she had to grit her teeth and wait in line like other young hopefuls. Her acting CV contained her role in *Dubplate Drama* and some radio presenting but that was it. She had an entry in *Spotlight*, the casting bible of the profession, in which she said she could do a London accent and an Essex one. It was a bit thin but Jonathan Shalit had big ambitions for her and, in the following months, she did more things outside the umbrella of the group to boost her profile.

For the most part she had to bear being introduced as 'Tulisa from N-Dubz' but that would eventually change. Shalit's company, ROAR Global, became a major shareholder in a leading theatrical agency called Cole Kitchenn, which promised to increase her opportunities greatly. The first job they secured for Tulisa was a small role in a film called *Bulla*, a gangster movie based on comedian Ricky Grover's popular stand-up character. Lisa Marriott from the agency said, 'It'll just be a real laugh for her. There are no lines to learn. She'll just ad lib and be herself.' Tulisa had to sing in a chaotic pub scene filmed in the Prince Regent, Limehouse, in the East End. Her fellow bandmate in the movie was played by Rochelle Wiseman from The Saturdays. By the time the film was released on DVD, it had been renamed *Big Fat Gypsy Gangster* and Tulisa's name was everywhere, even though her performance was little more than a five-second cameo.

N-Dubz, meanwhile, had ambitions to break into the US. Cracking the American market is an ambition for everybody who has ever had a hit in music. Since The Beatles had crossed the Atlantic to such hysteria in the sixties, practically everyone has tried and relatively few have succeeded. Some acts – Robbie Williams is a leading example – are just too British to succeed there. N-Dubz's blend of British grime and pop songs with their unique lyrics seemed at first glance to be unlikely candidates to interest the big American record labels.

What would Americans make of 'Duku Man Skit', for instance, a track from the latest album, which included the line that Tulisa would only shag a man if she loved him? There were also references to dickheads, balls and poo poo. N-Dubz even included a helpful glossary in their soon-to-be published autobiography. Tulisa, however, did not think their Britishness would be a problem. Her attitude was: 'How do they know they won't get it when they haven't heard us yet?'

Certainly, the Island Def Jam Music Group were curious enough to set up a meeting. N-Dubz had been noticed in 2009 by Senior Vice-President of A & R, Max Gousse, who flew to the UK to watch a couple of their live shows. He was impressed with the fan base they already had and likened them, as many did, to a teen version of the Black Eyed Peas. He brought them to the attention of his boss, L.A. Reid, one of the most influential people in popular music.

Before they could fly to Los Angeles to meet him, Tulisa had an important date with a surgeon. She was booked into the Bupa Cromwell Hospital in South Kensington for an operation to remove a lump from her nose. The procedure wasn't serious but she needed a general anaesthetic and she had some concerns that it might affect her voice even though it had nothing to do with her vocal chords.

For the first time Tulisa was able to use Twitter to keep her 'family', as she liked to call her fans, updated on how everything was going. Tulisa doesn't have a Facebook account; she was deleted from the site because she was thought to be a fake version of herself. Apparently there were sixty accounts pretending to be Tulisa. It would have been hilarious if it hadn't been annoying. She found herself having arguments with herself because the fake Tulisas wouldn't believe she was the real thing.

Instead, she turned to Twitter, which provided a fascinating insight into her life over the subsequent months. Her tweets revealed a young woman who robustly stuck up for herself. She took exception, for instance, to one user taking the mickey out of her for thinking that Argentina was in Europe. Her most polite tweet was: 'This is my twitter! U can't cum on ere violating me talkin like that and if u do u will get it back times 10.'

Her tweets from her hospital bed were much jollier as she kept everyone abreast of what was going on: 'Sooo scared! Have 2 do little op 2 day 2 remove a little lump, nothin serious but I hav 2 have general anesthetic. Don't like it.'

And then: 'Guna b in for 8 hours! Guna b a serious sleep! I hate needles, Id rather b punched in da face!'

Tulisa was proving to be a master of Twitter-speak. She was funny and informative at the same time. She told her followers that after the operation she wanted a big Capri Sun juice, her latest Martina Cole novel and a Nando's.

She wrote, 'Got my little gown on, never understood y ther open at the back lol. Cromwell is bangin tho. Got my own little room! Decent menu. Love jelly!'

The moment of most drama occurred when she had a panic attack, which gave her heart palpitations, and she needed Valium to calm her down. Fortunately Justin arrived, which helped make her feel better: 'Ok Valium kickin in now time for me 2 rest, da place is spinnin lol, if da fans wanna know how it went Ultra will let u no.'

Afterwards, as well as Justin, her best friend Nyomi Gray was there to hold her hand, keep her spirits up and cut up her chicken. Ny, often referred to as Lady Ny, had grown up near her in North West London. They had become friendly after Tulisa heard through mutual friends that she had a pet dog and rang her for advice about injections for her Staffordshire Bull Terrier called Romeo.

Tulisa and Ny were soul mates. They could relate to each other's childhood problems. Ny's life eerily mirrored Tulisa's own teenage emotional struggles. The *Guardian*, which has championed her music, revealed that at the age of thirteen she tried to kill herself and subsequently channelled her personal experiences into her song lyrics: 'I had a lot of emotional battles with myself. There were family arguments, my parents broke up and people around me had been murdered.' Her music became her emotional release: 'I'll sit in the dark and just write for hours, and I'll be in a zone – sometimes I'm not even conscious of what I'm writing at that minute until I stop and read it back.'

Music had always been her passion growing up in a house in Kentish Town. She was home schooled until she was ten and her strict mother wouldn't allow her to watch television. She started going to a play centre where one of the workers was a pirate radio DJ on Freak FM called XL Bass, who opened her eyes to the modern urban music scene before he was murdered in 2001.

At fifteen she was singing at raves at the Forum in Kentish Town. She was spotted by Ms Dynamite, who invited her to go on tour with her. Ny didn't perform but watched everything that went on and was persuaded that this was the career she wanted for herself. Her boyfriend at seventeen was Wiley, proving again that the music scene in North London was a small world. She moved in with him and started recording, earning the title from *RWD* magazine of 'the first lady of R & G' – Rhythm and Grime.

When she split from Wiley, she didn't have Jumbo Studios to fall back on and had to take any job cleaning or walking dogs to make enough money to finance her debut CD, an acclaimed mixtape called *Split Endz Vol 1*. She recorded it at a college where a friend was an engineer and flogged it on Oxford Street for a fiver.

Her career progression highlights how fortunate N-Dubz were that their hard work paid off in the end. Ny was a young artist, well known in her musical world and supported and used by top artists, such as Plan B, Professor Green and DJ Ironik, but unable to interest mainstream labels in a record deal. Tulisa knew the agony her talented friend was going through. Ny told *MTV*, 'Ask anyone up to their late teens or twenties and they know my name.'

She also likes to take a pop at politicians who have no idea about the importance of urban music, particularly to black youngsters: 'they don't understand, it's like therapy for these kids'.

Ny has a pure and soulful voice that contrasts neatly with Tulisa's more belting style. They love singing together and their spontaneous duets are all over YouTube, including one of them singing in the toilet. They were big users of Ustream, jokingly referring to themselves as losers for having a girls' night in and trying to remember the words to songs – just as any friends might do over a glass or two of wine. The a cappella version of 'Every Breath You Take' is a classic. Tulisa and Ny have the kind of bond that survives.

Some visa problems for Dappy and Fazer caused a delay in the trip to Los Angeles to meet L.A. Reid. It gave Dappy the chance to sort out his private life, which was fast becoming a soap opera. Just a week before they were due to fly out, he needed hospital treatment for a broken nose after reports of a bust-up with Kaye Vassell at their Crossharbour home.

They had apparently split up in the summer but were back together a few months later. The *News of the World* claimed that Dappy had called the police after the row. A search of their flat allegedly turned up some cannabis and a knife. A police spokesperson confirmed that Kaye, still only nineteen, had been taken in for questioning over a suspected assault and possession of a class B drug. Their one-year-old son Gino was not at the flat.

The newspapers reported the incident with great relish, one even claiming that Dappy had bite marks on his face. Tulisa, who despite their bust-ups has a lasting affection for her cousin, told the *Sun*, 'It takes a lot not to hit a girl back – I wouldn't have been able to control myself.'

No charges were brought against Kaye and neither she nor Dappy has spoken in public about the events of that night. Kaye may or may not have had enough of Dappy's notorious wandering eye. He was linked with a curvy singer called Jade Tibbs, who was a member of the girl group Fe-Nix, one of the support acts on the *Uncle B* tour. She called Dappy 'peng', a slang term for fanciable, on her Myspace page. Kaye would tell the *Sun* that she knew of six affairs he had confessed to but that she received messages every day from girls claiming they had slept with him: 'Dappy's shown me no respect. He's the father of my son, but he behaves like a child, not a man.'

Kaye also said she was upset by the song 'Shoulda Put

Something On', a powerful track on *Against All Odds* about the dilemma of unwanted teenage pregnancies. She claimed that Dappy had told her the song was about them. She was shocked, 'How do you tell your son that his dad wishes he'd worn a condom? I was in tears when he put that song on the album.'

Dappy responded, 'I'm standing by Kaye, our son and unborn baby. I will always be there for her.'

Much of the media attention about the album had focused on that track – not because of any suspected reference to a real-life situation involving Dappy but because it was dealing with such an important theme in society today. It was grown-up and responsible. Tulisa said it was their favourite track on the album.

What a threesome N-Dubz made when they finally flew out to California in February 2010! Tulisa was recovering from the operation on her nose, while Dappy was nursing his recently broken one. Fazer was fit and well but smarting over the recent police raid on his Chelsea home.

At least the news was favourable when they arrived. L.A. Reid was very keen to sign them after just one meeting. British urban acts were just beginning to cross the Atlantic with more success, thanks to Taio Cruz and, in particular, Jay Sean, whose American debut single, 'Down', had topped the *Billboard* Hot 100 – a first for a UK urban act. By the time N-Dubz flew home to start rehearsals for the *Against All Odds* tour, an agreement was in place with just the details to be sorted. Jonathan Shalit confirmed that an offer was made immediately after the meeting. Max Gousse said, 'I signed N-Dubz because they're great entertainers and speak to London's youth unlike any other band. We want to bring their message to the rest of the world.'

This was a serious breakthrough for N-Dubz. L.A. Reid is credited as the man behind the phenomenal success of Mariah Carey, Pink, Rihanna and Kanye West, along with many others. It was decided that Tulisa, Dappy and Fazer would return to the US in August, after their next UK tour, to record a new album with acclaimed songwriters such as Jim Jonsin, who had worked with some of the biggest acts in the world, including Katy Perry and Beyoncé. His involvement was a clear indication of Island Def Jam's commitment to N-Dubz. Fazer was especially pleased: 'We can't wait to get out to the States and have our music heard globally.'

The trio were so excited by the prospect of cracking America that they couldn't stop talking about it in their book *Against All Odds*. Publication was timed to coincide with their spring tour of the same name in the UK. Tulisa, we learned, had set her sights on going global and wanted to be as big a star as Beyoncé.

More down to earth but just as exciting was finding a house she loved in the village of Leavesden near Watford, not far from the Warner Brothers Studios, where they'd filmed much of the *Harry Potter* series. The four-bedroom detached house, with a freshly painted white door and a pretty driveway for her sports car, was a peaceful haven away from the hustle of the city, even though it was just a short drive to the M1 and straight into North London.

Tulisa, who paid £550,000 for her new house, couldn't wait to show it to her parents and promised her mother that she would have her own bedroom. She was also quick to reassure fans that Camden would always be home even though, strictly speaking, only Dappy had actually lived there.

The drawback was that she had to leave the house right away to go on tour but at least she would have Justin with her. He was one of the support acts, which was a slightly unusual scenario but it meant they could drive together to gigs and stay in the same room and avoid Fazer and Dappy as much as possible.

To coincide with the first night, Tulisa was a guest columnist in the *Sun*, filling in for Jane Moore, which guaranteed some good publicity. There was also a prominent mention of the new book, which we learned would be out the next day. The most noticeable thing at first glance was the byline picture, which revealed that Tulisa had gone back to her natural brunette hair.

Her lead story was about how neither she nor any of her friends would be voting in the upcoming General Election because they knew absolutely nothing about politics. She was embarrassed by her ignorance of the subject, particularly in interviews. It was typically candid: 'The only thing I know about Gordon Brown is that he is the Prime Minister and he usually looks like he has been slapped around the face with a wet fish.' She blamed politicians for a state of affairs in which most eighteen-year-olds would rather go to the pub than the polling station.

Elsewhere on the page she said she would never pay more than £100 for a dress because she would feel like she was being mugged. She also defended Cheryl Cole who, it had been suggested, was wearing hair extensions in a L'Oreal ad: 'Haven't people got better things to worry about?' While Tulisa may have had help from journalists to write the column, the views in the majority of articles reflected her developing public persona. She came across as a strong-minded, socially aware young woman with real opinions that she wasn't afraid to share. She called a suggestion that parents of children who cause trouble in school should have their benefits cut 'ridiculous'. She reminded us that such a course of action would have been the last thing her mum needed when she was ill.

In another article she backed banning the use of wild animals in circuses and said that, in hindsight, she wished she hadn't ridden elephants in a safari park during her trip to Bali. She observed, 'You can never really be sure if an animal is happy doing something like that.'

She also condemned the debate on whether the drug meow meow – mephedrone – should be banned. She was in no doubt. 'Teenagers are taking it and dying. *End of argument.*' She tantalizingly revealed that she had a friend 'whose whole personality has changed as a result of smoking weed for years.' She didn't say who it was but continued that meow meow sounded far worse and yet was legal, which was a dangerous temptation for young people. She concluded, 'Allowing mephedrone to be sold legally is like handing them drugs on a platter.'

There was just enough space left for Tulisa to talk about her own addiction – to Twitter: 'I have used it to talk to young fans about issues such as bullying, depression and abuse.' She wrote of a teenage fan who was suicidal after an illness meant she had to spend time in a wheelchair. Through Twitter, Tulisa had tried to find her help and the girl is now enjoying her job and her life much more. They are still in contact, demonstrating that Twitter can have a positive side and is not all about last night's partying.

Tulisa's hard-hitting views made a striking change from the daily menu of pop gossip served up in the tabloid newspapers. Dappy, however, didn't appear to have read her column. He was caught on CCTV in a back room of an Essex nightclub snorting meow meow through a rolled-up banknote.

The film made its way into the possession of the *Sun*, who published an account of the incident even down to the time he was 'devouring' the drug – it was 5.19 a.m. Fortunately for Dappy, he was filmed before the drug was made illegal in April 2009, so he wouldn't face another criminal investigation. The fallout was potentially very serious at a time when N-Dubz were about to press forward in the US. The last thing they needed was the authorities over there questioning his visa credentials. Dappy, who seemed to spend a lot of time apologizing for his behaviour, did so again – the day after publication.

This time Tulisa was sitting next to him on the GMTV red sofa, with Fazer to her right, when Dappy spoke about it: 'I want to say that I'm more than glad genuinely that they've banned this thing because I've seen how many people are dying of it and whatnot and it's just not a thing to be doing ... It was a night out and it fell into the wrong place at the wrong time and I don't think I'll ever touch any silly stuff again.'

Tulisa was the responsible voice of reason: 'I don't condone drugs. It's no secret that drugs are a very serious issue in the music industry and a lot more people than you know do it, and when it's become such a normal thing behind closed doors, it's easy to be tempted and get sucked in.'

Dappy almost ruined the whole damage limitation exercise by saying, 'You know you have to try things to understand that they're bad.'

Tulisa was quick to jump in sternly: 'Not always.'

The impression was gathering pace that Dappy was a trouble-seeking magnet and the press had realized this. It was one thing after another. No sooner had it been announced that Kaye Vassell was expecting their second child than she split with him again after allegations appeared that he was seeing a dancer called Georgia Amodu.

Tulisa was getting so fed up with it that she gave Dappy strict instructions that he was not to sleep with their backing dancers. The next time they were selecting dancers for a tour, she insisted they were chosen because of their dancing abilities: 'I wasn't having him choosing women just so he can shag them. We're choosing them because they're dancers.'

She couldn't keep an eye on Dappy all the time. The police were called yet again when he was messing around with a toy paintball gun before a concert at the O2 Academy in Newcastle and hit a fan on the bottom with a six-millimetre pellet. She called the police, who gave Dappy a stern talking-to and confiscated the 'weapon'. The pictures of them walking off with the bright blue toy gun were priceless. With Dappy, you never know whether to laugh or to cry.

While Dappy continued to make the wrong sort of headlines on the tour, Tulisa was making some important decisions. She dumped Justin. Only two months earlier she had been gushing about how much they were in love and would leave corny texts and messages for each other. In an interview with *Sugar* she revealed that he texted her all the time and, to prove it, had just received one that said 'Me luff ya.' It gave the impression of being quite intense.

She made the announcement on Twitter: 'Ok guys chill, yes me and Ultra have officially split.' The tour had only been going for a fortnight when she decided that she preferred to be on her own. She seemed to have a ruthless streak where men were concerned and at this time, with so many exciting things happening in her life, she didn't want the commitment.

Sources suggested that she was putting all her energy into her career, although Tulisa didn't confirm that. Instead she confided to *Bliss* magazine, which had been the first publication to put her on the front cover: 'We were really happy. I don't know what's wrong with me. It just wasn't right for me though – it felt too serious too soon. I got a bit claustrophobic and that was a bit too much for me.' She didn't say whether she returned his 'chick chip'.

The end of their relationship coincided with the tour, when they were spending so much time together, so perhaps that was the problem – the exact opposite of the old saying 'absence makes the heart grow fonder'. The situation might have been awkward if they had both used the same tour bus but Justin started driving himself to the gigs, going home to London between most performances while Tulisa stayed in hotels.

Justin, meanwhile, had high hopes for his own career. He was now represented by Jonathan Shalit and was preparing for the release of his first solo record, called 'Addicted to Love', which featured both Dappy and Fearless (FeFe). Justin has a light, soulful voice but the track itself achieved little. The video received nearly two million hits mainly thanks to the energetic antics of Dappy and Fearless, whose mid-record rap was probably the most interesting thing about it. A second venture with Agent X and Mutya Buena called 'Fallin'' failed to obtain a proper release and Justin's recording ambitions stalled.

Fortunately for Tulisa, being single didn't immediately make her the focus of media attention, although there was mild speculation even then that she had rekindled her romance with Fazer. Her career was going from strength to strength.

While N-Dubz were still together in the spring of 2010, Tulisa seemed to be operating in a parallel universe to the boys. Everything in her world seemed so positive. Everyone loved her new hair colour and she said it was bringing her much more attention from men. As proof of that, she was placed at number fifteen, a new entry, in *FHM* magazine's list of the hundred sexiest women in the world. Cheryl Cole was first.

The boys, however, were going through a negative phase. Fazer was mugged in North London and reportedly had a pendant worth £6,000 stolen, although he never confirmed the incident. Dappy ended a rotten April by being kicked out of Alton Towers for allegedly smoking cannabis. He was there with Kaye, who seemed to have forgiven his latest bout of bad behaviour, and his friend Fearless. Guests apparently complained of a funny smell coming from under the door of his hotel room. The hotel management were alerted and asked the three to leave. Afterwards a spokesman for the band said they had merely been smoking cigarettes. Tulisa reminded everyone that N-Dubz were still a young band and prone to making mistakes.

PART THREE

THE FEMALE BOSS

16

Tulisa in Lust

The split with Justin seemed to have no effect at all on Tulisa's triumphant journey across the UK for *Against All Odds*. Dappy also didn't have a care in the world as he engaged with the enthusiastic fans. 'Did you see us on Alan Carr's show?' he asked the audience at the O2 in Glasgow. They screamed that they had. 'Did you see us on *Jonathan Ross*?' They had seen that too.

An N-Dubz show was spectacular entertainment. *The Scotsman* said they performed with 'stage school vigour'. The show was sometimes more like *Glee* than a meaningful reflection on their urban roots. Their songs and the memorable videos that accompanied them had always been like mini dramas and they carried that sense of theatre with them on stage. On the infidelity anthem 'Ouch', Tulisa chased a pair of models dressed only in their underwear from a bed. During 'Playing With Fire', she lamped Dappy and Fazer with pillows.

Critics agreed that you couldn't take your eyes off her, whether she was dressed in a military uniform for the opening number, their Gary Barlow song 'No One Knows', or the lad-pleasing LBD and bang bang shoes. She also brought her acting skills to the table for a moving rendition of 'Comfortable'. The *Birmingham Mail* said she 'looked like she was holding back the tears'.

Tulisa believed that the difference between N-Dubz and other acts was that they were more spontaneous and not solely about the music. They kept the fans involved not just by inviting them to sing along but also by interacting with them: 'Between every song we're having conversations with the fans, and they love that. We do things differently. It's like one big party.'

One of the dancers in uniform at the start of the show was a former school friend of Tulisa's called Gareth Varey. He had danced and acted as choreographer on tours with DJ Ironik and Chipmunk, who were both good mates with Tulisa. He had been part of the dance team when N-Dubz filmed their advertisement for the Adidas House Party, part of the Adidas Originals promotion, and joined them for the full tour.

When Tulisa split with Justin, she found that Gareth was the best person to keep her spirits up and make her laugh. He had always been fun and outspoken. She tweeted that he used to make their teachers' lives a misery. They were never romantically involved. Instead, they became inseparable buddies and, along with Ny, who was not on this tour, he became an essential person in Tulisa's life. They were her original 'muffins', an affectionate term that was originally a corruption of the urban slang 'raggamuffin' – a street kid – but thanks to Tulisa has become an affectionate name for a good mate or partner in crime. She once tweeted about Gareth, 'I can function without any man but Gareth is something else – kind of like a mum & best mate & tiny tim combined.'

The tour itself was in two parts – arenas around the country and then a break in May before the start of the major festivals, including the Isle of Wight and Glastonbury and a summer trip to Ibiza. May also saw the release of 'We Dance On', the theme tune from *StreetDance 3D*, a film that celebrated British dance and showcased *Britain's Got Talent* winners Diversity, Flawless and George Sampson.

The credit for the song was N-Dubz featuring Bodyrox, who

were two electro house DJs, Nick Bridges and Jon Pearn. They sampled the famous Pachelbel *Canon in D Major* and the overall effect was to create a feel-good track. Neither act was in the video which, instead, captured the energy of the film and the theme of overcoming prejudice to pursue your dreams.

The track, which had a version of 'Strong Again' on the B side, made number nine on the charts, which was perfect timing for the tour. A new television project promised to raise Tulisa's profile even higher. Called *Being ... N-Dubz*, it was a six-part reality show sponsored by Adidas Originals for Channel 4 and promised to reveal what it was like to be Dappy, Fazer and Tulisa. The idea was that it would be a modern fly-on-the-wall documentary and make N-Dubz known to a wider audience.

Jonathan Shalit introduced the show wearing a white suit: 'Dappy, Fazer and Tulisa are modern Britain. They represent young people, what they think and what they do. The reason N-Dubz are successful – this is a message to all young people in Britain who are unemployed – work like N-Dubz do and you will be successful.'

Among other things, the programme revealed just how much time Tulisa spent on her hair, nails and generally getting ready, which meant the boys were always waiting for her. It's very easy to knock a programme like this and many critics did, calling the trio 'uncompromisingly stupid' and demanding the return of national service. But television can accelerate a mainstream career like no other medium and that is what it would do for Tulisa, as she stood out as a beacon of maturity when trying to deal with the mad antics of Dappy and Fazer.

One of the first 'events' filmed was a charity football match at which the 'Dynamite Trio' argued with the renowned rapper Lethal Bizzle. They had fallen out when Bizzle, real name Maxwell Ansah, claimed that he had sent Tulisa a demo for a song called 'I Need You', which would later bear a striking resemblance to the N-Dubz hit. The band said they had finished the song two months before receiving the demo.

During the charity six-a-side event at the Charlton Athletic football ground, Fazer spotted him and he and Dappy went over to confront him. A spokesperson for Bizzle, who was playing for another team, said, 'He was minding his own business. N-Dubz and ten of their entourage approached him while he was watching a match. Bizzle stood his ground and I could see they started backing off. But then Tulisa jumped in and started screaming abuse while security looked on.'

The press, of course, loved it, as the argument enlivened what might have been a dull if worthy event. They found an irate eye-witness who claimed N-Dubz yelled at Bizzle that they were 'gonna fucking do you' and it was all very menacing.

Afterwards N-Dubz made an official statement: 'The band remain understandably annoyed about the claims Lethal Bizzle has made against them. They take their music very seriously and wanted to set the record straight.'

Tulisa seemed worked up and told Bizzle she would pay a grand to take a lie detector test to prove she hadn't nicked his song. Onlookers said that after the confrontation Tulisa was in tears and her mascara was 'streaming down her face.' She seemed more annoyed than upset.

She had cheered up by the end of the afternoon, however, because her team won the ladies' event and she scored the winning goal. She was flanked by her players, including *Hollyoaks* actress Nathalie Emmanuel and the former Mis-teeq singer Su-Elise Nash, when she lifted the trophy. She said that as captain she would be taking it home to stick on her mantelpiece.

N-Dubz flew to Greece in mid-June to perform at MAD, the Greek equivalent of the BRITs and the *Being . . . N Dubz* crew went too. They were greeted by Tulisa's grandparents and Yaya told Dappy that he was not to go out at night.

Tulisa was late for jet skiing the following day, claiming she hadn't seen her bed until 7 a.m. and had just had an hour's sleep. She was in no mood for Dappy calling her 'unprofessional' and let him have it with both barrels. 'Everyone can fuck off,' she said succinctly. So Dappy, Fazer and some of their mates picked her up and chucked her off the jetty into the sea. She wasn't happy.

The f-word featured a lot in the television series, especially when a soaked and bedraggled Tulisa emerged back on dry land and made her feelings known to a sympathetic Gareth; she threatened to smash their faces in. The morning after the awards, Tulisa is nowhere to be seen. She had flown to Ibiza.

Before she left, Tulisa had been to see a fortune teller she always visited in Greece, who told her she would soon meet an Italian man. She remembered that foresight when she caught the eye of a tall, darkly handsome young man on the beach in San Antonio. He couldn't help noticing Tulisa's curvaceous figure in one of her favourite pink bikinis and sauntered over to strike up a conversation. It would be the start of a three-month love affair.

Her 'Italian' turned out to be a professional footballer from Manchester called Gianluca Havern who, although born and raised in North West England, told Tulisa all about his relatives back in Italy. That was good enough for Tulisa, who told him, 'You're the Italian stallion my fortune teller predicted I would meet.' Typical of Tulisa, who has always been unstarry, her first footballer was not some preening player from Manchester United or City but a defender with Stockport County on the outskirts of the city. She was able to tell him about her recent triumph in the charity football match.

Luca may have been a League Two player but, at 6ft 2in, he had Premiership looks and worked part time as a model. He was not only Tulisa's first love interest from the nation's favourite sport, but he was also the first man to spill the beans about a relationship with her. He would tell the *Sunday People* all about it in an account which, while disclosing that they had sex four hours after they met, spared Tulisa the embarrassment of too much graphic detail. Instead, he revealed a holiday romance of sun, sea and sex that seemed perfect for two young unattached people. He was impressed by Tulisa's great body, which he had admired so much in a bikini on the beach: 'It was even more lovely to look at once she had taken it off.'

Luca had travelled over to Ibiza for a summer break with his mates, who included the actor and budding R & B singer Lucien Laviscount, from the BBC series *Waterloo Road*, whom Tulisa had already met. She joined them when they left the beach to go to Café Mambo, one of the iconic bars along San Antonio's sunset strip, to watch the sun go down. Luca was still at Tulisa's side when she moved on to the Eden nightclub, where she went up on stage during a set by her friend DJ Ironik. In Tulisa's very small urban world Ironik, born and brought up as James Charters in North London, was a constant fixture, rather like Wiley. He was at most of Eden's TwiceasNice summer events.

According to Luca, Tulisa was more smitten than he was to begin with but as the evening wore on he realized that he felt the same way. They drank vodka and danced, breaking off frequently to slip to the side of the dance floor for a snog. Romance was taking an inevitable course and the couple went back to Tulisa's hotel for the night. She was staying at the Blau Park, a pretty hotel near the beach, with an outdoor pool that she loved.

Tulisa and Luca became inseparable for the remaining four days, ditching their friends to find some of the island's more secluded beaches, where they could dive from the cliffs into the sea. Luca found Tulisa very easy to talk to but with a quick wit, which she was always employing to make him laugh.

He was also struck by how she looked after her entourage when they went out in the evening, making sure the drunks found their way home safely to their hotel beds. Certainly the whole experience seemed wonderful – a world away from the cavalier escapades of Dappy and his friends. Touchingly, Luca recalled, 'She has a really beautiful face'.

Tulisa was back in Ibiza in July to celebrate her birthday. She flew out a group of her friends, whom she had dubbed the 'Ibiza foot soldiers', by EasyJet. They included Gareth and Ny, as well as Fearless and Dappy. Fazer couldn't make it but Zee was there with his camera. They all went to the famous nightclub Pacha, where they toasted the birthday girl with champagne and shots until seven in the morning. Zee filmed everyone, including Ny wishing a happy birthday to her 'little muffin' Tulisa. Dappy took the microphone to lead the dance floor in a chorus or two of 'Number 1'. A slightly the worse-for-wear Tulisa was reported to have tied her hair up with a thong as the sun rose.

Back in England her new home featured in *Being . . . N-Dubz* and she was obviously proud of owning her first house. She was filmed at her front door welcoming Fazer and Dappy. Viewers were treated to a glimpse of Tulisa's television room, complete with plasma TV mounted on the wall, and her display of platinum and gold discs. It seemed innocuous enough but four days later the house was burgled. The thief had smashed in three windows, including one of the panes in the front door.

Tulisa was not at home at the time, having already left for the N-Dubz show at the GuilFest pop festival in Guildford, Surrey. Afterwards she was due to go out and celebrate her twenty-second birthday with her friends at a London club. While she seemed casual enough about the burglary on Twitter, having a laugh at the thief's inability to remove the TV from the wall, she was clearly horrified that someone had been in her house and wondered whether she could continue to live there. After the excitement of fulfilling a childhood dream, it was 'heartbreaking' for this to happen. She had been living there for only two months but she decided that was long enough. She put the house up for sale and started looking for a new home with better security. Police were able to catch the burglar, who proved to be a local man from Watford, but that was no consolation to Tulisa, who never moved back in.

Surprisingly, she continued her affair with Luca over the summer. They texted regularly, sent picture messages and spoke on the phone. They met up when Tulisa's schedule allowed, including once at the luxurious Mint Hotel – now the DoubleTree by Hilton – in Manchester's city centre. She even dropped him off at football training the next morning, which wouldn't have done his reputation among the other players any harm, especially when she stayed to watch.

There was never any real danger of Tulisa becoming a WAG. She liked Luca but she was entering a phase in her life and her career when she would have little time for matters of the heart. Luca, to his credit, realized that they weren't going anywhere so they decided to call it a day when she went to the US to record the new N-Dubz album. Luca confirmed to the *Sunday People* that there was 'no big bust-up'.

Tulisa and Luca had an idyllic fling like thousands of young people enjoying a Mediterranean holiday that summer. They were unattached and nobody got hurt. Luca is still linked to Tulisa on Twitter.

While her career promised to scale new heights, his was going in the opposite direction. He was let go by Stockport at the end of August as part of the club's ongoing struggle to sort out its financial problems. He signed for Mossley, a Greater Manchester team playing in the Northern Premier League Division One North but only stayed a month before moving to rivals Ashton United. He moved again to Hyde FC in the Conference North League in 2011.

One of Luca's most interesting recollections of Tulisa is that she became upset when a story appeared in the papers that she was romantically involved with Fazer – something that she'd told him wasn't true and he believed her. She apparently was bothered because she thought a former N-Dubz dancer was the source of gossip about her.

She may have believed it was Dappy's former lover, Georgia Amodu, and there was certainly no love lost between them. They have had some blistering exchanges on Twitter, in which Georgia referred to Tulisa as 'fucking Tulisa' and the girl herself tweeted, 'WTF [what the fuck] do u do? Other than open ur legs?'

Away from Twitter, Tulisa was showing a caring and more

mature side. It was at this time she filmed a documentary about her relationship with her mother entitled *Tulisa: My Mum and Me,* an intimate account of growing up as her mother's carer and the problems young people face in that situation. The cameras were there as she showed off her new house to Ann and told her where her room would be. The seriousness of the subject couldn't have made a sharper contrast to the hi-jinks of *Being . . . N-Dubz.*

17

On Def Ears

Crossing the Atlantic was a huge challenge for N-Dubz but they were determined to keep their British identity despite working with American producers. Tulisa stressed that they wouldn't compromise and would continue to be involved in every aspect of their music. They didn't mind other producers being involved but only as part of a team that got together from the start. She observed, 'We'll always do what we want to do.'

The first compromise they made was dropping some of the language, which it was feared wouldn't be understood by an American audience, although Dappy said that he wouldn't be singing with an American accent. He always hated it when singers did that and thought they lost respect from their British fans.

Tulisa found the whole process difficult. She was used to the routine of being N-Dubz when they recorded songs. They had done the same thing since she was eleven and now she was being asked to change. She didn't enjoy the pressure of having to think up a lyric from nothing every day. She couldn't take her time as they had done all those years ago in Jumbo Studios or more recently at Fisher Lane. Dappy also found it difficult and Tulisa was having to shoulder an equal burden for once. In the past he had always started things moving, but in the US she confided there were days when he felt flat and uninspired.

Fortunately, Gareth was there to look after her. He had now been officially appointed as her personal assistant and was with her constantly. Rich Castillo also travelled over to make sure the trip went smoothly but, surprisingly, Fazer was left behind in London, ostensibly to work on 'tour production'. It's never been properly explained why he wasn't there but there were rumours of ongoing problems with his visa. Zee made the trip to make another of his *Behind the Scenes* videos, which had proved a fascinating record of the N-Dubz story.

Dappy seemed quite subdued to start with but became more buoyant whenever he thought a track was going well. Tulisa, typically, had tonsillitis, which she said she had picked up on the plane. A doctor was summoned to administer antibiotics. He cheered her up by telling her he treated Simon Cowell. She was worried her vocals were sounding like a strangled cat. She complained, 'My voice is fucked.' Her first vocal was on a track called 'Scream My Name', which would have been more accurately titled 'Croak My Name'.

She perked up when they travelled to Miami to work with the acclaimed producer Jean-Baptiste Kouame, the man behind hits for Rihanna, Chris Brown and Kelis. He produced the Black Eyed Peas hit 'Meet Me Halfway' and two tracks on Cheryl Cole's album *Messy Little Raindrops*, including the title track. He worked his magic on two for N-Dubz, 'Love.Live.Life' and 'Morning Star'.

Dappy and Tulisa also collaborated with Jim Jonsin on a song called 'Girls', which was very catchy and poppy. They played table tennis while the song was put together. Dappy was surprisingly good, presumably because he had wiled away time on tour playing the game with his mates. The highlight of Zee's film was Tulisa in a studio pretending to be an American girl – she was uncannily accurate in her vocal nuances, especially in the way she said, 'That is so cool.' Clearly she'd been spending too much time watching TV.

One of the songwriters on the trip was a stunning Norwegian called Ina Wroldsen, one of the most dynamic new talents in the business. Ina, a former singer, had written much of *Chasing Shadows*, the debut platinum album from girl group The Saturdays. Tulisa had become friendly with Ina and the girls, and in the album's acknowledgements sends big kisses to 'Aunty' Ina. Ina had written a song for N-Dubz called 'Love Sick' on which she shared the vocals with Tulisa.

The track seemed quite a departure from the usually more biting content of N-Dubz. The women's voices blended nicely together but there was the strong suspicion that this was more a girl group song than something from the streets of Camden. It was in the style of Girls Aloud rather than N-Dubz. Was that really Tulisa singing about being love sick and talking about dreaming of a boy and worrying about a broken heart?

The track was very catchy and revealed the direction Tulisa might take with her music when she left N-Dubz but one couldn't imagine that all her fans would be pleased at such wimpish sentiments. It sounded worryingly American after all her fine words of defiance.

It came as no surprise when Tulisa told the *Daily Star* that N-Dubz had changed their style to suit the US market after all. She explained, 'If you wanna sell records in America you have to be willing to change your style a little bit and accommodate them ... you either like it or lump it.' That didn't sound the same as her assurance when they left for the US that they wouldn't compromise.

One critic described 'Love Sick' as 'processed mulch'. If it had been the first single from the new album, then it would probably have been number one. Instead 'Best Behaviour' was chosen. This was a track they had written with Mr Hudson and would turn out to be the nearest to an old N-Dubz song. At least the theme of sleeping around seemed like a legitimate topic for the band. The idea was that it was time to change, forsaking one-night stands in favour of going home to someone who cared. Dappy said he wrote it about Kaye, who was expecting their second child in December 2010.

Fazer, in particular, had been very keen for this song, originally called 'Love Is All I Need', to be the single even though in the US they favoured 'Scream My Name'. A key difference between the two songs was that Fazer produced the former working with Mr Hudson in the UK, while the latter was an American production from Def Jam favourite Fuego assisted by Max Grousse. Everybody wanted to make the right decision because expectations were so high. In the end Fazer carried the day.

The critical reaction was just OK. Fraser McAlpine in his BBC Chart Blog thought it was trying to be an anthem when it was really a ballad. He thought the song 'quite nice' but needing a brush-up lyrically. 'Best Behaviour' reached number ten in the chart, which was a disappointing result for a completely new song after all the hype of N-Dubz's American connection.

The video was probably better than the song. Directed by the emerging hip-hip director Ben Peters, it was filmed over two days and he ensured that Tulisa has never looked better. She didn't actually do much as they performed on the tarmac in front of a private plane. At one point she had to look pensive on a garden lounger while she sang her verse. But Alison Jane Reid was impressed with the way Tulisa was styled in a pink drape dress: 'It pays homage to the idea of a Greek goddess and is very romantic and feminine. I think she is starting to look like an icon here. And the make-up is really beautiful, much more subtle, playing up to her eyes with their beautiful shade of blue. I'm still not keen on her shoes though, but the dress ... and that lovely dark hair. She doesn't look fake any more.'

Ironically, it was only ten months since the release of 'Playing With Fire', which had been nominated as Best Song at the 2010

MOBO Awards at the Echo Arena in Liverpool. Tulisa didn't think they were going to win so was very happy that they did. This time it was made particularly special because Fazer's mother Elaine had travelled up with them. As usual Dappy did most of the talking, dedicating the award to his father, Uncle B. He also gave this reason for loving the award: 'We write, mix, produce everything so it means more than a lot to us.' That might have been directed at the American connection. He also made a point of acknowledging JLS, which didn't sound like someone fanning the flames of a feud.

Tulisa was low key and said a simple thank you. She was more talkative backstage when she was interviewed by DJ Max, the presenter of the breakfast show on Choice FM, who had been a friend for years and with whom she always had a joke and a giggle. She confided that she was shaking throughout their performance of 'Best Behaviour' that evening: 'I haven't been that nervous for ages. I don't know why.'

For once she hadn't had a glass of wine to calm her nerves because N-Dubz had been on duty as backstage hosts for the BBC. Dappy and Fazer had put suits on for the occasion. It was further evidence that N-Dubz, and Tulisa in particular, were becoming more television friendly. Not having a glass of wine hadn't helped Tulisa, however. She told Max, 'I was on air, fully sober, hungover from the day before and I was just like, "Oh my God".'

Tulisa was also very candid about the difficulties they were facing working for the US market. She had softened her view, 'You do have to accommodate when you go over to America and we said we will compromise. We're not going to one hundred per cent change ourselves.

'There was a lot of days when I was just mind-blocked, 'cos I'd be coming up with all these ideas and they'd be like, "Oh well, that's great in the UK but it's not gonna work over here." And I'd be like, "Grrr, what do you mean it's not gonna work over here?" and it would just drive me mad.' The whole exercise didn't sound very enjoyable. You might have expected Tulisa to be more diplomatic and to gloss over any misgivings but that was not her way.

After a long night she met the boys for drinks at Circo, where they joined the US rapper Nelly and his huge American entourage. The night didn't pass without incident, however, because a bouncer thought they were trying to sneak out without paying and confiscated their car keys, which didn't go down well with Dappy or Tulisa, who told him in no uncertain terms that the drinks were complimentary. The police had to move on a crowd who gathered to witness the argument before the club management intervened to confirm that the drinks had indeed been free.

Tulisa's remarks to DJ Max about their US experience did little to boost confidence in the prospects for the new album, which was called *Love.Live.Life*, a bit of a tongue-twister. One of the most noticeable things when the album was released on 29 November 2010 was that the credits seem to list a million people involved in every song. About twenty producers were named, scattered throughout the tracks, which must have left Fazer gnashing his teeth. The title track listed six writers and not one of them was from N-Dubz.

Much of the fun, trademark N-Dubz was missing: there was no 'N-Dubz, N-Dubz' chanting at the start; the 'Ha Ha' from Tulisa was half-hearted. They had retained the 'Na Na Niiiii' but even that had lost its edge, sounding more like something from an American soul singer. The critics, who had been almost universal in their praise for *Against All Odds*, were divided about the new album. The *London Evening Standard* described their sound as 'hip-pop' and noticed the 'Americanization of their music.'

Metro thought there was 'something oddly endearing about the boundless enthusiasm of N-Dubz for enjoying a life they've grafted hard for.' Killian Fox in the *Observer* was worryingly to the point: 'This feels like a formula-driven move, and the insistence on having fun soon wears thin.'

Love.Live.Life smoothed some of the rougher edges off the N-Dubz sound. Was this enough to attract a wider audience and take it to number one? The answer was an emphatic no. It peaked at number seven and, although they were booked for their biggest tour yet in 2011, when they would play arenas around the UK, the suspicion remained that the wind had been taken out of the N-Dubz sails. The album was not a disaster by any means and eventually went platinum, but the question remained: would N-Dubz have become one of the biggest bands in the country with as loyal and devoted a young following if this had been their first album? The rough and gritty sentiments of the first two albums allowed their fans to identify with them and their music. The smoother grooves of their third album were more listener-friendly than built for audience chanting.

The fans were still there, of course. Even Prince Charles seemed to have heard of N-Dubz when he met them backstage at the Royal Variety Performance ten days after the album was released. The evening had begun traumatically for the Prince and his wife, the Duchess of Cornwall, when their Rolls-Royce was attacked by protesters, who splattered the car with paint and smashed a window as it made its way down Shaftesbury Avenue to the London Palladium.

N-Dubz were light relief after that ordeal. Tulisa was under the weather and had tweeted: 'Royal Variety Performance today! Throat and chest still not good but gotta make do I guess! At least I actually had more than 5 hours sleep!' She made it through a new version of 'Say It's Over' from *Against All Odds*, complete with orchestral backing. For some reason they didn't choose to perform a number from the new album. Perhaps that was wise because the next single, 'Girls', wouldn't have been suitable for a royal occasion because it contained the word 'fuck' in the first line.

After the show Prince Charles seemed to enjoy meeting the trio. The good manners that had been so important to the

Contostavlos brothers were back as Dappy chatted easily to him. Prince Charles asked, 'What are you guys doing here? Are you hip-hopping about?'

Dappy replied, 'No sir, we make great music for the masses.'

The Prince told him, 'So I've heard', which was probably true as his two sons are great fans of urban music.

The Prince then turned to Tulisa, who was wearing a full-length grey evening gown that Alison Jane Reid thought 'divinely elegant and grown-up without being too old for her. Long dresses are really hot for all age groups right now. They are so flattering, and create instant glamour. I like her hair too. It really suits her swept up and away from her face – very chic and alluring.'

Prince Charles obviously agreed and told Tulisa she 'looked amazing', before asking the boys about their suits. 'I love your suits. Did you get them tailored especially?' Fazer answered, 'Yes, sir, they're from Vivienne Westwood.'

The night couldn't have gone better and for the first time N-Dubz had moved from late night chat shows and their reality series into a big annual mainstream television event, rubbing shoulders with Kylie and Take That.

Afterwards they popped to a hotel round the corner to meet a young Wiltshire boy called Connor Robinson who was terminally ill from cancer. They were his favourite group and his single mum, Jenny, was determined to fulfil his dream of meeting them. 'He was so overwhelmed when Dappy walked over to him. It was amazing. I have never seen him react like that. It was great to see him so happy ... Tulisa is obviously his favourite, he loves her to bits. He still has a faint lipstick mark on his cheek and doesn't want to wash it off.'

Dappy had to dash off because Kaye had gone into labour and he arrived just in time to witness his second son, Milo, being born. He announced, 'This is the new Dappy, the family man – so long to all of the bad Dappy you've heard about.' Tulisa tweeted, 'I'm an auntie again. Aaaaawwww what a little muffin!'

She was apparently still single. She had, after all, just launched one of her anti-men broadsides. She told the *Sun* that only five per cent of men stay faithful and ninety-five per cent were 'absolute animals'. Nobody, therefore, took too much notice a couple of nights after the Royal Variety Performance when she and Fazer were out clubbing in the West End. Their evening would probably have passed without comment if they hadn't been refused entry to Studio Valbonne in Kingly Street, apparently because they weren't members. Tulisa argued with the doorman. When they weren't allowed in, the pair walked off glumly into the night.

As the year drew to a close it was time for Tulisa to take stock of her career. Acting remained very much on her agenda and she was anticipating making her feature film debut in 2011.

There was also still just a chance that 'Girls' might make a breakthrough but it stalled at number eighteen. The video revealed a new side to Tulisa's image: an empowered woman, not a victim, who sang about earning more than the men who wanted her to be their girl. As a glimpse of the future, she sings that she is the biggest female boss who ever lived – the first but definitely not the last time she would be linked with that slogan.

If you watch closely you can catch sight of Ny sitting on Tulisa's lap. Slightly lost in the song is Fazer, wondering why his girlfriend is always so late for everything. This may or may not have been a dig at Tulisa's bad punctuality and the way she always kept the boys waiting. Nobody at the time knew for sure if Tulisa and Fazer were a couple.

18

Simon Calling

It's all about connections. When Dappy rather endearingly referred to the 'big strings' that Jonathan Shalit could pull for them, he wasn't kidding. For many years Jonathan has spent his winter holidays in Barbados, where his parents had a house and where he now enjoys the sun in the company of many famous neighbours, including Simon Cowell. No agent, especially one as successful as Jonathan, could resist the temptation to chat about the virtues of his client list when enjoying cocktails with such an influential figure.

It may or may not be a coincidence that Kelly Brook is on the books of ROAR. She seemed a surprising Cowell appointment to the panel of his *Britain's Got Talent* in 2009 but she lasted only a week. She has had a fantastic career built around little more than a photogenic figure, which magazines and newspapers never seem to tire of showing. Konnie Huq, the former *Blue Peter* presenter, is another Shalit client to catch Cowell's eye and was hired to host the 2010 season of *The Xtra Factor*. The critics weren't that impressed with her efforts and she didn't return for another series.

Simon had already met Dappy at the beginning of 2010 when

Jonathan arranged for him to have a New Year's break in Barbados with Kaye. Dappy loved the glamour of the place, especially the jet skiing, and decided it was his new favourite destination. He was his usual cheeky self when he bumped into Simon in a bar. Apparently Simon congratulated him on the success of N-Dubz.

Dappy, while undeniably charismatic in a 'can't take your eyes off him' sort of way, was not a likely candidate for the judging panel of *The X Factor*. He had always been fearlessly outspoken about the shortcomings of the show. He was also proud that N-Dubz had made it without any help from Simon.

He did, however, receive some advice from Simon about breaking through in the US, which led to improbable stories that Simon had upset Jonathan by trying to 'tap up' Dappy. The reports were useful publicity, as they put Dappy's name in the same story as Cowell's – not a bad idea when you are trying to interest a major US record label. And, as was subsequently proved on the American version of *The X Factor*, Simon was a good friend of L.A. Reid.

The American version was on Simon's mind at the end of the 2010 season of *The X Factor* in the UK, but he was also fretting about the future of the British show. While the 2010 series was a ratings triumph, he realized that the show was in danger of losing touch with a younger audience. As far as ITV is concerned, the 16–24 age group is the one that it wants to attract because they bring in the money from advertising. Simon needed to shake things up. Surprisingly, the first person he earmarked for the chop was himself.

Simon was already fifty-one and would be fifty-two during the next series. He was at risk of being out of touch as he continued to bang on about yesterday divas Mariah Carey and Whitney Houston. Kevin O'Sullivan, television critic of the *Sunday Mirror*, observes, 'He deduced, quite rightly, that they needed somebody, at least one judge on the show who knew something about what was going on musically now. In other words, he needed someone to appeal to far younger viewers than he was reaching out to. Tulisa was his first choice and remained that.'

Ironically, the Mariah/Whitney middle-of-the-road quality of *The X Factor* had spawned the most successful act from the show when Leona Lewis won the third series in 2006. But trying to emulate her success with pale easy-listening imitations was proving frustrating. Instead, it was the younger, more current acts that didn't win the competition who ended up winning over the record-buying public. JLS were runners-up but were proving to be a phenomenal success. And in 2010 much of the interest revolved around two acts that finished third and fourth – a manufactured boy band, One Direction, and a white, sassy, rapping teenage girl, Cher Lloyd.

Cowell had let JLS slip through his fingers but he was quick to sign these two to his label, Syco Records. They rewarded his judgement with number one singles in 2011, which again demonstrated that it was the young fans who bought records. The older brigade might have voted for Matt Cardle, but after the dust had settled on *The X Factor* season, they didn't buy his single 'Run For Your Life', which only made it to number six in the charts.

Fortunately, Cowell didn't have to sack himself or anybody else to make way for new judges. Circumstances made changes relatively easy. His own mind was becoming firmly focused on launching *The X Factor* in America and there was intense speculation that Cheryl Cole, the darling of the British public, would go with him. Dannii Minogue had a young baby and was spending a great deal of time in Australia, so in early 2011 the only judge who seemed completely safe was Louis Walsh, the panto dame of the programme.

Despite being hugely popular with media and public, Cheryl was not exactly cutting edge. She looked great on the cover of *heat* magazine and every teenage girl aspired to be her but her glamorous image had taken the edge off her street credibility.

Cheryl may have been only twenty-seven but, in the UK, Cowell needed someone younger.

Fortunately for Tulisa, not everyone on *The X Factor* was listening to nineties pop. A member of the production team was a fan of *Being ... N-Dubz*. It was fun, lively and youthful but, more importantly, it was a shop window for Tulisa.

Kevin O'Sullivan observes, 'She shone out like a real star. I was stunned at how articulate and reasonable she was. That's the thing about her compared to the others in N-Dubz. They seemed to act like child-like morons. Every hotel they go into they seem to open up all the miniatures – just being really, really stupid. I remember them wanting to go and fire guns and Tulisa just stepping forward and saying, "What do I want to go and fire guns for?" You sort of thought that in this kind of moronic inferno of the band there is a girl who seemed like good news and was also intelligent.'

Simon had tried out a couple of possible contenders for the Cheryl chair when she was sick with malaria during the previous series but nobody had really come up to scratch. Pixie Lott was personality free, while Katy Perry's bubbly stage persona didn't translate well to the more static surrounds of television. The best of them seemed to be Nicole Scherzinger but Simon already saw a role for her in the US *X Factor*.

Kevin explains, 'Cheryl did appeal to younger viewers but not in the way Cowell wanted her to. He wanted someone with more serious street cred. He might have thought of Jessie J but, at the time, she was probably a bit young in the tooth.'

Simon already knew all about the success of N-Dubz but, after watching a couple of episodes of *Being ... N-Dubz* for himself, he had seen enough to recognize Tulisa's television potential and asked his team to approach her. A guest appearance on the panel of *Never Mind the Buzzcocks* also helped her cause. As well as being completely natural on screen, Tulisa correctly identified Dizzee Rascal's 'Holiday' from the tuneless humming of Phill Jupitus and Badly Drawn Boy in the intros round. That knowledge of current music was just what *The X Factor* producers wanted.

The actress Katy Wix, who was on the same show, looked good but was completely out of her depth musically. She inadvertently allowed Tulisa to shine. Tulisa slipped in to watch *The X Factor* live shows in October 2010 but it was never reported whether she met Cowell on that occasion. She also holidayed in the Caribbean over New Year but, again, any meeting with Simon was behind closed doors. Tulisa had one advantage over any alternative candidates: Simon was already in talks with Gary Barlow, who had admired Tulisa's talent when he worked with N-Dubz and was happy to be on a show with her.

Simon's interest in Tulisa is testament to his shrewdness and his willingness to take a gamble. She would probably not have been on a shortlist of a hundred if it had just been up to the public to decide who would replace Cheryl. Unsurprisingly, N-Dubz had yet to secure a guest spot on *The X Factor* despite being the UK's premier urban group. Tulisa is disarmingly frank about their appeal or lack of it: 'Half the country hated N-Dubz ... but the half that hated them were all probably *X Factor* fans.'

Simon Cowell may seem an unlikely champion for a girl from the Camden street culture. He grew up a world away in the tea and scones surroundings of Elstree in leafy Hertfordshire. But he did share the same dream as Tulisa – to make money and live in a big house. As a boy he would watch famous people arrive next door, where a film studio boss lived. He witnessed Elizabeth Taylor, Richard Burton, Bette Davis and Gregory Peck arriving for parties. It made a huge impression on young Simon: 'I thought, "This is very glamorous. I'd love to live in a house like that and have a party like that."' He has fulfilled that ambition totally.

Drive is not all Cowell shares with Tulisa. He too left school at sixteen with a very modest academic record and is an entirely self-made man. He began his path to success as a runner at

Elstree Studios, where his main job was making the tea. His father Eric was able to pull a few strings and young Simon moved to a job in the post room at EMI. He stood out because of his enthusiasm and his determination but there was an extra ingredient that placed him above the crowd – he would take a risk.

His first big gamble came when he borrowed £5,000 to back the debut single of a bubbly, black American dancer called Sinitta, whom he happened to be dating at the time. The song, 'So Macho', became a camp disco classic and sold nearly a million copies, reaching number two in the charts in the summer of 1986 – two years before Tulisa was born.

His next famous coup came when he signed the actors Robson and Jerome to the Sony BMG label. Robson Green and Jerome Flynn were two of the stars of *Soldier Soldier* and had sung a tepid version of the classic 'Unchained Melody' in one episode with no intention of becoming pop stars. Simon recognized a potential gold mine and persuaded them to release the track on S Records, which would later become his more famous Syco brand. It was number one for seven weeks, sold more than one million copies and was the biggest selling record of 1995. More importantly, it was the first example of Simon recognizing the power of television – something Tulisa's agent was also keenly aware of.

When *Pop Idol* began in 2001, one of the arrangements Simon put in place was that the winning song would be released on his label. He was keen to protect that investment and was persuaded to become a judge. By the end of the first series he was well on his way to becoming a television institution. His famous clash with the eventual winner, Will Young, was pure television gold. But Simon Cowell has always been primarily a businessman and not a television personality. Kevin O'Sullivan confirms, 'I don't think it's too controversial to say that Cowell doesn't do anything unless it's to his own financial advantage.'

That desire to make money led to the creation of *The X Factor* blockbuster and also motivated him to expand into the American market with *The X Factor USA*. Tulisa travelled to the States in early 2011 to finalize her deal, which was worth £500,000. The opportunity came at exactly the right time to ease her disappointment at failing to achieve a breakthrough in the US with N-Dubz. The first thing she did was phone her dad from LA to tell him the good news. He was thrilled for her: 'It was 4.30 a.m. and she was screaming down the phone. I thought something terrible had happened. But when she calmed down she told me she'd just come out of a meeting with Simon Cowell and she'd got the job. He told her he really liked her'.

Tulisa and Jonathan were keenly aware of the astonishing impact *The X Factor* had on the career of Cheryl Cole, transforming her from one-fifth of a girl group into a successful solo artist and one of the most famous faces in the country. If Tulisa did well on the show, then commercial opportunities would follow. Tulisa could become a brand just as powerful as N-Dubz, selling all sorts of products, including clothes and scent, which she was particularly keen to do – and a solo record by an *X Factor* judge would sell by the lorryload. When she signed her contract with *The X Factor*, Tulisa was given the money-making opportunity of her dreams.

Before she could begin to worry about that, however, there was the small matter of the next tour – N-Dubz's biggest so far. Rehearsals and preparations meant that she could spend some time in London settling in to her new home, which was in a secure gated community in Golders Green in North London. She had big plans for the house in Leavesden but perhaps this luxury apartment suited her current lifestyle better. The complex had a swimming pool and a gym and was safe from burglars and the paparazzi. She observed, 'I couldn't afford it at the time I bought my house but I can now so it worked out.'

She liked nothing better than to spend time there, watching TV curled up on the sofa with her two dogs, Raine, a

Pomeranian, and her new Rottweiler puppy, Prince, who wasn't exactly house trained. Sometimes Ny would come over and they would go out for a pizza in the Finchley Road or just have a drink. Ny recalled that often at least three tables of kids would come over to chat and have their picture taken with Tulisa. Sometimes they would go bowling together but more often than not they would just stay in, play with the dogs and put the world to rights. It was going to be a busy year so this was the time when Tulisa could relax and recharge her batteries.

Meanwhile, two more tracks from *Love.Live.Life* were released to keep the fans happy while rehearsals were taking place. 'So Alive' was one of the grittier songs on the album and featured their friend MC Skepta. It reached number ninety-nine in February.

The second release was 'Morning Star' which, thanks to the influence of Jean-Baptiste Kouame, had a much more American feel. The video was arguably their most boring to date, with the three of them doing little more than singing to camera with no apparent storyline. Tulisa, in a tight black and white dress with tumbling black hair and no hoop earrings, is looking progressively more polished and elegant. Alison Jane Reid observed that she was 'feline'.

The record, the last single released by N-Dubz to date, managed just fifty-two in the charts. The fact that N-Dubz have not had half a dozen top ten hits a year is one reason why *The X Factor* audience had little idea who Tulisa was when she was signed up. They had no conception of the popularity of the band or the relentless touring, frequently topping the bill over more established chart acts. Professor Green, for instance, was a support act on the new tour. Ny was also one of the supports, which gave her the chance to showcase her stunning voice and provide Tulisa with some much needed female company.

N-Dubz were an important part of a teenage culture that

Simon Cowell wanted to reach. The evidence of their teenage appeal was there on their 22-date arena tour, which began at the Ryde Arena on the Isle of Wight on 11 April 2011. The show began in spectacular manner. On the big screen behind the stage there was a film of a high-speed chase with some gangsters pursuing our three heroes, who are riding motorcycles. In a neat touch, the darkness lifts to reveal them on stage, still on the bikes, and they launch into the opening number, 'Took It All the Way', from the latest album.

Tulisa commanded everyone's attention right from the beginning because she was wearing a skin-tight unitard. The sharp-eyed reviewer from the *Daily Mail*, Sarah Bull, observed, 'There was no sign of any lumps or bumps underneath.' Sarah noted that the thought of wearing such an outfit 'would undoubtedly strike fear into the hearts of the majority of women', but Tulisa 'proved she is not most women as she bounded onto the stage ... flaunting her stunning figure in an eye-wateringly tight black all-in-one.' Squeezing her into the costume every night took a small army of backstage helpers and a great deal of talcum powder.

Tulisa's natural weight is just below eight and a half stone but can fluctuate up to nine stone when she is not touring and as low as eight when she is. The exercise she has through dancing around on stage for an hour and a half for a couple of months helps to keep her in shape.

The concert itself mixed all the old favourites with the new tracks. Halfway through, Tulisa sang 'My Name Is Tulisa', her version of the song from *Bugsy Malone* she had performed all those years ago at primary school. Lady Ny then joined her on stage to sing 'Love Sick', one of the highlights of the night because the two friends had been singing together for years.

They closed with 'Papa Can You Hear Me?' and then performed an encore of some of their best-loved songs, including 'Love For My Slum', 'You Better Not Waste My Time' and 'Ouch', before finishing with 'Number 1' and 'Best Behaviour'. Clemmie

Moodie in the *Daily Mirror* saw the show at the Doncaster Dome and described it as 'genius'.

The band put a great deal of money into creating a spectacular show. Fazer revealed, 'We've spent £1 million of our own money on this tour. We splashed fifty-six grand in one day. We don't care about profit. On a tour like this, we should be taking home £200k but instead we'll only make about nine grand each because we spent so much.'

The idea behind the spectacular was to prove that N-Dubz were now up there with the big boys – the acts like Britney Spears, Kylie and Take That, whose shows were epic. They were the first UK urban act to headline an arena tour and they wanted to show they were worthy of it. They had multiple costume and set changes. Tulisa, for instance, performed her *Bugsy* song in a Prohibition-style speakeasy, where all the dancers wore trilby hats and the girls wore basques. For the anthem 'Love.Live.Life', the audience were transported to a sci-fi world complete with an army of Stormtrooper-style backing dancers. Their last change was the most effective, donning tracksuits and trainers – all Adidas, of course – to sing their old Camden hits on a bare stage – a neat contrast between old and new N-Dubz.

Tulisa found the touring itself easier than previous years, thanks largely to Ny. They stayed in the best hotels, drinking wine and playing Scrabble. Ny said, 'We are obsessed with playing it. Some days we are really rubbish at it and we spend the time laughing at each other because it's so bad. The boys are boring. They don't play Scrabble, preferring video games on the bus.'

Fazer and Dappy practically lived in the bus for a month, watching DVDs, drinking, smoking and just chilling with their mates. They would even insist on obtaining a power supply for the bus so they could continue playing video games into the night. Tulisa liked to smoke but preferred to do so in five-star comfort.

The musical highlight of the tour was their first-ever night at the O2 in London, the premier arena in the country. The concert revealed how the three members of N-Dubz had developed individually. Fazer showcased his piano-playing on 'Papa Can You Hear Me?' and 'Best Behaviour'. He was growing musically all the time. Dappy, as ever, engaged with the audience, chatted to them and received the loudest screams. But Tulisa had taken by far the biggest stride forward during the past five years. An online review at *Urban Development* observed, 'Her vocal abilities appear to have improved incredibly over the years, and her stage presence is remarkable. The female boss was the highlight of the show.'

Rich Castillo called the concert at the O2 his proudest moment: 'Turning up at the arena and seeing 19,000 people screaming the band's name, knowing every word to every song and seeing everything we put on stage and everything we had thought about come to fruition was a real jaw-dropping moment.'

Between gigs, Tulisa was able to continue her acting career by filming her role in a new feature film called *Suicide Kids* alongside her old friend from *Dubplate* days, Adam Deacon. The director Arjun Rose had sent her the script to see if she was interested. He recalled, 'She asked whether I could make her part a little bigger, so of course I said "yes" and she was in!' The film was not a Hollywood blockbuster but a low-key British horror film about a group of seven 'suicide kids' who discover that a masked 'grim reaper' killer is doing the job for them. Tulisa's cameo was as the classmate who tries to persuade the police that they aren't suicides after all.

By the time the film premiered in October 2011, it had been renamed *Demons Never Die* and you could be forgiven for thinking that Tulisa was the star. All the promotional material mentioned her first and the rest of the cast nowhere. The actual female lead was the up and coming Emma Rigby, the former *Hollyoaks* actress who starred in *Prisoners' Wives* on BBC One in 2012. The reviews were generally lukewarm. *Total Film* called it 'unconvincing'. *Empire* said the 'the actual "horror" part is the let-down.' The most flattering review came unexpectedly from BRIT Award-winner Jessie J, who tweeted, 'I loved *Demons Never Die*. It was an amazing premiere. So proud of UK film.'

Dappy had a relatively quiet tour, perhaps brooding on what would happen to N-Dubz when Tulisa became a television star. A female fan bit him on the ear before the Doncaster gig and had to be marched out by security. Towards the end of the tour, a blonde model called Cassie Johnson claimed she had spent the night with him after a concert in Newcastle. She revealed to the *News of the World* that she had told him she didn't want to see him again when she left the next morning and refused to give him her telephone number. Amusingly, Tulisa had told the *Newcastle Evening Chronicle* before Cassie kissed and told that the band always had a 'wicked' stay in Newcastle, where the fans were always up for a good time.

After the tour ended at the Liverpool O2 on 21 May, Tulisa had a nail-biting week before the official *X Factor* announcement. Even though it was all settled, a new and surprise ingredient had been thrown into the mix when Cheryl Cole was ditched from *The X Factor USA*. Intense speculation immediately followed that she would be rejoining the British version. Tulisa couldn't help but be worried: 'When it was all going on, I tried to keep my head down but, yes, I was a little nervous she might get her old job – or my new one – back.'

Tulisa need not have been concerned. A source close to the programme revealed, 'It was all media drivel. As always, the flames were fanned by *The X Factor's* relentless publicity machine, which basically pumps out lies on an extraordinarily regular basis. So they said Cheryl was coming back, but she was never coming back.'

The beauty of the Cheryl story was that it was one that could be dusted off throughout the series – literally all the way to the final there was speculation that she would make a phoenix-like return to the panel. In publicity terms she was almost worth more to the show absent than if she had been present.

In the end it was no surprise that Tulisa was included along with Gary Barlow, Louis Walsh and Kelly Rowland when the official announcement was made on Twitter. Simon Cowell said, 'I think Louis and Tulisa will have slightly different points of view as to what the next star should look and sound like!'

Tulisa was enthusiastic: 'I'm so excited to be joining *The X Factor* and want to bring something fresh and new to the panel. I'm not going to be afraid to speak my mind and mix things up a little. I am hoping to find some hot new talent and mentor a winning category. It is always going to be great to get to know and work alongside the other judges. Let the fireworks begin!' She also revealed that she was a fan of the show and watched every episode.

Her selection for *The X Factor* opened a new door for Tulisa. Crucially, it also lifted a weight from her shoulders. She would no longer wake up worrying what Dappy had been up to. She told *Fabulous* magazine, 'The truth is, it was very stressful on a daily basis knowing my career was in his hands. Some mornings I'd wake up to find my future – the band's future – dangling by a thread because of something he had done.' She was no longer required to be the mother hen to him. It was up to others to deal with it if he got into trouble: 'People will realize we're two different people.'

She did, however, speak fondly of her cousin, with whom she had spent the greater part of her life for the past eleven years: 'Dappy is a loony tune, but he's a good lad with a big heart.'

19

Chavtastic

Chav is such a horrid-sounding word. It's perceived as an insult and, sure enough, as soon as Tulisa was confirmed on *The X Factor* the online abuse started. The most damning thing that anyone could say about Tulisa apparently was that she was a 'gobby chav'. Fortunately, Tulisa has never minded the title. She likes to be thought of as outspoken and being described as a chav doesn't upset her at all – she couldn't care less.

The origins of the word are confused. Intellectuals can find all manner of definitions and acronyms but the usual one is 'council housed and violent'. Mostly the word is used to describe women, often from London and the surrounding counties, who dress in a certain way, a uniform of conformity. The London fashion designer Lucy Tammam elegantly summed up what it means to be a chav: 'It is someone who manages to be underdressed and overdressed at the same time.'

To be described as a chav is all about fashion. Alison Jane Reid observes, 'White British kids adopted the street clothes and the slang of the American ghetto and wore status symbol trainers and baggy tracksuits, plenty of cheap gold bling and baseball caps. For the chav girl, it has to be pink and white, trackie bottoms and big, cheap gold earrings. I find the trend towards sportswear and shapeless street fashion deeply depressing.'

When she was with her friends as a young teenager hanging out in Camden Town, Tulisa desperately wanted to fit in and, to do that, you had to conform to the uniform. This was not an environment for pearl earrings and tea dresses in which there was no place to hide a baseball bat. Tulisa observed, 'I would say I'm from an urban, common area – the schools that I went to, people that I was brought up around, whatever you want to call it. I don't really care if you call it a chav – I really don't give a shit whatever you want to call it.'

She was still wearing that uniform when she started making videos. In her very first, 'You Better Not Waste My Time', she is dressed in white trousers and a lightweight puffa coat. Alison Jane observes, 'She's got permed hair, the hooped trashy jewellery and it's an absolute chavtastic look. And then in "Ouch" she has even more jewellery on. She is just dripping in bling mixed with designer sunglasses, white stretched jeans and an Adidas top.'

These were the early days when Tulisa shied away from spending money and would shop in markets or High Street chains. The important thing about her look then was that the target audience for N-Dubz music could relate to what she was wearing – it's what they wore to school or on nights out. Tulisa could have been one of them.

As her confidence grew and N-Dubz achieved more success and financial reward, she was able to become more individual in her style, although throughout her adult life she has adopted the urban look for young women – very short, tight dresses that reveal every curve. Nobody in their right mind would ever have described Tulisa as an ugly duckling but she emerged into the spotlight of *The X Factor* as a swan.

To celebrate her good fortune she had her teeth fixed. They weren't exactly bad before but by the first audition the entire judging panel could have been exhibits at a conference on cosmetic dentistry – and Simon Cowell, king of the veneers, wasn't even there. Tulisa loved her dental work, especially since, it was revealed, she hadn't paid for the procedure, which cost an estimated £12,000, even though that was little more than petty cash for her these days.

She had a gum lift and twelve porcelain veneers fitted over a two-month period by Dr David Bloom at the Senova Dental Studios in Watford. In return, Tulisa tweeted that she loved them and featured on the company's website explaining why she wanted the treatment: 'My original teeth, I just hated them. I didn't notice how much I hated them until I started being in the public eye, being photographed and on television.'

Tulisa revealed that in her previous TV appearances she was thinking about her teeth every five seconds, trying to remember not to smile too much and remembering that her left side of her face was her best profile. Now she couldn't stop smiling. She had recommended the treatment to two of the girls from The Saturdays, so the publicity was already demonstrating what a smart marketing move it was by the dental firm.

Later on, when she was well established on *The X Factor*, there was some half-hearted controversy in the media about her plugging Senova but it's not exactly a secret that celebrities endorse products. Tulisa was very upfront about it and told the *Radio Times*: 'These are things I work to afford, and I don't have to pay for them. It's ridiculous! I could sell half the free things I have and be able to put a mortgage down on a house.'

Tulisa needed to be confident in her smile when she turned up for the first *X Factor* auditions in Birmingham on 1 June 2011. Cheryl Cole sent her a bunch of flowers, which was a complete surprise. Tulisa was touched, and said it was 'a pretty amazing gesture. To be going through all that she is, well, that's a very kind, thoughtful gesture.' They brightened her dressing room but they did not calm the butterflies and she admits she was the most nervous she had ever been. She had been an entertainer for half her life, appeared before royalty and performed in front of thousands of fans at festivals and arenas but she was 'absolutely terrified' when she took her seat on the judges' panel.

Nobody could tell how nervous she was as she posed for photographs, wearing a demure lip-print jumpsuit from DKNY with matching red platform heels and lipstick, her hair swept back as if she were a secretary in the mould of Christina Hendricks in the television series *Mad Men*. *Glamour* magazine loved the look and said 'Bravo!'

The *X Factor* propaganda machine was determined to portray Tulisa as a young woman prepared to speak her mind. She had to live up to that on the first morning when an aspiring girl rapper offered a Nicki Minaj track at her audition. Nicki Minaj is one of Tulisa's favourite hip-hop performers and she snapped at the contestant, 'It's a singing competition, not a rapping competition. And that is someone else you are rapping. It's a no!'

In the first publicity shot from the show, Tulisa is sitting next to Gary with Kelly on her other side and Louis on the end. By the time the TV series began the order had changed: Kelly and Tulisa had swapped places for a reason that was never explained. It may have been obvious very early on that Louis and Tulisa had a rapport or that the producers were hoping for a little flirting between Gary and Kelly. Simon Cowell was wrong about Louis and Tulisa – they seemed to agree on almost everything.

One of the odd things about *The X Factor* is that all the auditions and Bootcamp are concluded by the time the series is shown at the end of August. Tulisa had a busy summer with a schedule of N-Dubz concerts at the major summer festivals, including T in the Park in Balado, Scotland before dashing down to Weston-super-Mare the very next day for T4 on the Beach, a concert she loved. She tweeted: 'Smashed it! No miming! U know how we dooooo! Off home to feed the dog n cook dinner.'

She had time to accept an invitation to Cheryl's twenty-eighth birthday party at the Sanderson Hotel just off Oxford Street – a further indication of a growing friendship between the two women. Cheryl, too, had been singing professionally since she was fourteen and faced the accusations that she was a chav before she starred in *The X Factor*. Making it in such a male-dominated industry is very hard for women and the two had much in common.

Tulisa had her own birthday to celebrate at the fashionable Movida nightclub in the West End in July. All the usual suspects, including Dappy, Kaye and Fazer were there. Tulisa arrived in a chauffeur-driven red Mercedes while Fazer drove himself. Nobody knew for sure if they were arriving from the same address but speculation was growing that they had been an item since the previous year, although Tulisa adamantly refused to talk about her love life, mindful that she'd revealed far too much when she was with Justin Edwards.

She wore a very tight beige bandage dress and a pair of snakeskin shoes. The dress had arrived the same day, just in time for her to change into it. She revealed that it was free, proving that her comments to the *Radio Times* about gifts were completely true. She looked a million dollars, although she continued to show acres of both cleavage and leg – a combination that always meets with disapproval from fashion commentators. Alison Jane Reid observes, 'Short, very tight dresses only look good on stick insect supermodels. Tulisa is a very healthy, curvaceous girl and this makes her look as if she is trying too hard. The maxim for the truly stylish woman is that you never reveal too much.' This is a view with which most men would disagree.

The X Factor cashed in on Tulisa's birthday by presenting her with a muscle-bound topless butler for the day at the Liverpool auditions. She played along with it, knowing it would make excellent television when the series started. She was wearing bright red lipstick and a matching dress from Alexander McQueen, the design house that made Kate Middleton's wedding dress and further proof that Tulisa had long forgotten her rule about never wearing a frock worth more than £100.

From chavtastic to fantastic – Tulisa's changing look . . . All blonde curls and big hoop earrings at the Pinktober Women of Rock Charity Concert at the Royal Albert Hall in November 2009.

No curls, but even blonder at Capital FM's Jingle Bell Ball at the O2 Arena a month later. Does she sleep in these hoops?

Back to black but still can't give up the earrings – at the launch of the N-Dubz book *Against All Odds* at the Lakeside shopping centre.

At last – no hoops, no frills, no curls – just understated glamour for *The X Factor* auditions in Liverpool in June 2011.

Tulisa's agent, Jonathan Shalit, tries to interest Simon Cowell in his new client at a charity auction in Barbados.

Tulisa and Kelly Rowland are all smiles as the new *X Factor* judging panel is pictured at the press launch at the O2 Arena, London, in August 2011 – the smiles wouldn't last.

The hours of practice were worth it. Tulisa shows off her *X Factor* salute for the first time before the auditions begin in Birmingham.

Tulisa takes her Rottweiler puppy Prince on a visit to see her groups at *The X Factor* house in October 2011.

There was never any rivalry. Former judge Cheryl Cole sent Tulisa a bunch of flowers on her first day on *The X Factor* and they were happy to pose together during the Pride of Britain Awards at the Grosvenor House Hotel, London, in October 2011.

A rare photograph of mother and daughter when Ann Byrne came to watch Tulisa at *The X Factor* semi finals. Tulisa called her 'my idol'.

Tulisa and her little muffins – 'Little Mix'.

Tulisa refused to name her steady boyfriend during *The X Factor*. It wasn't Chipmunk, although she showed the rapper what he was missing at his twenty-first birthday party at Jalouse in the West End.

And it wasn't her ever-present PA, Gareth Varey, whom she helped celebrate his twenty-third birthday at fashionable Mahiki.

It was Fazer – although the whole world already knew their secret by the time they finally showed themselves in public as a couple at *The X Factor* wrap party at DSTRKT in December 2011.

Now that everyone knew, she and Fazer were open and loving during a New Year holiday to the idyllic Maldives in the Indian Ocean. Ten days later it was all over.

After a break-up, a girl needs her mates. Rochelle Wiseman (left) and Vanessa White of The Saturdays show solidarity as Tulisa leads the way on a night out clubbing at the end of January 2012.

One of the new men she was linked to was actor Jack O'Connell, and they became closer in the weeks after she was devastated by a sex tape scandal. Here they pop outside a Soho pub for a quick cigarette.

Tulisa didn't seem to be down about Fazer when she visited LA to work on her solo album in February 2012. She was happy to be photographed on a daily basis in her sunniest clothes: she changed into shorts (left) as soon as she checked into her hotel but didn't forget her Lipsy Pocket Dome Bag, which cost £45. She packed a variety of Lipsy playsuits including this plunging nautical print number, which also cost just £45.

Good vibrations: having a giggle on a visit to the Hustler sex shop in Hollywood.

More hard work in Miami, where she shot the video for her first single. Tulisa strolls along the beach with her best friend, singer Ny Gray.

Tulisa in a retro one-piece swimsuit – simply fabulous.

The one sour note in a sublime summer took place the following week when reports surfaced of a row between Kaye Vassell and Tulisa after one of the N-Dubz concerts. Apparently Kaye had accused Tulisa's best friend Ny of sleeping with Dappy, which she denied. Tulisa was said to be upset that Ny was being accused of something she hadn't done. According to the *Sun* she was even more annoyed when Kaye allegedly spat at Ny, prompting Tulisa to shout at her, 'Get the fuck out of here.'

Before the eighth series of *The X Factor* began on ITV on 20 August there was just one more loose end for Tulisa to deal with – the end of N-Dubz's American dream. It's impossible to say exactly when it died. The probability is that the beginning of the end was when *Love.Live.Life* – or any of the singles from it – failed to make number one. The plan had been for them to travel back to the US at the beginning of 2011 to add some tracks and do some re-recording to make certain songs more agreeable to the American audience. It didn't go well.

The news that they had parted with Def Jam came out officially in August 2011 but it was obvious that the American hype had calmed down long before then. One of the biggest ironies of the whole debacle was that the album was never even released in the US. All the worry about compromising N-Dubz was completely unnecessary.

The exact course of events was a grey area just as it was in the old days when they parted company with Polydor – did they jump or were they pushed? Some reports suggested that Def Jam had informed N-Dubz that their five-album contract had come to an end. A spokesman for the label said, 'N-Dubz have left the Def Jam imprint in the USA due to creative differences over musical direction. This was one hundred per cent the band's decision and they remain signed to Universal worldwide.'

Dappy wanted to make absolutely sure everyone knew it was their decision: 'We were never going to co-operate with them when they decided to change what we are. If we had co-operated we would still be signed. But I stuck my finger up at them when they wanted us to make another *Being . . . N-Dubz* TV show. Tulisa thought we should do it because we could make some money out of it, but I said no. They should've stuck with the band they came to see at the Shepherd's Bush Empire.'

The most interesting titbit regarding the split was the news that Tulisa had a solo deal with Island Records and that Def Jam had an option to be her US label. It seemed a game plan for Tulisa's future was already firmly in place.

First, though, she had to be accepted by the great British public, the *X Factor* viewers who had never heard of N-Dubz or listened to hip-hop or grime. The very first time they saw Tulisa on 20 August 2011 she was wearing a shiny silver mini dress. Fellow new judge Kelly Rowland was wearing something remarkably similar and together they looked like cheerleaders at a Roman gladiator afternoon.

This was an important episode for Tulisa because it would create a first and maybe lasting impression with the viewing public. Her opening words to the nation, in one of those rapid compilations that whizz by at the start of each episode, were 'What is *WRONG* with you!' while gesturing with her hands. It soon became clear that Tulisa uses her hands quite a lot when she talks – a mannerism she has always had but one that can become more noticeable when she's nervous.

These opening programmes are slickly edited so Tulisa and the other judges are really at the mercy of the producers, who can manipulate the footage however they want in order to create good television. There always seems to be one hopeful who is surprisingly good, another who has a sob story and a third who insults the judges: it's a formula but it works.

The editing favoured Tulisa in the first episode, in which she was heavily featured. She wore ten different outfits as they cut and pasted the show together. One of her opening exchanges was with some tone deaf girls whom she tells, 'none of you can really sing.' The cutting reply was: 'It's a bit rich coming from you.'

Tulisa is introduced as a 'member of Britain's biggest hip-hop band, N-Dubz'. The older viewers would have little idea what hip-hop was or have heard of N-Dubz so Tulisa set out her manifesto for the show as if she were working an audience at a political rally: 'This year I would like to bring some fireworks to the judging panel. I have been in N-Dubz since the age of eleven. We have worked our butt off to get where we are today. We script our own videos and we write our own songs. I know what I'm talking about.

'This isn't just about finding a star; it's about finding something fresh, something new. I know talent when I see it and that's my job. I'm here to judge. I'm young. I'm feisty. I'm current and I'm opinionated. Would I say I'm gobby? Yeah!'

The first contestant we meet in London is a teenager, Frankie Cocozza, who has the air of a cheeky rascal about him and the producers decide can be a bit of a character on the show. He shows the panel his backside, which is tattooed with girls' names. Tulisa laughs and tells him, 'It's quite clear the girls already love you. After that audition it's going to get a whole lot worse.'

We didn't know at the time – although we could have guessed – that the first four hopefuls were in the final selection of sixteen that some weeks later would be chosen for the live shows. Frankie is followed by Kitty, Goldie and Janet. Tulisa told Kitty, a Lady Gaga impersonator, 'People will either love you or hate you. I hope they love you. With that vocal you really touched me. It was very haunting as well. It was a brilliant audition ... you do like to talk a lot.' She thought Goldie, a slightly bonkers singer from Thailand, was 'so refreshing'. Janet Devlin, a young Irish singer, performed the old Elton John chestnut 'Your Song', which Tulisa found 'very moving' and thought was a 'recording vocal'.

So far Tulisa had said all the right things without revealing any of the spirit she had promised. That changed with the obligatory pantomime villain, a young hopeful called George from North London who had been on the show before, in 2009, when he had thrown a wobbly. He told us he had matured, which didn't bode well. Sure enough, he was terrible and proceeded to show that he hadn't matured at all.

For some reason it was Tulisa with whom he had a confrontation, as if to prove she wasn't kidding about her feisty nature. While Gary was funny with his scripted one-liner that George had 'matured like a bad curry', Tulisa was more direct: 'I don't think your attitude has changed at all. You came and stood right next to me, and I felt a lot of aggression off you.' The exchange became heated, especially when George called her a 'scumbag trying to replace Cheryl.' That was the signal for Tulisa to let rip, 'Don't come in my space!' Some swearing from George prompted Tulisa to respond, 'You've just embarrassed yourself to the whole nation. I've worked my way up from Camden Town. That's why I'm here today.'

Offstage, George hadn't finished and said of Tulisa, 'No dogs allowed. I would have brought my Alsatian ...' At that point, host Dermot O'Leary, resembling an embarrassed geography teacher, stepped in: 'Watch your mouth, George. Don't call girls that.'

All in all, it had been a brilliant first episode for Tulisa. On *The Xtra Factor*, the companion show, Simon Cowell, chewing gum and looking terrible, was clearly delighted: 'She's like a lippy brat. I like that. She's bolshie and I like that.'

The Xtra Factor, which in 2011 was presented by Caroline Flack and Olly Murs, was much more fun than the main show and viewers were able to learn more about the judges. Tulisa, for instance, revealed her abilities as a mimic with a very funny impersonation of Kelly's accent and American manner. She also chewed on Refreshers, referring to them as the best 'old school' sweet.

Olly asked her some questions so that we would know more about her. She said she liked boys who were confident and cocky 'jack the lad' types. He also asked her where she would like to be in five years' time. Her answer revealed that her ambitions hadn't really changed from when she was a young girl: 'I want to be married and I want to be one of the most successful businesswomen in the UK – as a celebrity and household name in business. I want to get into everything from nightclubs to fashion that people want to invest in. That's the plan.'

The plan was already in motion. In that first episode of *The X Factor* she revealed the tattoo on her outer right forearm: 'The Female Boss', which she had drawn by Craig Bain Joseph (CBJ), one of London's best-known tattoo artists, at his Ink Lounge in Palmers Green. She said, 'Finally getting it done after about 100 fans have got it done before me. Feeling all right. Few glasses of wine to ease off the pain, um, yeah, it's going good.'

She first revealed it to N-Dubz fans on the video for 'Morning Star'. The beauty of this tattoo was that it could be a walking advertisement for Tulisa's business in the future. It was literally a living brand and Tulisa could promote herself during every episode of *The X Factor* provided she never wore a long-sleeved dress.

Tattoos have moved on a great deal from the days when they were confined to sailors with a Popeye anchor on one forearm and 'Mum' on the other. Tattoo originates from ta-tau, a Polynesian word meaning mark. Captain Cook, the famous explorer, came across the body art in Tahiti in 1769 and noted it in his journal, adding that it was common practice among both sexes on the island. Marking the skin is frowned upon in the Bible and, with the advent of Christianity, was banned in Europe until Cook's discovery.

Now, popularized by celebrities like Robbie Williams, David Beckham and Angelina Jolie, it has become an important part of modern culture and self-expression for young people. CBJ, originally from Granada in the Caribbean, was one of a growing band of renowned tattooists who were regarded as serious artists. He was responsible for the elaborately beautiful tattoos that Fazer has on his arms, one of them a painstakingly drawn money tree that says money is the root of all evil.

Dappy has many tattoos besides the famous 'RIP Dad' on his

neck. He even has '2lisa' inked on his arm. Tulisa returned the compliment with 'Dappy' drawn on her neck. It's very close to the hairline so is only visible when she wears her hair up. She explained why to Simon Hattenstone in *RadioTimes*: 'Everybody I know has a tattoo of the guy they're dating or their first boyfriend, and I was like, all the guys I've dated have come in and out of my life and have meant nothing to me. If there's one guy I have a strong bond with, who's been there for me, it would be Dappy.'

By far her most visible tattoo is the giant winged unicorn on her shoulder, which was boldly on display when she wore a blue, jungle print dress for the London auditions. The size of the drawing seems over the top until you realize that it is cunningly covering up an old tattoo. The old drawings that she had inked one teenage holiday to Greece weren't of an embarrassing former lover but her birth name, Tula, spelt in Greek capitals. She wasn't Tulisa then, which was a pity as it would have been cool to have that on her shoulder in Greek lettering. Underneath were some cheesy yin and yang images that definitely needed concealing. She had the new work done at a studio in Los Angeles during her first recording visit there in 2010. Afterwards she couldn't stop looking over her shoulder to check that she liked it. She called it Pegasus after the divine horse of Greek mythology.

Gone are the days when tattoos, particularly on girls, were frowned upon. Alison Jane Reid observes, 'They are hugely important to young women. They use tattoos to communicate who they are and what they stand for.'

20

The Role Model

Michelle Barrett was a 31-year-old mother of four with a winning yet hesitant smile as if she was not quite sure if she had a right to be on stage. She chose to sing the poignant 'All The Man That I Need' by Whitney Houston. The first few bars, when it became clear that she could sing nicely, were enough to start Tulisa quietly weeping. Gone was her feisty image and in its place was an emotional young woman thinking about the mum she loved. She confessed to Michelle, 'You remind me of my mum ... Just like you, she had such a beautiful voice and she didn't do anything with it.'

The auditorium was hushed for a minute as Tulisa and Michelle exchanged what she said was a 'mummy and daughter thing': 'You guys are going to think I'm nuts. It's just, you know, like standing in the kitchen listening to her sing. She just had the most amazing voice ... and I wish she would do something like this and get up.' At this point her tears were too much to cope with and she couldn't say any more.

The crowd cheered as Michelle got a resounding yes from all four judges. It was one of the best moments of the whole series but, in the strange world of *The X Factor*, we never saw her again.

She did have a moment of fame in the Sunday papers when she was revealed to be an underwear model.

The same thing happened to a maths teacher from Aberdare in South Wales called John Adams, who resembled Superman and whom the panel loved after his rendition of the Damien Rice song 'Cannonball'. Gary Barlow told him it was his favourite song and that he had 'nailed that vocal'. Tulisa shyly eyed him up as if he was the talent on a night out in a club: 'If I may say so, you're rather handsome.' We would hear the song again on *The X Factor* but not sung by John, who disappeared without trace.

The important aspect of these exchanges – and the one with George in the first episode – was that they were showing different sides of Tulisa. They were giving her a personality. As she described herself, 'I've got a hard exterior, but I'm mushy on the inside.'

Tulisa created a good first impression. Her friend DJ Max said, 'Tulisa is lovely, funny, honest and down to earth. She's had no media training, speaks from the heart and shoots from the hip.' Kevin O'Sullivan confirmed the most important thing for Tulisa: 'Simon Cowell is thrilled with her.' Louis Walsh was equally struck, gushing, 'I can't believe how much I like her.'

The only downside to her new mainstream fame was that the media were on the lookout for stories that might make a headline. They appeared less interested in her love life with Fazer and more eager to expose her early life. Her former stepmother Mel Vondrau was quick to print with 'The troubling truth about Tulisa' but so, surprisingly, was her father, Plato, who revealed in the *Daily Mail* and the *Sunday Mirror* 'The very upmarket reality behind the new *X Factor* bad girl's street image' in which he was quoted as saying, 'Money was never a problem' and spoke of giving her £500 in cash for her seventh birthday.

Perhaps Plato, unused to media attention, had been naive in speaking to the press. His intentions were almost certainly well meaning, without thought as to how his comments might look

in print. Tulisa was careful not to stir things up further by con-
ducting a public row about her upbringing. All she would say in
numerous interviews on the subject was that her father was a
'very proud Greek man', that he had glamorized her childhood
and that she did not agree with what he said. 'People can
choose to believe what they want.'

Any embarrassment or ill feeling caused by the article was
quickly forgotten because there is a deep bond between father
and daughter and he loved turning on his television on a
Saturday night to watch. For her part, she was quick to invite
him to one of the live shows when they began in October.

Another unsatisfactory headline came from the outspoken
Tory MP Nadine Dorries, who had read Tulisa's account of
youthful sex and drugs in the neighbourhood where she'd
hung-out as a teenager and said: 'Providing strong mentors who
young, impressionable people can look up to should be what *X
Factor* is and what it's about. The choice of Tulisa, unfortunately,
falls way short of the mark.'

Ms Dorries was involved a couple of months later in some
headlines of her own concerning a new relationship with a married man – albeit one she said had left the marital home after
suffering twenty years of strife. Anne Atkins, writing in the *Daily
Mail* was unimpressed: 'Just when you thought MPs couldn't
sink any lower, just when you thought going to jail for fraud is as
tacky as it can get, middle-aged Tory MP Nadine Dorries smirks
inanely that she is "in a romantic relationship". A relationship,
that is, with another woman's husband —, a devout Catholic
and father of two daughters.'

Tulisa was not pleased with Ms Dorries' criticism: 'She's a
pompous ****. I'm an honest person. I'm not going to lie. And
I feel that your past is what made you who you are today.' She
certainly did not accept that she wasn't a role model and
believed her success was an inspiration to other kids who were
smoking weed, having sex too young and becoming involved in
crime. She told *You* magazine, 'It makes these kids go: "She's

just like us. If she can do it, we can do it." That's the point. It drives me nuts when people say that's not a role model.'

One further unwelcome distraction was a story that Tulisa had made a sex tape on a BlackBerry. Apparently, an unidentified man was trying to sell the video to the *Sun* for £500,000. Tulisa's spokesperson said, 'The tape is one hundred per cent fake and is just someone trying to cash in on her *X Factor* role. She is horrified that someone would go to extreme lengths to fabricate a video. It is absolutely not her.'

Tulisa had enough to worry about on the show itself by being given the groups to mentor. They had never won the competition and this series seemed to have a particularly lacklustre line-up. The situation was so dire by Bootcamp that producers created so many new groups it was almost impossible to keep track of who they were.

Four out of the eight acts who made it from Bootcamp to Judges' Houses were 'manufactured' by the show. It was even more complicated than that because one, Rhythmix, was formed from two groups who had already been put together – Jade and LeAnn from Orion were mixed with Jessie and Perry from Faux Pas. The thinking behind the mix and match groups appeared to be to try and find one or two who might conceivably find a place in the hugely popular urban market. Simon Cowell had been paying attention when teenage rapper Cher Lloyd had done so well the previous year.

It seemed that the show had no qualms whatsoever in tinkering with things to try and come up with a section that would, at the very least, be competitive. The majority of the band members who flew off to Judges' Houses didn't really know each other at all. Before then they needed to know which judge would be their mentor.

Tulisa may have had an inkling she would be put in charge of the groups, but when she opened the door to the room where those remaining were waiting excitedly, and revealed that it would be her, she jumped up and down as if she had received the news that she had passed her GCSEs. Everyone seemed ecstatic, with lots of squealing and hugging.

Not everybody was delighted though. Aaron Welby, one half of singing duo Girl v Boy observed, 'We knew it was going to be an uphill battle from the start with Tulisa; you could tell from her face as we were walking on that she didn't like us.' In his opinion she was only interested in urban groups.

The big talking point before Judges' Houses began was who would be Tulisa's co-judge and there was much speculation that it would be Dappy. Tulisa did her best to persuade the producers that he should be involved. She told the *Daily Mirror*, 'I want him as a mentor for one of the groups. He will be so funny, out of control. I really want him to be involved. I don't know if it will happen but it's something I am fighting for. I think all the contestants will love him.' The producers were not keen. Dappy told Kiss FM, 'Tulisa said to me that she begged them. But they knew I would cause madness. You don't want to get me on that as a judge – if you're crap, I would tell you you're crap!'

While it would have been entertaining for Dappy to have been involved, the producers obviously considered it to be too much of a risk to have someone who might cause mayhem on a mainstream, family show. He was, however, upset at being denied the chance to appear with his cousin: 'It devastated me. I can't lie. I wanted to be on there with Tulisa.' He was bitter when he was interviewed by Radio 1's *Newsbeat* programme: 'I've got a point to prove to them lot, they make me feel like I'm some idiot, like I'm not good enough to go and judge someone. Have they seen me in the studio? I'm a monster in the studio.'

Dappy had been outspoken about *The X Factor* – and would continue to be so – which couldn't have helped his cause. The biggest acts in the world, including Lady Gaga and Rihanna, treated the show as a promotional tool without feeling the need to analyse its place in the music industry. Commercially, Dappy knew the power of *The X Factor* and said he couldn't compete with acts from the show like One Direction and JLS.

He did his best, however, by reaching number one with his first solo single, 'No Regrets', knocking One Direction off the top spot in the process. Tulisa was 'so proud of him' and the man himself said he had waited for this moment all his life.

In the end the producers chose Jessie J to help Tulisa at Judges' Houses, which in her case would be a villa in Mykonos on the Aegean. It was a shame that she wasn't nearer her grandparents. She flew out with the eight groups but, at this stage, it was all business and definitely not a Club 18–30 package. Aaron Welby recalled that Tulisa wasn't allowed to speak to them on the plane and he later revealed that they only saw her twice at the villa after they arrived.

Tulisa had never met Jessie J before but the two hit it off and ended up picking three of the put-together groups, The Risk, Nu Vibe and Rhythmix, as well as the lovable duo 2 Shoes, who seemed to have stumbled into the show by accident when they were looking for the set of *The Only Way Is Essex*.

Fazer had jetted in to help and enjoy the glorious Greek weather. We never saw him on camera but he gave some advice behind the scenes. He was very taken with Rhythmix and observed, 'When they started singing, it got me.'

The biggest story during Tulisa's stay in Mykonos was when she was reported to have ditched one of the girl groups for being more interested in sneaking off for sex with the boys than in being professional and trying to further their careers.

This was never confirmed, although it is just the sort of unfocused behaviour that would have met with her disapproval. She said, 'I'm all for love and romance. But if they're just mucking about, just for fun to have a s*** when they should be rehearsing then I'm not into that. At all. There's a time for partying, but only when the hard work has been done.'

On arriving back in this country, Tulisa had some important business to attend to, plugging her 'first perfume', TFB (The Female Boss), with a series of interviews and a discreet mention of the product, which cost £19.95 for a 100ml bottle. Apparently you put the scent on and you immediately become TFB just like Tulisa.

Nobody realized at the time why the name of the perfume was so inspired: every week at the start of the live shows Tulisa would bare her forearm to the camera, revealing her tattoo of the same title, 'The Female Boss'. It took a while for the media to catch on that this was blatant advertising. Gareth, who was always guaranteed to keep Tulisa smiling, announced tongue-in-cheek that he too was going to release a perfume – a combo of Silk Cut Purple and wine.

Dappy, meanwhile, 'celebrated' the beginning of the live shows by spending twelve hours in police custody on suspicion of assaulting Kaye. The *Daily Mirror* reported that he had become violent towards her at the West London home of her mother. He was released without charge and the Metropolitan Police said that no further action would be taken. Kaye denied there had been any violence and Dappy tweeted, 'I love Kaye the mother of my kids and my 2 beautiful boys. We are a unit. Nothing comes between family..NaNa x.' He later added that he had never attacked his girlfriend.

21

Tulisa v Kelly

Both Kelly and Tulisa knew that the producers would try to create a rivalry between them – the elegant black American singing star against the down-to-earth Londoner. They had talked about it from the very beginning so that they were prepared for any flak. In particular they expected 'frock wars', in which their respective outfits would be cruelly dissected by the fashion experts. They checked with each other the day before filming to find out what colours they would be wearing the next day to avoid any embarrassing clashes. If Kelly was wearing white, then Tulisa would wear black – it was simple. That only worked well while they were speaking to each other, however.

Almost all judges' rows on these sorts of programmes are entirely fabricated to whip up some publicity for the show. Only very occasionally do they turn out to be real. The producers of the 2011 X Factor must have thought it was Christmas when Kelly and Tulisa started a proper feud.

Kelly Rowland is a thorough professional from the moment she jumps out of bed at 6 a.m. – not for her the long lie-ins after the late nights favoured by Tulisa and her friends. Louis Walsh observed, 'From the second she's up, she's in diva mode.' She is a fitness fanatic and probably spends more time in the gym than any other celebrity. She seems obsessed with achieving a perfect body shape and revealed that she suffered from OCD (obsessive compulsive disorder): 'Everything has to be lined up.'

She was rumoured to do two hundred sit-ups before bed every night. Even after a thirteen-hour day on *The X Factor*, she would happily hit the gym at 1 a.m. to keep her body in shape. And she was fitting in frequent nine-hour transatlantic flights to and from her palatial mansion in Miami. Complete with marble floors, swimming pool and its own jetty, it was definitely the sort of home Tulisa craved.

Kelendria Rowland may have settled in the Florida city but she was born in Atlanta, Georgia. Her father was largely absent when she was growing up and her parents split when she was seven. Her mother, Doris, was a live-in nanny, and when Kelly was eight she re-located to Houston, Texas. She would later admit that she was no longer in contact with her father but insisted it was not a 'pity party'.

Kelly was the same age as Tulisa – eleven – when she started on the long road to fame. At school, she heard about auditions for a group called Girls Tyme through her friend LaTavia Roberson, who introduced her to Beyoncé Knowles. It was the start of a close and enduring friendship. There were six girls in the band when they performed on *Star Search*, then the premier talent show in the US. They failed to impress the judges, so Kelly and Beyoncé matched the failure of Justin Timberlake and Britney Spears in that particular competition.

Three of the girls left and they were joined by another friend, LaToya Luckett. The quartet would practise in Beyoncé's backyard and at her mother's hairdressing salon. They had a manager but, when he left, Beyoncé's father, Mathew, stepped in. He quit his job selling medical equipment and put the girls through a series of hard boot camps as they stepped up their quest for stardom. They even learned to dance in wedge heels, striving to copy the great girl groups of the past like The Supremes and En

Vogue. The philosophy was very similar to that of N-Dubz – if you don't work hard, you won't achieve anything. During the summer holidays, Kelly moved in with Beyoncé and her family because it was easier for her mother, who found it too difficult to take her to practise.

In 1993 the group changed their name to Destiny's Child, a name taken from the Book of Isaiah in the Bible. They then spent four long years on the road before being featured on the soundtrack of the hit movie *Men in Black* in 1997, which set them on the path to success with their self-titled debut album released the following year. More personnel changes followed until, at the end of 2000, they were a trio – Kelly, Beyoncé and Michelle Williams – and became arguably the most successful girl group of all time. They sold more than fifty million albums around the world before a final split in 2005. Kelly had already released her first solo album, *Simply Deep*, which was a UK number one in 2002 and enjoyed worldwide sales of 2.5 million.

Her early success was soon eclipsed by Beyoncé, who established herself as one of the biggest stars in the world. Kelly's career stalled a little and her second album, *Ms Kelly*, which was released in 2007, failed to make the top twenty in the UK. Her third album, *Here I Am*, was ready for release during *The X Factor*. While it was never acknowledged that Kelly joined the series only to plug her album – and tour with Chris Brown – it would make perfect commercial sense for that to be the case.

You might be forgiven for thinking that she and Tulisa would forge a friendship based on their shared experience of a broken home, childhood unhappiness and success achieved through hard work. They also had not enjoyed much luck with men. Kelly's fiancé, an American football player called Roy Williams, called off their wedding eight weeks before she was due to walk down the aisle. She picked herself up from that by immersing herself in work and personal training.

At first, there was no sign that Tulisa and Kelly wouldn't be on speaking terms during *The X Factor*. They said all the right things about each other in public. Kelly said, 'Tulisa's so nice'. Even Beyoncé commented, 'Kelly tells me Tulisa is a lovely person as well as a talented artist. She is on one of Simon's shows while only being in her twenties. You don't get to that level unless you're doing something right.' Tulisa remarked, 'I call Kelly the Professional Bitch because she's so professional. She is a mean machine – she's got me exercising. Now I do warm-ups before I go on stage.'

Privately, however, Tulisa, who is seven years younger, felt no connection. A source close to the show observed, 'She really hated Kelly's faux ghetto style – all that "Put it down, girl". She does impressions of Kelly's faux ghetto talk and has everyone in stitches.' Tulisa thought the whole American vibe was fake especially as, growing up, she was aware of the struggle black families had in her neighbourhood. 'Kelly travelled with a massive entourage while Tulisa had Gareth and I think she thought the whole thing was slightly ridiculous.'

Louis Walsh had actually predicted a falling-out well before the live shows when he said, 'There is no way Tulisa and Kelly are going to get through the series without a major row . . . and they won't have to fake it.'

Whatever was simmering beneath the surface between the two women came bubbling out into the open during what became popularly known as 'Mishagate'. On week three, Tulisa apparently called a young black singer from Manchester, Misha Bryan, a bully – except she never did. It was Louis who used the b-word. But it was Tulisa who had opened the debate by commenting on Misha B's feisty nature, which 'can come across quite mean to certain contestants'. She went on, 'I've been told by a few contestants this week that there's been a few mean comments towards them. I am not putting you down but take that feistiness and that energy and bring it on the stage. When you get off stage leave the war behind.'

Louis took things further by saying that he had heard that Misha had been bullying one of his contestants backstage, which had Kelly frantically saying, 'We are not going to go there.' The host, Dermot, prolonged the row by asking Tulisa if she thought it was fair to make such comments about Misha. She was not in the mood to back down: 'When it affects other contestants, then I am sorry but I am going to say something.'

While she was saying something, Kelly and Louis were bickering behind her back. Apparently Louis spent thirty minutes after the show soothing Kelly's hurt feelings. On the results show, the following night, he apologized for using the word bully. This was genius in a way because it reminded everyone that he had used it about Misha in the first place and let anybody who missed it catch up with what had happened. The media cleverly spun the story to make it seem that Tulisa had been the instigator of the bullying claim – after all, nobody really cared what Louis thought.

Misha B, who was unquestionably one of the best singers in the series, was quoted in the tabloids as saying, 'Being called an *X Factor* bully on national TV was not fair. I know I am not a bad person. Tulisa hurt my feelings because there are always two sides to every story.' Misha herself gave the story oxygen. She said, 'At school I was bullied – and I did bully people myself, but I am a different person now.' In the fickle world of celebrity to have been bullied is an asset, to have bullied is not.

One far-fetched theory put forward in the media was that Tulisa had instigated the whole row because she was annoyed at text messages between Misha and Fazer, who had volunteered to produce a record for her.

Kelly and Tulisa were not on speaking terms. The *Sunday Mirror* reported that Kelly had told a friend, 'Tulisa and I have no relationship, the show has become a living hell.' The *Daily Mirror* said that Tulisa had been overheard 'bitching' to a friend, 'I don't care about Kelly and don't even want to look at her.' That was painfully obvious from the body language on the judges' panel. Tulisa was supposedly upset at being painted as the villain when all she was doing was sticking up for her acts.

Tulisa was also reported as telling Kelly to 'fucking stay out of it' when she tried to offer advice on her acts. A source said, 'They definitely don't like each other and a lot of the dislike is coming from Tulisa.' Kevin O'Sullivan observed, 'To be fair to Tulisa, she doesn't turn up with an entourage. She is what she is.'

The irony of the whole bullying saga was that Tulisa could relate to Misha in a way that the majority of *X Factor* viewers could not. Misha was raised by a foster carer, never knew her father's name and was abandoned by her mother. As a teenager, most of Tulisa's friends were black, from poor families and either in gangs in the Camden area or associating with people who were.

Racial prejudice has always been a big issue with N-Dubz, particularly with Fazer. As the only black member of the group he was more aware of it growing up than the other two. Tulisa has had a number of black boyfriends, including Fazer, and the posse she has taken with her on holidays to Ayia Napa and Ibiza reflects her wide circle of friends across the ethnic spectrum. Her best friend these days, Ny, is black, as is Su-Elise Nash, who has been on several holidays with Tulisa. The Camden estates where Dappy and her teenage friends lived were mainly black neighbourhoods and her two closest mates then, Mercedes and Solly, were both black.

It's impossible to say how much damage to Misha's chances of winning *The X Factor* was caused by the row but the early favourite with both the bookies and the voting public was the Irish singer Janet Devlin, who didn't win either. Misha went out at the semi-final stage and Tulisa was seen apparently mouthing the words 'I'm sorry' to Kelly, which may have been a reference to 'Mishagate' or just a more general commiseration.

After the exit, the *Daily Mail* revisited the story and wrote, 'In October, *X Factor* judge Tulisa Contostavlos very publically accused Misha of bullying her fellow contestants.' She hadn't. It was Louis, but history has recorded the event differently. Misha B herself didn't appear to bear any lasting grudge. She said, 'I'm very grateful for the experience I had with Tulisa because it has helped me to grow as a person ... I think Tulisa is incredible, very inspirational.'

Tulisa appeared to make up with Kelly with a hug on the show but they hadn't really. At the launch for Kelly's latest album in November, she said they were 'doing good' and 'pretty much back on track.' Kelly also appeared live in a bikini top and hot pants, performing a new single, 'Down For Whatever', from *Here I Am*, which was largely produced by Jim Jonsin, who had been involved in the last N-Dubz album. While the single reached number six, the album failed to chart in the top twenty.

Tulisa announced that she would not be releasing a record during *The X Factor*, as both Kelly and Cheryl, more successfully, had done. She wanted to concentrate on the show and release an album in 2012. N-Dubz had a greatest hits album coming out for Christmas so she didn't want to be in competition with that or become involved in any contractual difficulties as a result.

The 'bullying' controversy managed to steer the spotlight away from what the two women were wearing throughout the series. Fashion experts seem to agree that whoever was wearing a long gown won the evening. Kelly seemed more settled in her style, perhaps a reflection that she had been in this world for several years more than Tulisa.

The X Factor fashion parade changes so rapidly. Just when you think you like an outfit, then it's the following evening and you can't bear what either lady is wearing. Most weeks both *heat* magazine and *Glamour* preferred Kelly's look, while Tulisa seemed to be searching for a style, finding designers that suited her, like Vivienne Westwood and Alexander McQueen, and making a few mistakes on the way. She certainly didn't need to be styled like Cheryl Cole.

Alison Jane Reid observed, 'The idea of making her look like a Cheryl clone is a shame. It just shows a lack of imagination –

why would she have to look like someone else? Tulisa is beautiful in a completely different way. She has absolutely stunning hair and lovely pale skin.

'Basically she needs to be more restrained. I think with her body shape she needs to wear slightly longer dresses – not the short skin-tight numbers. A lot of the dresses are overfrumpy – a bit like the fairy on the Christmas tree.'

All the worst ingredients came together in week five with a short white gladiator dress with fussy black accessories. Cheryl might just have been able to carry it off but *heat* called it an 'overloaded ensemble' and Tulisa's worst fashion week.

Alison Jane observed, 'I really feel for Tulisa in this dress. It is truly awful. She clearly knows it too! She looks very uncomfortable. The dress is too short and too fussy for a girl with such a curvaceous body. It makes her thighs look big. As for the dress – did she mean to audition for the film *Gladiator*? She looks as if she has raided the fancy dress shop and thrown on everything but the kitchen sink.'

It wasn't all bad news for Tulisa. *Glamour* magazine thought the Alexander McQueen tribal print dress she wore to the London auditions was 'amazing' and definitely gave her the edge. Pulling her hair back from her face suited the whole look. The dress that ticked all the boxes for Tulisa, however, and made her the clear winner on the night in all the magazines was the turquoise lace dress designed by Matthew Williamson she wore in week seven of the live shows. While the dress was well above the knee, it wasn't hip-hop short.

Alison Jane enthused, 'She looked absolutely gorgeous and she is only showing her legs. Her hair is lovely and, combined with her pastel-coloured make-up, gives her a really natural look. Restrained prettiness is great for Tulisa.

'The same night, Kelly wore a very short rah rah number that looked more like a Tulisa choice and didn't suit her at all.' The only slight drawback with Tulisa's dress was that it had long sleeves and you couldn't see the 'Female Boss' tattoo.

Fashion is all about opinions and the very next week Tulisa wore a leopard print short dress in black and gold complete with 'fetish' footwear. Alison Jane thought she looked ready for a bondage session.

For the live final Tulisa chose a royal blue fishtail dress by up-and-coming designer Fyodar Golan. *Sky Living* called it her 'most dramatic choice yet.' The only problem was that it was so tight she couldn't really move in it and Louis had to help her dutifully to her seat. *Heat* was not impressed but did think her hair and make-up 'looked very glam'.

Throughout the series Tulisa's outfits may have been a bit hit and miss but they all revealed one characteristic – she had no fear. She wore a leather catsuit complete with little cat's ears on Halloween night.

Alison Jane observed, 'I love the catsuit. Wow! She looks feline and adorable, like a latter-day Pussy Galore in the Bond films. Tulisa looks like a twenty-first century icon when she plays up her delicious, sex kitten curves with a dash of wit and va, va voom. When she gets it right, she looks extraordinary.'

22

Woman of the Year

Tulisa began the eighth series of *The X Factor* being described by Simon Cowell, in a nice way, as a 'brat'; she ended it as Woman of the Year. She said the award from *Now* magazine was going to go straight onto her mantelpiece: 'A year ago the only time I would get in *Now* was when I looked chavtastic in a tracksuit. This means so much.'

The newly crowned Woman of the Year knew exactly what to say to be gracious – another sign of how far she had come in a short time. She was no longer 'Tulisa from N-Dubz'. She observed, 'Getting away from the band and finding out what I want to do has given me confidence ... Now I can enjoy life.'

Tulisa was given the award just before *The X Factor* final in which Little Mix were crowned series winners. It had been quite a journey for the girl group: they had been 150–1 outsiders when the live shows began. They had even had to change their name from Rhythmix to the much catchier Little Mix. A children's charity called Rhythmix had objected and probably had done the girls a favour. It was almost the first time anyone had noticed the four unassuming girls and they never looked back after they sang Katy Perry's 'E.T.' on the Halloween show.

They were dressed as dolls and gave one of the most memorable performances of the entire series. Tulisa joined them on stage during finals weekend to sing a mash-up of Alicia Keys' songs 'Empire State of Mind' and 'If I Ain't Got You'. She stood in the middle of the girls, wearing power heels that made her taller and more striking. Little Mix in flat trainers, by comparison, seemed like a group of schoolgirls who had won a prize to duet with a superstar.

Before she went on, Tulisa admitted to being nervous because it was the first time she had ever sung with girls. Little Mix were excited too: 'If it wasn't for Tulisa believing in us from the start, we wouldn't be here today. We cannot wait to stand on the stage in front of 10,000 people and sing it with Tulisa. We have to go out there tonight and give the best performance we have ever given.' Even Simon Cowell liked Little Mix and thought they had 'won the night'. He added, 'Little Mix are a revelation.'

The performance was a triumph for Tulisa and immediately prompted everyone to start talking about her upcoming album and the type of music that would be on it – that, of course, was the point. The mainstream audience had no idea what Tulisa sounded like or, indeed, if she could sing at all. This was conclusive proof that she could. Being an active part of the final meant that Tulisa's performance was one of the lasting memories that the audience would take away from *The X Factor*.

The winners' song this year was 'Cannonball', which we knew from the auditions was Gary Barlow's favourite. It didn't suit Little Mix nor the other finalist, Marcus Collins, and one couldn't help but wonder if it had been chosen with Janet Devlin in mind, as she had been the most popular act in the early weeks.

Tulisa continued to be diplomatic and considerate, and said of her group, whom she always referred to as 'my little muffins': 'I really have met friends – such true, genuine, talented young ladies who deserve this more than anyone I know.' When Dermot O'Leary announced that Little Mix had won,

Tulisa was overjoyed. Ny, who had been waiting in the wings, was so excited she rushed on stage to give her 'muffin' a hug.

After the victory night, Tulisa tweeted that the evening had shown her that if you really believe in something and want it badly enough, then it can happen. 'U just need 2 believe,' she wrote. She also revealed that after the win she would be going to her local kebab shop to celebrate. Then it was home to watch it all again with Fazer, Ny and stylist Abuk Joseph, who had become one of her inner circle. It was just as exciting the second time around.

Two nights later and it was time for the more 'public' celebration – the series wrap party at the DSTRKT club in Soho. Tulisa managed to command most of the attention from photographers in a supremely tight metallic gold bandage dress. The look was definitive Tulisa, complete with glossy tumbling curls, long lashes, a nude lipstick and killer heels. Fashion commentators might have thought she had overplayed the traditional female urban look but an online poll in the *Huffington Post* showed that it met with public approval. An impressive 82.5 per cent thought it was 'fun, festive and fierce'.

Tulisa arrived with Fazer, who was dressed in a cool black suit and sunglasses. He hung back slightly while she took the brunt of the paparazzi interest, but there was no pretence any more. They were very much together.

Dappy, however, was nowhere to be seen. He had 'celebrated' his cousin's victory on the Sunday night by telling his audience at a solo gig in Manchester: 'This is what fame is, not standing for hours outside to audition for *X Factor*'. He was also reported as saying 'F*** Simon Cowell.'

Dappy's solo career continues to go well and his follow-up single to 'No Regrets' was a collaboration with the Queen guitarist Brian May called 'Rockstar', which meant he featured on MTV just as much as he did at the height of N-Dubz. His continued ranting about *The X Factor* means he is unlikely to claim a guest spot any day soon but you never know – it would certainly gather much publicity for the show. Fazer and Tulisa, meanwhile, had come a long way in just a few months. When *The X Factor* began in August, it was an open secret that they had been in a relationship for a year. She resolutely refused to confirm he was her boyfriend in any interview. She was very frank talking with the renowned journalist Chrissy Iley for *Glamour* magazine but wouldn't name him: 'I don't want to confirm who I'm with. It causes less hassle.'

While she was still being discreet, elsewhere there was speculation that the couple were about to become engaged and Fazer planned to whisk her off to the Caribbean to propose. Eventually they had to venture out together or else become total hermits, which would have been ridiculous. They were first seen as a 'couple' in late September when they went to a party at Movida to celebrate Dappy's single 'No Regrets' reaching number one. They both posed happily for pictures outside the club, although Fazer was clutching a dodgy-looking cigarette that grabbed the attention of the newspapers.

Behind the scenes, Fazer would often pop down to the *X Factor* shows and hang out in Tulisa's dressing room. It was all very low key. Tulisa apparently hadn't changed since her days with Justin Edwards. She was still very insecure. She told Chrissy Iley, 'I get jealous. If he's seeing his girl mates, I want to know them. I say, "What friend? You don't need female friends. Why didn't I know her before. Introduce me. Let's go out for dinner." I don't stand for any shite.' She admitted, with her usual disarming honesty, that she was selfish, stubborn and possessive but could be snuggly at times: 'One minute I'm the puppy dog, the next I'm the ice queen.'

Fazer, who is more laid back, seemed to take it all in his stride, confirming, 'I would never cheat on her.' He was quoted as saying that they would definitely have kids one day and that he had always wanted children. He also said he loved it that 'guys fancy her' and didn't seem to mind her going out to enjoy herself.

Just before Christmas she hosted a birthday celebration for her PA, Gareth, at Mahiki in Dover Street. Many of the usual suspects were there, including DJ Ironik and Abuk Joseph. She warned on Twitter when the evening began that she was pouring the first drink of the night and 'this could get messy'. The five-hour drinkathon reportedly cost Tulisa £9,000 and she was looking a little the worse for wear when she and Gareth were bundled into a taxi outside the club. She later tweeted, 'It got soooooooo messy!'

Fazer and Tulisa left wintry London after New Year for a romantic holiday in the Maldives in the Indian Ocean. Tulisa deliberately avoided the Caribbean, wanting to make sure that she was well away from that celebrity playground. Instead she and Fazer stayed at the £1,000-a-night five-star Coco Palm resort, where they were just like any other couple enjoying a romantic holiday – except that their every move was being photographed. They splashed around happily in the warm ocean, and Fazer gave his girlfriend, who was wearing a pink, purple and gold Lipsy bikini, a playful piggyback. They went kayaking in the tranquil waters and lazed about on sun loungers drinking cocktails and champagne. Tulisa was pictured snuggled up in Fazer's arms while reading Martina Cole's bestseller *The Jump*.

They appeared very natural together and very much in love. The online gossip from their fans was all positive and glowing. Here were two young people happy to be with each other and clearly going from strength to strength. Ten days later and it was all over. The split was no slow-burn saga with weeks of speculation proving correct, as had been the case with Katy Perry and Russell Brand. Tulisa and Fazer went from love's young dream to zero practically overnight.

Instead the speculation started after the break-up and most of it seemed to point the finger at Fazer and his party-loving lifestyle, which wasn't something he had been known for up to that point. A source told the *Daily Mirror* that nobody else was involved and they didn't want to 'stick the knife' into one another.

They were both seen out clubbing in the West End separately. Tulisa was escorted by Gareth to Movida, where they joined a bunch of her girlfriends, including Rochelle Wiseman and Vanessa White from The Saturdays, who were rallying round. Fazer was at the Aura Club and, a few nights later, in Club 55. He was linked to clothing tycoon Philip Green's daughter Chloe, who appeared in *Made in Chelsea* and was apparently at both clubs. Chloe denied there was anything between them and maintained that 'girls can have friends that are guys.'

Neither Fazer nor Tulisa seemed that upset about their split. It was ironic that after keeping their relationship secret for so long they should split after such a public demonstration of their affection while on holiday. The timing is interesting because Tulisa was about to start the next phase of her career by travelling to Los Angeles to work with top American producers on her solo album. By far the most likely cause of her split with Fazer was that she was beginning a busy, exciting year in her life that hopefully would see the launch of a glittering solo singing career. There was no time for thoughts of settling down.

She had already started recording the album with Fazer while *The X Factor* was still going on. But when she flew into LA at the beginning of February 2012, Max Gousse from Def Jam was on hand to mastermind things. Def Jam, it seemed, were more interested in Tulisa than they had ever been in N-Dubz.

Tulisa had her own posse of paparazzi following her around day to day, usually capturing her walking down Sunset Boulevard near her fashionable hotel, the Mondrian, in the Lipsy mini dress du jour. The first thing she did was forget to apply her sunblock and the resulting sunburn looked very painful. The pictures showed her with a scarlet face and a big red blotch on her arm, which was not a good look.

Every day of her six-week trip the British newspapers were treated to a picture of Tulisa and an update on her social life.

Other than the sunburn disaster, Tulisa has never looked better, glowing with health, vitality and happiness. She didn't appear to be the least bit upset about her 'devastating' split from Fazer.

The man himself was branching out, making his catwalk debut at a James Small menswear fashion show at the Corinthia Hotel, London, where, looking slightly bashful, he was cheered on by Kate Moss, whom he later joined for drinks with Rihanna.

Tulisa, meanwhile, was determined to enjoy herself. She went out for dinner with Rochelle and Vanessa, who were on a flying visit to LA, went drinking with The Wanted, turned heads at various Grammy events and partied with Jessie J, who had flown in for the awards and was now a firm friend. The pair had exchanged a series of flirtatious tweets in which Tulisa wrote, 'Stop enticing me 2 cum over 2 the dark side. I'm intrigued.' The openly bisexual Jessie J replied, 'That dress your wearing would look great on my hotel floor.' It was all good fun and was shared with a combined Twitter following of nearly five million people.

Most of the time Tulisa's playmates were Gareth and Ny, who had flown to California with her. Their 'fun' included a trip to Paramount Studios and to Hustler, a Hollywood sex shop, where Tulisa dissolved into fits of giggles. They also went to a local tattoo parlour, where Gareth had the name of his employer inked on the inside of his right leg, just above his ankle.

Tulisa wrote a series of tweets on Valentine's Day, which would soon come back to haunt her, in which she told all her single followers to hook up with the girls before going home to 'ya wabbit'. She didn't mention whether she had bought one of the famous sex toys after browsing at the LA store.

Aside from the drinking, partying and paparazzi, there was a serious point to Tulisa's LA trip – the music. The songwriters and producers brought in to help were serious players in the American music business and Tulisa had just six weeks to finesse a sound that would be acceptable to American audiences. Gone were the old N-Dubz concerns about compromise and retaining her Britishness – Tulisa had global domination in mind.

She wrote one song called 'Does Anyone Believe In Love' with Jean-Baptiste Kouame, whom she already knew from his work on *Love.Live.Life.* She was sure it would be a hit. She was also thrilled to work with Diane Warren, one of the biggest names in the music business and famous for her nineties' power ballads, including 'Because You Love Me' for Celine Dion, the LeAnn Rimes number one 'How Do I Live' and the Toni Braxton classic 'Un-Break My Heart'.

To record with Diane Warren is to have arrived and, hopefully, Tulisa was cutting down on the cigarettes to do justice to one of her songs. Tulisa called Diane the original female boss and she returned the compliment by tweeting that Tulisa was a badass bitch. More seriously, she thought Tulisa was going to have a massive record.

Other big hitters that Max Gousse brought in to work with Tulisa included LA-based British singer Rachel Rabin, producers Tydolla$ign and Corey 'Chorus' Gibson, who became an instant friend when he bought her a hotdog. Best of all was studio time with The-Dream, real name Terius Youngdell Nash, who co-wrote two of the most famous tracks of the past few years, 'Umbrella' by Rihanna and the Grammy-winning Beyoncé track 'Single Ladies (Put A Ring On It)'.

If this talented bunch can't sort out a number one for Tulisa, then nobody can.

After Los Angeles, it was a five-hour flight with Gareth and Ny to Miami, where she would be filming the video for her debut single, which she let slip would be called 'Young'. They stayed in the penthouse at the Shore Club, one of the most beautiful hotels on Miami's South Beach and a perfect location for Tulisa to model all the bikinis she had bought. Gareth tweeted simply, 'The shore club hotel is the tits.'

A week of high living included being driven round the resort by The-Dream in his scarlet Ferrari. Her entourage joined his for a champagne night out at Tootsie's Cabaret, a well-known Miami lap-dancing club that promises 'full nudity and full friction.' A trip to Disney World seemed very tame by comparison but at least it kept the photographers happy.

On her last night in the US she went out to dinner with Chipmunk, who had flown in, and then they went on to the Liv Nightclub at the Fontainebleau Hotel. The next morning she was feeling like 'death warmed up' – perfect, in fact, for a day's filming.

The serious purpose of the trip was a little lost between partying and sunbathing but Tulisa did have a video to shoot for her first single. Back home, Fazer was happy to talk about the track that he had produced. He enthused, 'It's going to be a really big dance record.'

The video itself involved a number of costume changes on or around the beach, including a pair of tight pink shorts for a spot of rollerblading with Ny and Gareth. She wore a floral one-piece, fifties-style Ted Baker swimsuit, which proved quite a contrast to the revealing bikinis she'd been favouring in her leisure time. The fashion critics much preferred it. Alison Jane Reid observed, 'It's fabulous. She has the perfect body to carry off the retro glamour of the fifties – a tiny waist and curves in all the right places. Her flowing hair just completes the modern, romantic goddess look.'

After filming it was time to pack for the journey home. Everything was going well until one of her bags started vibrating at check-in. A security guard approached and said, 'Ma'am, can you open your case and turn whatever that is off?' It was a Rampant Rabbit sex toy. Tulisa wanted the ground to open up and swallow her. She told the *Sun*, 'I only bought it as a present for a mate, but the joke ended up on me.' One had to wonder why the newly purchased present had batteries included and connected. Tulisa did say it was the 'most cringe moment of my life' when she told her Twitter followers all about it. The amusing postscript was that a leading retailer of sex toys offered to pay her £200,000 to design her very own Tulisa Torpedo.

The incident gave Tulisa one last hurrah of publicity for a trip that had been a masterful exercise in promotion. You would have to be on Mars not to know that she had been in the US recording her new album.

Not quite so welcome were the stories claiming that she had enjoyed a fling with Mark Wright of *The Only Way Is Essex* and *I'm A Celebrity Get Me Out Of Here*. He had apparently been on a photo shoot in Miami and they had met up because they were both managed by Jonathan Shalit. The story sounded like a publicity snog that had got out of hand.

The stories that she had a 'steamy' one-night stand with the ex-TOWIE 'hunk' seemed to offer him more publicity oxygen than her. She hadn't needed to be linked to anyone to get her name in newspaper headlines for the past six weeks. She was not amused and tweeted, 'I have definitely not shagged mark wright and I can swear that on my Uncle B's grave!'

Tulisa would not take Uncle B's name in vain under any circumstances so that pretty much closes the door on the story, although the papers will probably add her to the list of Mark's conquests for eternity. She did admit that she was seeing someone, who turned out to be the actor Jack O'Connell.

They had been introduced by Gareth, although her diary was so crowded it's difficult to see how she could have begun a new relationship since her break with Fazer. Jack had become well known through his role as the unpredictable James Cook in the teenage drama *Skins*, which covered many of the issues explored by *Dubplate Drama*. Tulisa, however, had first noticed him on television playing Eamonn in Sky's adaptation of one of her favourite Martina Cole novels, *The Runaway*. She mentioned him in a tweet in June 2011 when she writes that she had watched three episodes of *The Runaway* and that Jack was a 'certified ledge'.

The reaction of the 'ledge' to being outed by the media as the man in her life was to protest that he and Tulisa were just mates. He was about to fly out to Los Angeles but before he left he took Tulisa to watch a football game for the first time: a first division match between his favourite team, Derby County, and Midlands rivals Nottingham Forest. It was just the thing mates would do – if they were men.

She couldn't have been prepared, however, for the media storm when the sex tape stories began again. This time they were more than just rumours that could be brushed aside. A tape appeared online that was available for download for £3.90 and seemed to show Tulisa engaging in oral sex with a man whose face is not shown.

Tulisa's lawyers moved swiftly to obtain an injunction preventing anyone 'using, publishing or communicating or disclosing to any other person all or any part of the film'. But in the modern world of social networking and Internet access, an online genie is impossible to put back in the bottle when he is causing mayhem.

Tulisa decided to confront the embarrassment publicly by posting a five-minute monologue on YouTube during which she admitted that it was indeed her performing the sex act and pointed the finger of blame at her former boyfriend Justin Edwards for leaking the video.

She held up two pictures of them together and said, 'I practically moved in with him. I loved him deeply, had a lot of respect for him. We talked about kids and marriage. I got my record label to give him a singles deal. I never expected a scenario like this.'

She continued, 'As you can imagine, I'm devastated. I'm heartbroken. I've been in bits for the last few days.'

Her admission was generally well-received including, importantly, by Simon Cowell, who said it made no difference to her coming back to *The X Factor*. He stressed, 'I mean, God, if I said no to her coming back, it's allowing every sleazebag in the country to wreck somebody's career when she didn't do anything wrong.

'The public are very, very a) forgiving, and b) understanding. But I hope they don't forgive the person who did it.'

Tulisa also began legal proceedings against Justin for breach of privacy. In an early hearing at the High Court in London he denied that he had released the footage, stating it would have been 'un-gentlemanly'. The saga will be continued by lawyers, although there was more unwelcome news for Tulisa when the tape was spotted for sale in a Soho sex shop.

At least it didn't have a negative effect on her blossoming relationship with Jack O'Connell and they were pictured in *heat* magazine with her head leaning affectionately on his shoulder. The magazine said that Jack had told Tulisa 'he didn't give a s**t about the tape and she shouldn't give it a second thought'.

Her new notoriety also guaranteed maximum publicity for the release of the video for her debut single 'Young'. The song was one of those that stuck in your head for hours after the first listen. Much of the media interest was focused on the line in which Tulisa asked for forgiveness for what she had done, and the film revealed an energetic and carefree Tulisa in Miami.

The 2012 trip to the US proved just how far Tulisa had come since she began appearing on *The X Factor*. Moving away from the umbrella of N-Dubz, she had been transformed from a mother hen to two boys into a confident young woman finding her own style. She didn't always get the fashion right but she looked comfortable in her Lipsy playsuits and the bikinis that revealed her shapely figure to the world. She is clearly proud of her body and likes the way she looks – some proof of that shows in her make-up, which is much lighter than it used to be in her blonde street days when she shovelled it on with a trowel.

Alison Jane Reid observed, 'The natural make-up she favours at the moment is a breakthrough for Tulisa. It is so much more flattering. She is lucky. She has almond-shaped eyes, pale skin and long flowing hair – she's a natural siren.'

Tulisa is still in her early twenties and is allowed to make mistakes as she moves further away from her teenage years. Her mantra repeated almost annually has always been to make money, buy a big house and a fast car. She is already a million-aire and can afford almost any luxury she desires. She is likely to pocket a million for the next series of *The X Factor* and a similar figure for her autobiography.

Her story is very different from the other leading female stars of her generation. Jessie J, Leona Lewis and Adele, for instance, all had their talents fostered at the BRIT School for Performing Arts & Technology and graduated together in the same year. They weren't getting drunk on cider on a menacing housing estate or bunking off school to catch a Tube to a studio in a grotty building in Dollis Hill.

It's easy to scoff at her tales of the mean streets of Camden and the urban world that spawned N-Dubz but her experiences growing up gave her, Dappy and Fazer the motivation in their lives. Not everyone can leave the street life behind.

In the week of *The X Factor* final, a musician called Leon Baker was sentenced to eight years in prison after being found guilty by a court in Bristol of possessing a firearm and ammunition. He was arrested in an armed police operation targeting drug dealers in the city. He had a gun in his boxer shorts. He is better known as Baker Trouble, who sang with Dappy and has a co-writing credit on 'Love For My Slum', which featured on the first N-Dubz album and remains one of their best-loved songs. His fate, serving his time while Dappy is a number one solo recording artist, is a reminder that the latter wasn't joking when he said he would have ended up in jail if it hadn't been for Uncle B and N-Dubz.

Tulisa's stories of sex at fourteen, smoking weed and having a bottle smashed over the back of her head in a fight are the reality of this life. She was lucky that she had talent, looks and the support she needed to leave it behind. But, as she freely admits, her life then defined who she is. She presents herself as a tough girl to the outside world. One of my favourite Tulisa tweets is her in aggressive mode: 'Some people just need a high 5 ... in the face ... with a chair.'

But behind that front there is also a sensitive girl who doesn't know what to do with herself when she is alone. She hates being on her own, a legacy of nights spent staring at the walls of her childhood bedroom. Now there's always Gareth or Ny or, if they're not around, she can pop round and see her dad or her mum. They remain a very close family.

Her mum's mental illness helped to shape her early years and increased her feeling of isolation. But it also meant that she grew up quickly. One of the most memorable photographs from her first *X Factor* series is nothing to do with frock wars: it's a simple, touching picture of Tulisa with Ann after the live results show in December 2011. She has a protective arm around her mother, who is squeezing her hand. Her love for Ann is unconditional: 'She's always been an amazing mother. She really inspired me to get where I am today and is definitely my idol.'

Family is very important to Tulisa, which is why any falling-out between her and Dappy is unlikely to last for long because they are 'blood'. Dappy's solo career could scarcely be going better. Fazer too is branching out: he had a triumphant night appearing at the Barbican with the 85-strong BBC Symphony Orchestra – a night of urban classics that also featured Ms Dynamite, Devlin and Skepta. The orchestra can't have performed too many concerts at which the audience shouts out 'We love you, Fazer.'

Tulisa first solo performance will be at the Wireless Festival in Hyde Park at the beginning of July. After months of speculation, the N-Dubz demise was finally confirmed in March 2012. And so for the foreseeable future all three will be solo artists with little prospect of a reunion.

In the aftermath of the sex tape scandal, Tulisa is going to have to get used to even more persistent media scrutiny in the future. She's not that keen on the paparazzi at the best of times. Her private view is best expressed in a tweet of December 2011: 'I think its disgusting that paps r allowed 2 open ur car doors and take pictures of ur knickers.'

She is likely to have to suffer mischief and innuendo for some time to come, but both the public and the media will probably move on when a new series of *The X Factor* gets under way.

At the start of this book, I asked why Tulisa turned left on Haverstock Hill towards rough, unpromising neighbourhoods when she could have turned right towards the easier streets of Hampstead. Why, I wondered, would anyone choose to do that? The answer, I believe, has to do with the need to belong. She felt alone and needed a group of people she could fit in with – a big family of her own.

Tulisa has 1.7 million followers on Twitter and every one of them is her 'family'. She will talk about everyday things like shopping in Tesco – which she does a lot – dealing with her dog Prince making a mess in the hallway or sharing the chicken recipe she is trying out that evening. She cares about feminist issues, climate change and bullying but has no time for the rioters of the summer of 2011, who damaged property and were harming their cities. She has a bawdy sense of humour and uses the sort of language the majority of people use all the time in real life. And she can laugh at herself: 'This year I shall be sporting a new tat saying "Chavtastic" on my forehead.'

It's as if she's at home with you, chatting in the kitchen.

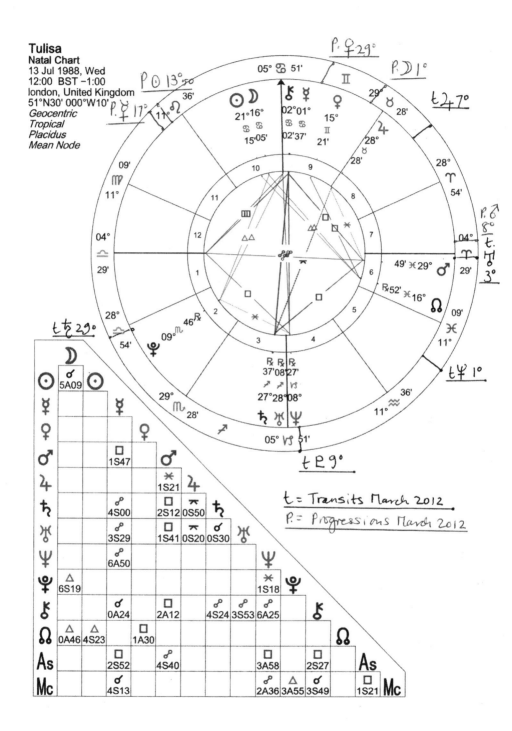

Tulisa
Natal Chart
13 Jul 1988, Wed
12:00 BST −1:00
london, United Kingdom
51°N30' 000°W10'
Geocentric
Tropical
Placidus
Mean Node

P. ♀ 29°
P. ☽ 1°
♄ 2+ 7°
P. ☉ 13°50
36'
P. ☿ 17°
P. ♂ 8°
t. ♅ 3°
t ♆ 1°
t ♇ 9°
t ♄ 29°

t = Transits March 2012
P. = Progressions March 2012

05° ♋ 51'

☉ ☽   ♄ ☿   ♀
21°16'   02°01'   15°
♋ ♋   02'37'   ♊
15'05'   21

♉ 29°
28'

2+ 28°
♂ 28'

♈ 28°
54'

09'
♍ 11°

04°
♎ 29'

♂ 49' ♓ 29°
℞ 52' ♓ 16°
☊ 09'
♓ 11'

04°
♈ 29'

28°
♎ 54'

♇ 09° ♏ 46' ℞

29°
♏ 28'

37'08'27'
♐ 27°28°08' ♑

♄ ♅ ♆
05° ♑ 51'

36'
♒ 11°

Tulisa's Stars

Tulisa – Matriarchal Goddess

Feelings dominate the way Tulisa operates in this world. It is through her feelings that she will understand people. It is her feelings that will prompt her actions. It is her feelings and the ease and grace with which she communicates these that will connect her so immediately to others. Tulisa has a startling number of planets in watery signs, including the ruler of her birth chart, the Moon. This planet, which speaks of our instinctive needs and our emotional world, was in a position of strength at her birth, in the sign it rules, Cancer. Here is someone who, above all else, will live in accordance with the dictates of her heart and the intuitive wisdom of her instincts.

This signature of emotional depth is further emphasized by links between other planets in Cancer and Pluto, ruler of the underworld, Lord of Forced Maturity. Those who have Pluto dominant in their birth chart will inevitably grapple with issues of survival, facing trials that will eradicate the superficial and acquaint them with their own regenerative instincts. She will have encountered, and will continue to be drawn to, total make or break circumstances.

Tulisa's birth chart strongly supports the idea that when the gods dish out problems, they also give the tools to deal with them, provided one is prepared to accept and use these gifts. The position of Chiron, known as the Wounded Healer, in the sign of Cancer suggests problems around the mother and her ability to nurture her child. One consequence of this is that

Tulisa may have experienced a level of insecurity and feelings of unworthiness. Few would doubt that this could be crippling unless one has the ability to face the wound courageously and use the insights gained constructively.

Chiron's story is of a centaur, wounded by a poisoned arrow, who attempts to heal himself through his knowledge and experience of medicine, learned from the god Apollo. This proves impossible but the wisdom he gains is then used to help others, finding solutions that give life. Tulisa's Chiron is linked very positively to Pluto, indicating the regenerative force she can draw upon to help others, although she will never, of course, be able to change the experiences she has had.

Tulisa can turn straw into gold and this planetary gift from the gods will always come to her aid and will be needed. Tulisa's need to live intensely, her desire to walk near the edge, form part of her magnetism, a curious quality that can repel some while attracting others. She simply has extraordinary survival skills that will be evident from her ability to 'read' those around her and make the right calls. Such a wealth of planets in water signs (Cancer, Scorpio, Pisces) inclines her to hypersensitivity and her reactions will often seem unpredictable and original but her instinct for self-protection is second to none.

Although the presence of Chiron in the parental sign of Cancer suggests problems with heredity, the fact that both the Sun and Moon are also here is reassuring, an indication of the togetherness of her parents at the time of birth. This often translates as parents who have similar values or background and will be expressed positively in terms of Tulisa's ability to integrate the assertive and receptive drives within her character – she will know when to use charm and when to flex muscle in order to achieve her goals.

Her background, moreover, is not something she will reject. Aspects of it will make her feel curiously safe and she may later find herself replicating parts of this, perhaps taking on a caretaker role. This is ideal as long as it is part of a public and authoritative position, making use of her protective, mothering instincts brilliantly. However, she should avoid personal relationships where a needy partner manipulates her into finding solutions for his weaknesses. This is a situation that could easily come about, as Tulisa is a young woman whose sometimes fragile (although hidden) sense of self-worth leaves her vulnerable to those who play the victim role.

The presence of Uranus, planet of the rebel, next to Saturn, often a significator of the Father, hints at several issues Tulisa will have absorbed with her baby milk. One of these is how to integrate with a group and belong, at the same time as having one's uniqueness acknowledged. Those with this planetary pairing often hate the idea of being ordinary, have a strong drive (especially when linked, as in this chart, to Mercury) towards the expression of their originality and yet feel uncomfortable standing apart from the crowd. This problem for Tulisa may have come to prominence in those years when peer pressure exerts such a horrible force to fit in and she will have made some progress then in accommodating her conflicting drives. A further obvious way to use this energy is through voicing the discontent of those who feel excluded. However, she will meet the same adversary in different forms many times along her life's path and each time her courage will be tested.

The other point of interest is the nature of Father suggested here. The paternal symbol Saturn, in the sign of freedom-loving Sagittarius, suggests someone keen to find faith in the universe and a set of rules worth living by. He would also have worked consistently to provide material wealth. Saturn linked to planets that suggest wilfulness hint also at someone who would resist constraint. Tulisa would have learned how to live with risk, with the excitement it brings and the insecurity.

In terms of relationships, Tulisa wants someone to talk to. Venus, the planet that defines what we value, is in the communicative and cerebral sign of Gemini. She will enjoy game-playing and the exchange of ideas. Her qualities of wit and liveliness will make her a sociable companion, attracting others easily, allowing great pleasure in flirtation. This desire to find mental stimulation and variety, to encounter difference frequently, is slightly at odds with a need for great emotional security. Of course, this can be incorporated in a lifestyle – a wide circle of friends can provide companionship and a mix of minds – but Tulisa, with a charismatic link between Mars and Neptune, is both seductive and open to seduction. She is likely to be idealistic about potential partners and fall for those who embody the illusion of strength. Much of her life will be led under the influence of male figures with whom she will struggle with issues of power and control. Ultimately her tendency towards possessiveness and exclusivity will win out. These battles are partly a way of living out that conflict within herself between the need for adventure and freedom and an equally strong wish for security. Tulisa, in embracing the drama of passion, will be sensitive to the evolutionary process of destruction and regeneration.

Tulisa has a particular pattern in her birth chart that reveals much in terms of her career. It involves more than half the total number of planets that sit linked awkwardly to each other. Misused, Mars and Saturn often result in violence or rage. Directed properly, they provide the energy, commitment and strength to produce something worthwhile; Tulisa has the initiative, drive and stamina to succeed. Uranus added to this group allows for a quirky alternativeness, originality and impulsiveness. Tulisa is decisive, ruthless even, knowing exactly what she wants and the fastest way to achieve it. Creative Neptune and Mercury, planet of the voice, provide the vehicle for this volcanic force, allowing energy to take inspirational form. Fear, too, is part of the mix that drives her quest – which, in some way, is to heal the family or a hereditary shadow. On this journey she will go beyond any personal circumstances and become something of a crusader for those whom Chiron represents – the abandoned outsiders and those who are wounded.

Tough planetary aspects build character, deepen the soul,

develop the spirit – but too much, as the gods know, can just grind a girl down and we all need a little munificence. Tulisa has both Jupiter and Venus, known as the greater and lesser benefics (or planets of pleasure and luck), tapping into the turbulent and hardened planetary forces already mentioned. Jupiter, well placed and linked in Taurus (the sign associated with singing), promises success and steady growth of assets. Venus occupies a degree of Gemini linked with fame and wealth. Curiously though, there is a warning here, shown through a tense connection this planet makes, that Tulisa must not be seduced by glamour and wealth away from the more serious purpose of her life.

The recent past has seen the transit of Jupiter in the sky, planet of Fortune and Growth, linking to Mars and the dominant planetary grouping in Tulisa's chart. In May and September 2010 and January 2011, Tulisa would have experienced opportunities that may have demanded calculated risks but would have reaped a rich harvest of success. The beneficial influence of this planet will continue until June 2012, when it will complete its twelve-year orbit, returning for the second time in her life to the point that it occupied at her birth. A particular cycle of success will have ended and something new will be about to begin. Tulisa will meet those who will introduce her to a much broader understanding of the world and who will help her towards greater accomplishment. Opportunity for travel and furthering her knowledge will simply be a part of a very positive time, although she should be careful not to overextend her interests.

A foretaste of success will have occurred earlier, in March 2012, as Jupiter positioned opposite Pluto, in her birth chart, planet of power and control. This will be an intense period, as Tulisa may become obsessive in pursuit of her goals and find that her style of coercion provokes strong opposition. The energy here is best used by aligning her interests with those of others.

Late June and again late July, sees an awkward link made

between Uranus, planet of unexpected change, and Tulisa's Neptune. There may be some problem connected to a parental figure or she may find herself in circumstances in which she is led astray.

The movement of Saturn, the great taskmaster, must also be considered – where Jupiter promotes and expands, Saturn restricts and thwarts. The most significant link made by Saturn will be in January 2013, when this planet of endings meets up with Pluto, the planet of irrevocable change. Certain structures in Tulisa's life will change forever. With her natal Sun and Moon in Cancer, a sign that draws sustenance from the past, there may be difficulty here as she struggles to hold on to that which is really over. But even at this early stage of the game, Tulisa has learned the old must give way to the new and the new is what carries life forward.

Tulisa's Saturn Return, that astrological marker that separates the child from the adult, occurs in March 2017. That this lies a good five years away is a tribute to the remarkable achievements of this gifted woman. Her successes have been as much to do with facing personal trials and surmounting them with courage as with the way she has directed negative emotions into positive creative endeavours. Her extraordinary ability to inspire and nurture are her greatest strengths and ones that have yet to see their fullest deployment. She is a gifted performer but with five out of eleven planets placed in signs associated with parenting, one would expect an emergent role as someone with something to say about society.

Madeleine Moore
March 2012

Life and Times

5 Feb 1987 Richard Rawson (Fazer) born at the Royal Free Hospital in Pond Street, Hampstead.

11 June 1987 Costadinos Contostavlos (Dappy) born at the Royal Free Hospital.

13 July 1988 Tula Paulinea Contostavlos (Tulisa) born at the Royal Free Hospital. Her parents, Ann and Plato, are living at his family's six-bedroom house in Cricklewood but soon move to Belsize Park.

June 1999 Stars as Tallulah in the Rosary Roman Catholic Primary School's Junior Musical, *Bugsy Malone*. Plato says it made the hairs on the back of his neck stand up when she sang.

Sept 1999 Begins senior education at the Catholic girls' school La Sainte Union in Highgate but is bullied about her mother's mental health issues and leaves after one unhappy year. She agrees to become the girl singer in Dappy and Fazer's group, the Lickle Rinsers Crew.

Sept 2000 Joins Dappy and Fazer at Haverstock School, where she makes friends but is also bullied. Later alleges girls as young as twelve were shagging in the toilets. Loses virginity at fourteen. After two years at Haverstock, spends a year out of school.

Sept 2003 Enrols in her last school, Quintin Kynaston School in St John's Wood, but leaves without taking her GCSEs when she reaches sixteen.

Nov 2005 At seventeen, she writes in her diary that her mother has had a panic attack and a seizure. Tulisa is finding it too difficult to cope with; she self-harms and wipes the blood on the open page of her diary.

May 2006 Films the video for the N-Dubz track 'You Better Not Waste My Time' around the streets of Camden. It becomes their debut single on digital download in August.

April 2007 Fazer and Dappy discover Uncle B – Tulisa's Uncle Byron and mentor to N-Dubz – dead after a heart attack on the sofa at home in Camden Town. He is fifty-three. Tulisa is told on the set of *Dubplate Drama*.

Sept 2007 N-Dubz are named Best Newcomer at the 2007 MOBO Awards at London's O2 Arena. Afterwards she says they would have broken up if they hadn't won. The second series of *Dubplate Drama* begins on Channel 4 with Tulisa in a small role as singer Laurissa.

Oct 2007 N-Dubz sign with Polydor and re-release 'You Better Not Waste My Time' but it peaks at a disappointing ninety-six in the chart. Tulisa says they should have brought out a fresh track.

Dec 2007 Dappy appears on *Never Mind the Buzzcocks* wearing his trade-mark Dappy hat. N-Dubz perform at the ceremony to switch on the Christmas lights in Gosport, Hampshire; Keith Harris and Orville the Duck top the bill.

Jan 2008 Goes back to Haverstock School with Dappy and Fazer for a concert to raise awareness of gun crime.

Aug 2008 N-Dubz leave Polydor, sign with All Around the World and release 'Ouch'. The video gets ten million hits on YouTube in five months.

Sept 2008 Involved in a scary, violent incident in Finchley Road, North London, which leads to her boyfriend, DJ Adam Bailey, facing criminal charges after a man is found stabbed. Tulisa is arrested but released without charge.

Nov 2008 N-Dubz's debut album is finally released on All Around the World label and reaches number eleven in the UK chart. It is called *Uncle B* as a tribute to their late mentor. Seven singles are released from the album, including 'Papa Can You Hear Me?', Dappy's song about his father.

Jan 2009 *Uncle B* goes platinum, selling more than 300,000 copies. Is present at the birth of Dappy's first son, Gino, and says, 'I officially don't want kids till I'm about thirty-five.' Dappy, Fazer and DJ Maze hauled off BA flight for 'disorderly behaviour'.

March 2009 Denounces cyberbullying in an interview with *Newsbeat*. She says bullies are sad people with a lot of hate and anger.

April 2009 'Number 1' by Tinchy Stryder featuring N-Dubz goes to number one in charts in debut week, selling 87,000 copies. Collapses on a flight to Greece and is rushed to hospital on outskirts of Athens with suspected swine flu.

May 2009 Given the all-clear after six days in isolation. Supports 'Spit It Out', a competition sponsored by ChildLine in conjunction with *Dubplate Drama*.

June 2009 Has major role in third series of *Dubplate Drama*, playing drug addict singer Laurissa, who has a violent and abusive boyfriend. N-Dubz give memorable performance at Isle of Wight Festival, which starred Jay-Z and Sir Paul McCartney.

July 2009 Celebrates her twenty-first birthday at a West End restaurant. Calls off engagement to Adam Bailey. N-Dubz win Digital Award at the thirty-fourth annual O2 Silver Clef Awards.

Aug 2009 Turns down £250,000 to pose nude for *Playboy* magazine. N-Dubz headline the St Helens Live Music Festival with Chipmunk as support.

Sept 2009 N-Dubz win two MOBO Awards as Best UK Act and Best Album for *Uncle B*. Tulisa leads all-star group Young Soul Rebels in stage performance of 'I Got Soul', a charity record for War Child.

Nov 2009 N-Dubz break from nationwide tour to appear at the Crompton House School, Oldham, after pupils win radio competition. Second album, *Against All Odds*, released and reaches six in the chart. It is certified platinum within two months. In the album notes, thanks new boyfriend Justin Edwards for making her happy. Single 'I Need You' makes number five, outselling Britney Spears and Sugababes.

Dec 2009 Gives evidence at the trial of former boyfriend Adam Bailey. He is cleared of wounding with intent to cause grievous bodily harm and dangerous driving. N-Dubz appear at Jingle Bell Ball at the O2 in London along with Westlife, Lady Gaga and JLS.

Jan 2010 N-Dubz dropped from anti-bullying campaign by Beatbullying after Dappy sends threatening text messages to single mother who texted *The Chris Moyles Show* that the band were 'losers'. With Nick Grimshaw, Tulisa co-hosts BBC *Switch* on Radio 1.

Feb 2010 Has an operation at London's Cromwell Hospital to remove a lump from her nose. After 'Number 1' fails to win Best Single at the BRITs, Tulisa complains that N-Dubz are being ignored in favour of American acts.

March 2010 Is guest columnist in the *Sun* and writes that she would never pay more than £100 for a dress. Supports a ban on drug meow meow.

April 2010 Is placed fifteenth in *FHM*'s annual list of the 100 sexiest women in the world poll. Cheryl Cole is first for the second consecutive year. Launch of N-Dubz autobiography *Against All Odds: From Street Life to Chart Life*, in which Tulisa describes two occasions she tried to kill herself. Splits from Justin Edwards, who was supporting N-Dubz on tour.

May 2010 N-Dubz sign with Island Def Jam label to launch their US career. 'We Dance On' featuring Bodyrox from the soundtrack of the film *StreetDance 3D* reaches number six in the charts.

June 2010 Captains the winning ladies' team at a Soccer Six charity tournament at Charlton's Valley Stadium. N-Dubz headline the East Dance Stage at Glastonbury before dashing to another gig at Whitehaven in Cumbria. *Being . . . N-Dubz* starts on Channel 4. Enjoys holiday fling with footballer Luca Havern in Ibiza.

July 2010 Her new home in Leavesden, near Watford, is burgled but the thief fails to remove TV from the wall. Tulisa puts house up for sale.

Aug 2010 Documentary *Tulisa: My Mum and Me* is shown on BBC Three, in which she reveals her problems growing up with a mentally ill mother and the difficulties faced by young carers.

Sept 2010 Reveals new unicorn tattoo on her back at the MOBO nominations at London's May Fair hotel. She had it inked in Los Angeles to hide an existing tattoo of her real name, Tula. 'Playing With Fire' featuring Mr Hudson wins Best Song at the awards ceremony at Liverpool's Echo Arena.

Oct 2010 Appears on *Never Mind the Buzzcocks* on BBC 2 alongside team captain Noel Fielding and writer Howard Marks.

Nov 2010 Banned from Facebook after complaints that her real page is one of sixty fake Tulisa pages. Third N-Dubz album, *Love.Live.Life*, released, peaking at number seven in the chart.

Dec 2010 Prince Charles tells her she looks 'amazing' when he meets her backstage at the Royal Variety Performance. N-Dubz perform 'Say It's Over' during the show. Dappy becomes a father for the second time when son Milo is born. Tulisa moves into new home, a luxury apartment in a secure block in North London.

Jan 2011 Has tattoo 'The Female Boss' drawn on her right forearm at the Ink Lounge in Palmers Green.

March 2011 Has her teeth fixed with new set of veneers, giving her 'VIP smiles'. Gets new Rottweiler puppy called Prince.

April 2011 N-Dubz spend £1 million of their own money on three-month *Love.Live.Life* tour. Tulisa sings a version of 'Tallulah's Song' from *Bugsy Malone*. They play the O2 Arena in London with Professor Green as support.

May 2011 Confirmed as new judge on *The X Factor* alongside Gary Barlow, Louis Walsh and Kelly Rowland. She will earn £500,000. Tweets that she has always 'loved the show'.

June 2011 Cheryl Cole sends a bunch of flowers to her first *X Factor* auditions in Birmingham. Admits to being the most nervous she has ever been.

July 2011 Attends Cheryl's twenty-eighth birthday party at the Sanderson Hotel off Oxford Street. Holds own twenty-third party at Movida. *The X Factor* gives her a topless butler for her birthday.

Aug 2011 The eighth series of *The X Factor* begins and the viewing public are introduced to Tulisa. Tells one contestant he has embarrassed himself in front of the whole nation. Tory MP Nadine Dorries criticizes show bosses for hiring Tulisa, whom she says falls 'way short of the mark' of what a good role model should be. N-Dubz leave Def Jam label without ever releasing a record in the US.

Sept 2011 Movie career begins with *Big Fat Gypsy Gangster*. She has a small role with her friend Rochelle Wiseman of The Saturdays. The film goes straight to DVD. Attends first party in public with then current boyfriend Fazer to celebrate Dappy's solo debut, 'No Regrets', going to number one. Jessie J is co-judge in Mykonos for the Judges' Houses part of *The X Factor*, but Fazer goes along to help too.

Oct 2011 Sparks an *X Factor* row by telling contestant Misha B about hearing complaints that she has been mean to other contestants backstage. Plays cameo role in British horror movie *Demons Never Die*. Launches her perfume TFB (The Female Boss) at The Perfume Shop in Oxford Street. It has 'top notes of subtle spices, gentle rose and sweet jasmine to create a feminine floral heart'.

Nov 2011 *Greatest Hits* reaches only number thirty-five in the album chart.

Dec 2011 Is photographed with her mother Ann, who visits her at *The X Factor* live show. Sings 'Empire State of Mind' and 'If I Ain't Got You' with Little Mix during final, which they win. Named Woman of the Year by *Now* magazine.

Jan 2012 Flies to Maldives with Fazer for a romantic New Year break. The couple are pictured strolling along the beach and playing in the surf. Breaks up with him when they return to UK.

Feb 2012 Puts finishing touches to solo album in Los Angeles and is pictured in a series of sundresses. Films video for single in Miami with best friends Gareth Varey and Lady Ny.

March 2012 Confirms on Twitter that N-Dubz have split. Denies fling with Mark Wright from *TOWIE*. Is linked with *Skins* actor Jack O'Connell. Admits she is the girl in a sex tape circulating online and blames former boyfriend Justin Edwards' who denies he's responsible for the leak. Releases video for debut solo single 'Young'.

Acknowledgements

I used to live in North London near where Tulisa was brought up and it was fun to return to old haunts – the bars and restaurants of Haverstock Hill, Finchley Road and Swiss Cottage and the fascinating stalls of Camden Market. Thanks to everyone who spoke to me on my travels and who helped me with this book.

Thank you to the team at my publishers, Simon & Schuster, for their continued support. My editor, Carly Cook, has brought enthusiasm and insight to the project. Thanks to editorial assistant Emily Husain for sorting out author problems; Jo Whitford for project editing; Jo Edgecombe for overseeing production; Lizzie Gardiner for her striking jacket design; Emma Harrow for publicity; and Rumana Haider and Gill Richardson for looking after the all-important sales.

Thanks to my agent Gordon Wise, who continues to make such a difference to my career, and his assistant at Curtis Brown, John Parton. I am grateful to my research team – Catherine Marcus, Ellie Sigman and Alison Sims. My thanks to Jen Westaway for transcribing my interviews and to Arianne Burnette for her superb copy-editing skills.

My old friend Kevin O'Sullivan provided witty and incisive comment about *The X Factor*. Alison Jane Reid is one of the UK's leading fashion commentators. She is currently a contributing feature and fashion writer to *The Lady* magazine as well as a regular writer for *Coast*, *High Life* and *Illustrated London News* Group. When not interviewing famous people, she has her own 'English eccentric' magazine online: www.ethical-hedonist.com.

I wanted to say a special thank you to Ray Dorset, the founder of Mungo Jerry, the writer of so many great songs and one of the nicest men in pop. Some people who spoke to me wanted to remain anonymous because of the very small world nature of the record business and I have respected their wishes. Thanks also to Kyle Forrester, Isobel Gaffney, Róisín Ghadelrab, Nicola Myers and Jo Sharkey.

Madeleine Moore has produced a fascinating birth chart for Tulisa. I urge you to read what she says about Tulisa's stars. You can also read more about my books at www.seansmithceleb.com.

Finally, thank you to Jo Westaway for her patience, cheerfulness and research – and coming down the pub with me to discuss it.

Sean Smith is the UK's leading celebrity biographer and the author of the number one bestseller *Cheryl*, the definitive biography of Cheryl Cole, as well as bestselling books about Robbie Williams and Kate Middleton. His books about the most famous people of our times have been translated throughout the world. His subjects include Kylie Minogue, Justin Timberlake, Britney Spears, Victoria Beckham, Jennifer Aniston and J.K. Rowling. The film *Magic Beyond Words: The J.K. Rowling Story* was based on his biography of the Harry Potter author. Described by the *Independent* as a 'fearless chronicler', he specializes in meticulous research, going 'on the road' to find the real person behind the star image.

Select Bibliography

Jessie Grace Mellor, *Before They Were Dubz*, unauthorized DVD (Victrix Films, 2011)

N-Dubz, *Against All Odds: From Street Life to Chart Life* (HarperCollins, 2010)

N-Dubz, *Behind the Scenes*, DVD (ZeeTVD, 2009)

N-Dubz, *The Making of* Love.Live.Life, official DVD (ZeeTVD, 2011)

Picture Credits

© Big Pictures: 1, 2, 3, 4, 5, 6, 7, 8, 9, 24, 31, 37
© Rex Features: 12, 13, 14, 19, 20, 21, 23, 35, 38
© Xposure Photos: 15, 36, 39
© Livity: 11
© PA Images: 16, 17, 29,
© Splash: 18, 34, 40, 41
© Mirrorpix: 25, 28
© Getty: 10, 22, 26, 27, 30, 32
© Flynet: 33

Index

Aaliyah, 22–3, 101, 143
Abbot, Russ, 12
Adabra, Michelle, 60, 100
Adams, John, 208
'Addicted to Love', 160
Adele, 104, 235
Adler, Larry, 78
Adulthood, 66
Age Ain't Nothing But a Number, 23
Agent X, 160
Agorou, Zoi 'Zoe', *see* Contostavlos, Zoi
'All About Eve', 41
All Around the World, 96
Against All Odds (album), 97, 133, 135–7, 144
  recording of, 141, 145–6
  release of, 138, 147
  reviews of, 147
  tour, 155–6, 160, 165–6
Against All Odds: From Street Life to Chart Life, see N-Dubz: Against All Odds
'All the Man That I Need', 207
'All These Things That I've Done'/'I Got Soul', 130
Allen, Lily, 146
AllMusic, 36
Ama, Sadie, 88, 90
Ama, Shola, 51
Amodu, Georgia, 158
  Tulisa's Twitter exchange with, 172
Amstell, Simon, 93–4, 117
Andrews Sisters, 12
Ant, Adam, 50–1
Ascot, Mavis, *see* Byrne, Mavis
Ashton United FC, 172
Atkins, Anne, 209
Aura Records, 8

'Babylon Fi Get Shot', 118
'Bad Man Riddim', 42
Badly Drawn Boy, 186
Bailey, Adam, 111–16
  and Finchley Road fracas, 111–15
  Tulisa's engagement to, 111
  Tulisa's split from, 115
Baker Trouble 84, 235

Balls, David, 101
Balls, Ed, 118–21
Barlow, Colin, 82
Barlow, Gary, 145–6, 187, 195, 199, 208, 224
  on Tulisa's voice, 145
Barnes, Elaine, *see* Rawson, Elaine
Barrett, Michelle, 207–8
Basement Jaxx, 67
BBC Chart Blog, 95, 177
BBC Music, 147
BBC Symphony Orchestra, 236
'Beat Again', 133
Beatbullying, 28, 119
  N-Dubz dropped by, 121
Beatles, The, 150
Beckham, David, 205
Beckham, Victoria, 103–4
Before They Were Dubz, 46–7
Behind the Scenes, 102–3, 133, 175–6
Being . . . N-Dubz, 167–8, 171, 173, 186, 202
BeMOBOs, 131
  see also MOBOs
Berridge, Larry, 7–9
'Best Behaviour', 176, 191, 193
Beyoncé, 23, 99, 106, 125, 129, 156, 215–7, 230
Big Brovas, 81
Big Fat Gypsy Gangster, 150
Biggins, Christopher, 80
Billboard Hot 100, 155
Birmingham Mail, 166
Black Eyed Peas, The, 91, 101, 145, 151, 175
Blazin' Squad, 64
Blind, Robin, 9
Bliss, 70, 160
Bloom, Dr David, 198
Bodyrox, 166–7
Bono, 130–1
Book of Five Rings, The (Miyamoto Musashi), 33–4, 42, 65
Boyz II Men, 23, 70
Branigan, Laura, 23
Breakbeat, *see* Fagan, Aaron
Bridges, Nick, 167

BRIT Awards, 68, 72, 125–6, 148
  and War Child, 130
BRIT School for Performing Arts &
  Technology, 235
Britain's Got Talent, 166, 183
britishhiphop.co.uk, 60, 65, 98
Brook, Kelly, 80, 183
Brown, Chris, 175, 216
Brown, Gordon, 157
Brown, Justin, 59–60
Brucknell, Kitty, 203
Bruno, Frank, 89
Bryan, Misha, 217–20
Buena, Mutya, 88–90, 160
Bugsy Malone, 22, 191
Bull, Sarah, 191
Bulla, see Big Fat Gypsy Gangster
Bunjee, DJ, 41
Burger, Paul, 79
Burke, Alexandra, 125–6
Burt, George, 57, 59–60, 95
Burton, Richard, 187
Butler, Jean, 11
Byrne, Ann (mother), 4, 11–15, 156, 172
Byrne, Brian (uncle), 11
Byrne, Goldmund (cousin), 12, 41
Byrne, Hollis (cousin), 41
Byrne, Jack (cousin), 41
Byrne, Louise (aunt), 11–3, 15, 28–9
Byrne, Mavis (aunt), 11
Byrne, Mick (uncle), 11
Byrne, Moira (aunt), 10–13, 15–6
Byrne, Niamh (cousin), 41
Byrne, Oisin (cousin), 41
Byrne, Paula (aunt), 11–13
Byrne, Phelim (cousin), 41
Byrne, Tommy (maternal grandfather),
  10

Camden New Journal, 65, 85
Cannon and Ball, 12
'Cannonball', 208, 224
Cardle, Matt, 185
Carey, Mariah, 70, 155, 184
Cartoon, 16
Castillo, Rich, 81–3, 96, 175, 193
Chairworks, 142–3
'Chakanoori Tango', 9
Chambers, Charlotte, 85
Channel U (later Channel AKA), 59, 61–2,
  64, 83, 91, 95
Charles, Prince of Wales, 180–1
chavs, 196–7, 200
Chegwin, Keith, 93
Cher, 78
Cheung, Goldie, 203
ChildLine, 108–9
'Chip Diddy Chip', 132

Chipmunk, 123, 129–30, 132, 166, 231
Church, Charlotte, 77–80, 82
Church, Maria, 78–9
Ciao!, 63
Classic BRITs, 80
Clay, Jeremy, 68
Cleary, Thomas, 34
Clinton, Bill, 79
Clothier, Michelle, 67
Cocozza, Frankie, 203
Coldplay, 130
Cole, Cheryl, 125–6, 145, 146, 157, 161,
  175, 185–6, 220–1
  Tulisa sent flowers by, 198
  twenty-eighth birthday of, 199–200
  and *X Factor USA*, 185, 194
  X Factor's effect on career of, 189
Cole Kitchenn, 150
Collins, Marcus, 224
Collins, Phil, 38
'Comfortable', 115–16
  divorce of, 19, 26
  'Earth Mix' backing vocals sung by,
    26
  finally diagnosed, 85
  in *Go For It*, 12–13
  hospitalization of, 17–18, 28
  Ireland visits of, 10
  mental-health problems of, 13, 16,
    17–18, 19–20, 28–9, 47
  mimicry and impersonations by, 12
  panic attack by, 55
  Plato marries, 14
  Plato meets, 10
  Tulisa begins to lose respect for, 54
  and Tulisa's secondary education, 28
  Tulisa's unconditional love for, 236
Contostavlos, Byron (uncle) (Uncle B),
  6–10, 16–17, 22, 33–4, 41–2, 44–5, 50,
  59, 61
chain smoking of, 71
Dappy taken to gigs by, 30
Dappy taken to recording studio by,
  39–40
and Dappy's early musical interest, 38
death of, 70–1
and 'Every Day of My Life' video, 59
Fazer meets, 35–6
Fazer steals phone from, 35–6
in 'Feva Las Vegas' video, 69
fishing loved by, 34
and Greek holidays, 33
hairdresser training of, 7
in Hi Fi, 7–9
and Hitt Studios, 26
and Jumbo Studios, 25–6
marriage of, 15
and martial arts, 33–4

Contostavlos, Byron (uncle) – *continued*
  MOBO dedication to, 178
  MOBO thank-you to, 130
  MOBOs, remembered at, 89
  musical beginnings of, 6–7
  new studio envisaged by, 70
  NW1 projects bankrolled by, 59
  and Polydor deal, 64
  raises money cutting hair, 57
  refuses to be negative over Lickle
      Rinsers Crew's future, 56
  remembered at MOBOs, 89
  solo single released by, 9
  song tribute to, 72
  T-shirt image of, 101
  Tulisa and Dappy guided by, 9
  Uncle B album tribute to, 97
  van bought by, 49
  Westbound formed by, 26
Contostavlos, Costadinos
      ('Dino'/'Dappy') (cousin), 39, 126
  a capella rapping of, 40
  aeroplane incident concerning, 117
  on *Against All Odds* tour, 165–6
  Alton Towers eject, 161
  anger at injustice shown by, 9, 39
  on arena tour, 192–3, 194
  assault conviction against, 116–17
  and 'Babylon Fi Get Shot' video, 118
  Beatbullying criticizes, 121
  in *Behind the Scenes*, 102–3
  birth of, 15, 30
  and Byron's death, 70–2
  Charles, Prince of Wales, meets, 181
  Cowell meets, 183–4
  'Dappy' nickname of, 30
  distinctive singing style of, 43
  in documentary, 46–7
  and *Dubplate Drama, see Dubplate Drama*
  early keyboard talent of, 39
  father worries about, 34
  Fazer meets, 34–5
  fighting by, 30–1
  and Finchley Road fracas, 112, 113,
      114
  first son born to, 117
  fishing loved by, 106, 142
  football loved by, 34
  hat obsession of, 31, 40, 93–4
  at Haverstock School, 30
  Haverstock School left by, 57
  height of, 31
  and JLS, 132–3
  Kaye's allegation against, 201
  Kaye's reported bust-up with, 154–5
  Kaye's split with, 159
  and 'Love For My Slum' video, 84
  'Manufactured Bands' rant of, 63–4

  May's collaboration with, 225
  and meow meow, 158
  at MOBOs, 89–90, 129, 132–3
  on Moyles show, 120–2
  N-Dubz formed by, 9
  in N-Dubz TV show, *see Being . . . N-Dubz*
  on *Never Mind the Buzzcocks*, 93–4, 117
  number-one single of, 212
  own accommodation found by, 141
  paintball-gun incident concerning,
      159
  in Rage's video, 144
  'RIP Dad' tattoo of, 72, 205–6
  schooling of, 30–1, 35
  second son born to, 181
  solo career of, 225, 236
  and 'Spit It Out', 109
  Stryder's fallout with, 126
  suspected of assaulting Kaye, 213
  tattoos of, 72, 205–6
  timeline of, 245–50
  tinnitus suffered by, 126
  at Tulisa's Ibiza birthday celebration,
      170
  on *Uncle B* tour, 123–5, 126–7
  video acting talent shown by, 83
  visa problem for, 154, 175
  at WAC, 57–8
  words and rhymes loved by, 39
  writing routine of, 143
  X Factor criticized by, 44, 211, 225–6
  see also Lickle Rinsers Crew; N-Dubz;
      NW1
Contostavlos, Gino, 117–18
Contostavlos, Milo, 181–2
Contostavlos, Plato (father), 4, 6–7, 14–17,
      18–19, 208–9
  Ann marries, 14
  Ann meets, 10
  and Adam Ant, 50–1
  and Byron's death, 72
  divorce of, 19, 26
  fishing loved by, 34
  hairdresser training of, 7
  in Hi Fi, 8–9
  and Hitt Studios, 26
  and Jumbo Studios, 25–6
  Mel divorces, 46
  Mel marries, 27
  Mel meets, 26
  musical beginnings of, 6–10
  Steve Contostavlos name of, 9
  technical expertise of, 89–90
  Tulisa moves in with, 55
  Tulisa withdrawn from Haverstock by,
      49
  and Tulisa's secondary education, 28
  Westbound formed by, 26

Contostavlos, Spiros (cousin), 15, 34
Contostavlos, Spyros (paternal
    grandfather), 4, 6, 7, 18–19
Contostavlos, Tula ('Yaya') (paternal
    grandmother), 5, 14–15, 18, 127,
    168
Contostavlos, Tulisa:
  Aaliyah's similarities to, 23
  and Adam, see Bailey, Adam
  admits to 'naughty things', 53
  on Against All Odds tour, 165–6
  on arena tour, 191, 192–3
  arrested, 111–12
  autobiography of, 235
  BBC documentary about, see Tulisa: My
      Mum and Me
  in Behind the Scenes, 102–3
  birth of, 14
  birth chart and stars of, 238–44
  breakdance lessons for, 42
  in Bugsy Malone, 22
  burgled home of, 171
  Byron teaches karate to, 33
  and Byron's death, 71–2, 73
  Charles, Prince of Wales, meets, 181
  chronic mistrust of men by, 139
  and cyberbullying, 119–20
  Dappy defended by, 94
  debut single of, 230, 234
  in Demons Never Die, 193
  disappearances of, 50
  and Dubplate Drama, see Dubplate Drama
  early singing of, 22–3
  Elly Jackson's feud with, 146–7
  engagement speculation concerning
      Fazer and, 226
  and Facebook, 151
  false ID card of, 46
  and Fazer, speculation of romantic
      relationship between, 172, 182,
      200
  Fazer's relationship with, revealed, 226
  Fazer's romantic holiday with, 227
  Fazer's split from, 227–8
  and female empowerment, 104
  fighting by, 46
  film role for, 150
  and Finchley Road fracas, 111–15
  first dream car bought by, 138
  first perfume of, 212
  first solo performance of, 236
  gaining confidence, 92
  Georgia's Twitter exchange with, 172
  Greek holidays loved by, 33
  in Greek hospital, 127–8
  at Haverstock School, 30–2, 45
  height of, 31
  house bought by, 156

  Ibiza birthday celebration of, 170–1
  Island Records solo deal of, 202
  and Justin, see Edwards, Justin
  at La Sainte Union school, 27–8
  'Lady T' stage name of, 47, 60
  and Little Mix, 3
  and Luca, see Havern, Gianluca
  massive Twitter following of, 237
  maturing vocal style of, 116
  midflight illness of, 127–8
  at MOBOs, 89–90, 129–33 passim
  N-Dubz formed by, 9
  N-Dubz role of, 41
  in N-Dubz TV show, see Being . . . N-Dubz
  on Never Mind the Buzzcocks, 186
  nose operation on, 151
  online abuse against, 196
  personal diary of, 29
  and Plato and Mel's relationship, 26–7
  at Quintin Kynaston school, 51–2, 54
  in Rage's video, 144
  receptionist, job of, 56
  at Rosary RC Primary, 20–4
  self-harm by, 50, 55
  sex toy in luggage of, 231–2
  solo album of, 149, 228, 229–30
  and 'Spit It Out', 108–9
  struggling with despair, 45
  suicide attempted by, 47–9
  Sun column of, 156–8
  tattoos of, 205–6
  teeth of, 197–8
  The Female Boss, 104, 205
  timeline of, 245–50
  tonsillitis suffered by, 175
  'Tulisa' name of, 15, 60
  twenty-first birthday of, 115
  twenty-second birthday of, 171
  and Twitter, 151–2, 158, 160, 171, 227,
      231
  on Uncle B tour, 123–5, 126–7
  in US to work on solo album, 228–32
  Valentine's Day tweets of, 229
  video acting talent shown by, 83
  and War Child, 131–2
  weight of, 55–6, 191
  West End birthday party of, 200
  Woman of the Year, 223
  wrists slit by, 55
  writing routine of, 143
  and X Factor, see X Factor
  on Xtra Factor, 204–5
  see also Lickle Rinsers Crew; N-Dubz;
      NW1
Contostavlos (née Agorou), Zoi ('Zoe')
    (aunt), 15, 30, 70, 101
  Fazer meets, 35
Cook, Captain James, 205

Cornwall, Duchess of, 180
Cowell, Eric, 188
Cowell, Simon, 44, 60, 175, 183–9, 199, 204, 208
  Dappy meets, 183–4
  Dappy's alleged insult to, 225
  Little Mix liked by, 224
  Tulisa's *X Factor* deal with, 189
Crazy Titch, 84
Cruz, Taio, 104, 155
cyberbullying, 119–20
CyberMentors, 119–20

Daily Mail, 13, 16, 26, 28, 55, 191, 208–9, 219–20
Daily Mirror, 142, 192, 211, 213, 218, 227–8
Daily Record, 96, 125, 128
Daily Star, 143, 176
Daily Telegraph, 147
Dappy, *see* Contostavlos, Costadinos
David, Craig, 38, 104
Davis, Bette, 187
Day One, 41
Deacon, Adam, 66, 193
Dee, Donna, 40, 42, 47, 49–50
Deekline, DJ, 42
'Defeat You', 123, 132, 135
Demons Never Die, 193
Dennis, Les, 12–13
Dermot, Fr, 21
Destiny's Child, 216
Devlin, 236
Devlin, Janet, 203, 219, 224
Digital Spy, 101, 148
Dingwall, John, 96
Dion, Celine, 230
Diver, Mike, 147
Diversity, 166
Diverzion, 83
Dizzee Rascal, 105, 299, 186
'Does Anyone Believe in Love', 230
Doonican, Val, 10
Dorries, Nadine, 209
Dorset, Ray, 6–7, 16–17, 25–6, 30, 43, 64
'Down', 155
'Down For Whatever', 220
Dream a Dream, 79
Duang, Folora, 109–10
Dubplate Drama, 66–8, 69–70, 73, 85, 99, 132, 232
  and ChildLine, 108
  Tulisa's starring role in, 110–11
'Duku Man Skit', 150
Dylan, Bob, 11

Edwards, Justin ('Ultra'), 138–40, 152, 156, 200
  Tulisa drops, 159–60

Egere-Cooper, Matilda, 137
Elstree Studios, 188
EMI, 106, 188
Emmanuel, Nathalie, 168
Emmet Spiceland, 11
Empire, 194
'Empire State of Mind', 224
En Vogue, 215–16
Enter the Wu-Tang: 36 Chambers, 36–7
Evening Chronicle, Newcastle, 194
Evening Standard, London, 179
'Every Day of My Life', 57–9

Fabulous, 195
Face Killa, 89, 118
Facebook, 143–4, 151
Fagan, Aaron ('Breakbeat'), 133–5
'Fallin'', 160
Faux Pas, 210
Fazer, *see* Rawson, Richard
Fe-Nix, 154
Fearless/FeFe, 112–3, 160–1, 171
Female First, 95
Ferdinand, Rio, 105
'Feva Las Vegas', 68–9, 83, 123, 136
FHM, 125, 161
Fielding, Noel, 93
'Fill Me In', 38
Fisher Lane Studios, 142
Flack, Caroline, 204
Flashdance, 23
Flatley, Michael, 11
Flavour, 100
Flawless, 166
Flynn, Jerome, 188
Forrester, Kyle, 20–1, 28
Foster, Jack, 105
Foster, Jodie, 22
Four Ramblers, 10
Fox, Killian, 179
Freak FM, 153
Fuego, 177
Fugees, The, 88, 127
Future Sound of London (FSOL), 26

Gaffney, Isobel, 21–2
Gallagher, Liam, 27
Gates, Gareth, 64
Geldof, Bob, 11
Genius/GZA (Gary Grice), 37
George (*X Factor*), 203–4
Gestetner, Henny, 77
Ghostface Killah, 37
Gibson, Corey, 230
Girl v Boy, 211
'Girls', 175, 180, 182
Girls Aloud, 176
Girls Tyme, 215

Glamour, 199, 220–1, 226
'Gloria', 23
GMTV, 158
Go For It, 12–13
Goldie (*X Factor*), *see* Cheung, Goldie
Gousse, Max, 151, 155, 177, 228
Gray, Nyomi ('Ny'), 152–4, 170, 182, 190, 192, 219, 225, 229, 230
    Kaye's allegation against, 201
Green, Chloe, 228
Green, Robson, 188
Gringo's Revenge, 8
Grover, Ricky, 150
Guardian, 51–2, 91, 99, 152
gun crime, 109–10, 235
GZA/Genius (Gary Grice), 37

Hair, 11
Hankerson, Barry, 23
Harnett, Ricci, 110
Hattenstone, Simon, 206
Havern, Gianluca ('Luca'), 169–72
Haverstock School, 30
    alleged racism in, 35
    free concert at, 109
    Tulisa withdrawn from, 49
Heat, 185, 220–1, 234
Heawood, Sophie, 122
Here I Am, 216, 220
Hi Fi, 7–9
    split of, 8
Hill, Lauryn, 127
Hitt Studios, 26
Holman, Tommy, 60
Horwell, Richard, 114
Houston, Whitney, 184
Huffington Post, 225
Huq, Konnie, 183
Hustler, 229
Hyams, Luke, 69
Hyde FC, 172

I Am . . . Sasha Fierce, 99
'I Got Soul'/'All These Things That I've Done', 130
'I Need You', 130, 143–5, 167–8
'I Swear', 62–4, 95, 123, 135–6
    favourable online reviews of, 63
'If I Ain't Got You', 224
Iley, Chrissy, 226
I'm a Celebrity . . . Get Me Out of Here!, 66–7, 80, 232
Imbruglia, Natalie, 123
'In the Summertime', 26, 43
Independent, 84, 136–7
Independent on Sunday, 122, 141–2
IndieLondon, 146
Inspectah Deck, 37

Ironik, DJ, 153, 166, 170, 227
Island Def Jam Music Group, 150–1, 156, 177, 228
    N-Dubz part company with, 201–2
Island Records, 202

Jackson, Elly, 146
Jam, 8
Jamelia, 81–2, 88
James, Sarah-Louise, 143
Jay-Z, 37, 101, 105–6, 148
Jeep, 10
    split of, 13
Jessie J, 186, 193, 212, 229, 235
Jesus Christ Superstar, 11
JLS, 132–3, 145–6, 178, 185, 211
John, Elton, 78, 131
Johnson, Cassie, 194
Johnson, Wil, 89
Johnston, Sheriff Johanna, 134–5
Jolie, Angelina, 205
Jonsin, Jim, 155–6, 175, 220
Joseph, Abuk, 225, 227
Joseph, Craig Bain ('CBJ'), 205
Jumbo Studios, 25–6, 58
Jupitus, Phill, 93, 186

Kelis, 175
Kelly, Loraine, 80
Kelly Marie, 26
Kensit, Patsy, 27
Keys, Alicia, 224
Killers, The, 124, 130
King, Kanya, 87–8
Kirsty (school friend), 21–2
Kiss 100 FM, 64
Kitty (*X Factor*), *see* Brucknell, Kitty
Klass, Myleene, 80–2
Knight, Gladys, 23
Knowles, Beyoncé, *see* Beyoncé
Kouame, Jean-Baptiste, 175, 190, 230

La Roux, 146–7
La Sainte Union school (LSU), 27–8
Lady Gaga, 211
Lamb, Archie, 105
Laviscount, Lucien, 169
Lawrence, Eddy, 92
Leicester Mercury, 68
Lemon, Billy, 7
Lethal Bizzle, 94, 167–8
Levine, Nick, 148
Lewis, Leona, 145, 185, 235
Library Journal, 33
Lickle Rinsers Crew (later N-Dubz), 39–45, 49–50, 56–7
    documentary about, 46–7, 98
    first public performance of, 42

Lickle Rinsers Crew (later N-Dubz) –
  continued
  first studio get-together of, 41–3
  others' jealousy of, 49
  record companies' lack of interest in, 56
  renamed NW1, 56
'Life Is Getting Sicker By The Day', 42–3
Lister, David, 88
Little Deeper, A, 68
Little Mix, 3, 223–5
Liu, Gordon, 37
Live Aid, 130
Livity, 67
Lloyd, Cher, 185, 210
Lloyd Webber, Andrew, 11
London Tonight, 88
Lott, Pixie, 130–1, 186
'Love For My Slum', 83–5, 98, 112, 118,
  191, 235
'Love Is All I Need', 177
'Love.Live.Life', 175, 192
Love.Live.Life, 133, 136, 179–80, 190, 201
  release of, 179
  reviews of, 179
'Love Sick', 176, 191
LRC Records, 60
  N-Dubz's last single on, 83
Luckett, LaToya, 215

McAlpine, Fraser, 95, 143, 177
McBride, Paul, 134
McCartney, Paul, 27, 131
Macpherson, Alex, 99
MAD Awards, 168
Manfred Mann, 11
'Manufactured Bands', 63–4
Marquee Club, 8
Marriott, Lisa, 150
Martin, George, 78
Marxman, 41
'Mary from Dungloe', 11
Massive Attack, 41
Max, DJ, 178, 208
May, Brian, 225
Maze, DJ, 53, 70, 89, 117, 135–6
  arrested, 135
'Meet Me Halfway', 145, 175
Mellor, Jessica, 98
Men in Black, 216
meow meow, 157–8
Mercedes (friend), 219
Messy Little Raindrops, 175
Method Man, 37
Metro, 179
Middleton, Kate, 27–8, 120
MIDEM, 16
'Mighty Quinn', 11
Miliband, David, 30

Miliband, Ed, 30
Mill, Ian, 79
'Million Love Songs, A', 146
Minaj, Nicki, 199
Minogue, Dannii, 185
Minogue, Kylie, 181, 192
'Misha B', 217–20
Mr Hudson, 115, 129, 147–8, 176, 177
Mobb Deep, 37
MOBOs, 87–90, 129–33, 144, 178
  and War Child, 130–2
  see also BeMOBOs
Modlin, Monty, 12
Monica, 22
Moodie, Clemmie, 191–2
Moody, Chloe, 121–2
Moore, Jane, 156
Moore, Madeleine, 244
More!, 47, 139
'Morning Star', 175, 190, 205
Moss, Kate, 229
Mossley FC, 172
Moyles, Chris, 120, 122
mph, 109
Ms Dynamite, 68, 153, 236
Ms Jade, 22
Ms Kelly, 216
MTV, 153
MTV Base, 64
Mungo Jerry, 6–7, 17, 25–6, 30
Murs, Olly, 204–5
Musashi, Miyamoto, 33–4
Music Magazine, 146
My Big Fat Greek Wedding, 14
'My Name Is Tulisa', 191

Nagle, Mark, 112–4
Nash, Su-Elise, 219
National Centre for Social Research, 120
Nas, 37
Naz (product manager), 103
N-Dubz:
  Adidas deal with, 103
  All Around the World deal with, 96
  on *Against All Odds* tour, 165–6
  anti-bullying single released by, 120
  and Anti-Bullying Week, 119
  arena tour of, 191–3, 194
  autobiographical songs of, 48, 61
  Barlow works with, 145–6
  Beatbullying drops, 121
  in *Behind the Scenes*, 102–3
  Best UK Act MOBO award for, 130
  book by, 32
  Bugsy footage in live shows of, 22
  Charles, Prince of Wales, meets, 180,
    181
  NDubz Christmas Party tour of, 136–7

and *Dubplate Drama, see Dubplate Drama*
first album of, 97
formation of, 9
greatest-hits album of, 220
at Haverstock School concert, 109
HD video promo of, 59
Island Def Jam part company with, 201–2
and Maze, 135
MOBO nominations for, 87–9, 129
MOBO wins for, 89–90, 129–30
most controversial record of, 83–4
new tour manager for, 73
NW1 become, 60
Polydor deal of, 64, 70
Polydor quit by, 94–5, 201
as positive role models, 83
postcode association with name of, 60
pro-education, 58
Radio 1 list upgrade for, 101
on ringtones, 102
at Royal Variety Performance, 180–1
school gigs by, 83, 92–3, 142
serious press wake up to, 137
Shalit chosen by, 77, 82
and 'Spit It Out', 108–9
and strong language, 36
Stryder's collaboration with, 104–5
summer dates by, 141
timeline of, 245–50
TV show featuring, *see Being . . . N-Dubz*
on *Uncle B* tour, 123–5, 126–7
US ambitions of, 150–1, 201
US arrivals of, 155, 174
and War Child, 130–1
writing routine of, 143
see also individual song and album titles;
Lickle Rinsers Crew; NW1
*N-Dubz: Against All Odds – From Street Life to
Chart Life* (N-Dubz), 32, 35–6, 48, 116, 156
Tulisa's description of her early life in, 53
'N-Dubz vs NAA', 83
Nelly, 179
Never Mind the Buzzcocks, 93–4, 117, 186
New Nation, 100
News of the World, 154, 194
Newsbeat, 119, 211
'No One Knows', 146, 165
'No Regrets', 212
Notorious B.I.G., 37
Now, 56, 223
Now That's What I Call Music!, 101
NSPCC, 108
Nu Flow, 81
Nu Vibe, 212
'Number 1', 104–6, 123, 133, 170, 191

credits row over, 126
MOBO nomination for, 129
Nuttall, Cris, 96
NW1, 58–61
become N-Dubz, 60
Lickle Rinsers Crew become, 57
musical styles of, 58

Observer, 99, 179
O'Connell, Jack, 232–4
Offside, 41
Ol' Dirty Bastard (Russell Jones), 37
O'Leary, Dermot, 117, 204, 218, 224
One Direction, 185, 211
'One in a Million', 23, 143
'One Sweet Day', 70
Only Way is Essex, The, 232
Ordinary Man, 41
Orion, 210
Osafo-Jones, Krystle, 61
O'Sullivan, Kevin, 184–6, 188, 208, 219
O2 Academy, Newcastle, 159
O2, Glasgow, 165
O2, Liverpool, 194
O2, London, 88, 193
O2, Sheffield, 127
'Ouch', 95–6, 123, 135, 165, 191, 197
ten million hits for, 95

'Papa Can You Hear Me?', 72, 97, 100, 102, 112, 123, 130, 136, 191, 193
Paramount Studios, 229
Pearn, Jon, 167
Peck, Gregory, 187
Peel, John, 8
Perry, Katy, 156, 186
Peters, Ben, 177
Pink, 155
Plan B, 104, 153
Platt, Darren, 84, 96
Playboy, 126
'Playing With Fire', 147–8, 165, 177–8
Police, The, 38
Polydor, 64, 70, 82, 91
Dappy criticizes, 91–2
N-Dubz leave, 94–5, 201
Pop Idol, 64, 188
Portishead, 41
Presley, Elvis, 68
Professor Green, 153, 190

Queen of the Damned, 23
Quintin Kynaston school (QK), 51–4

'R U Cyber Safe?', 120
Rabin, Rachel, 230
Rachel (Dappy's class friend), 39–40
racism, 35, 219

Radio Times, 198, 200, 206
Raekwon, 37
Rage, 144
Rantzen, Esther, 108
Rawson, Dean, 130
Rawson, Elaine, 35–6, 127, 178
Rawson, Lewis, 130
Rawson, Phil, 35–6
Rawson, Richard (Fazer):
  aeroplane incident concerning, 117
  on arena tour, 192
  with BBC Symphony Orchestra, 236
  in *Behind the Scenes*, 102–3
  and body popping, 42
  branching out, 236
  and Byron's death, 70–1, 72–3
  catwalk debut of, 229
  Charles, Prince of Wales, meets, 181
  cooler name sought by, 37
  Dappy meets, 34–5
  in documentary, 46–7
  driving ban for, 136
  and *Dubplate Drama, see Dubplate Drama*
  early drumming talent of, 39
  engagement speculation concerning
      Tulisa and, 226
  'Fazer' name adopted by, 38
  fishing loved by, 106, 142
  and Misha B, 218
  at MOBOs, 89–90, 130
  mugged, 161
  in N-Dubz TV show, *see Being . . . N-Dubz*
  own accommodation found by, 141
  phone stolen by, 35–6
  piano playing of, 193
  police search flat of, 136
  racism suffered by, 219
  in Rage's video, 144
  and 'Spit It Out', 109
  tattoos of, 205–6
  timeline of, 245–50
  and Tulisa, speculation of romantic
      relationship between, 172, 182, 200
  and Tulisa's midflight illness, 127–8
  Tulisa's relationship with, revealed, 226
  Tulisa's romantic holiday with, 227
  Tulisa's split from, 227–8
  on *Uncle B* tour, 123–5, 126–7
  visa problem for, 154
  writing routine of, 143
  and *The X Factor* contestants, 212
  at *The X Factor* wrap party, 225
  see also Lickle Rinsers Crew; N-Dubz;
      NW1
reality TV, 63
Reid, Alison Jane, 61–2, 102, 144, 148, 177,
    181, 190, 197, 200, 220–2, 231
  on chavs, 196–7

  on make-up, 234
  on tattoos, 206
Reid, L.A., 151, 154–5, 184
Rhythmix, 210, 212
  change name to Little Mix, 223
Richie, Lionel, 88
Rigby, Emma, 193
Rihanna, 89, 155, 175, 211, 230
Rising Stars, 12
Risk, 212
Riverdance, 11
ROAR Global, 150, 183
Roberson, LaTavia, 215
Robinson, Connor, 181
Robinson, Jenny, 181
Robinson, Kane, 104
Robson and Jerome, 188
Roc Nation, 106
'Rockstar', 225
Rocky Horror Show, The, 11
Roll Deep Crew, 109, 105
Romeo Must Die, 23
Rosary RC Primary School, 20–3, 49
Rose, Arjun, 193
Rotblat, Dr Joseph, 5
Roussos, Demis, 17
Rowland, Kelly, 195, 199, 214–22
'Run For Your Life', 185
'Run, Run', 8
Runaway, The, 232
Ruth (schoolfriend), 21–2
RWD magazine, 153
Ryan, Lee, 93
Ryan, Louise, 78
RZA (Robert Diggs), 37

Saatchi & Saatchi, 78
Sampson, George, 166
Saturdays, The, 150, 176, 228
'Say It's Over', 180
Scherzinger, Nicole, 186
Schuter, Jo, 51
Scotsman, 165
'Scream My Name', 177
Sean, Jay, 155
'Secrets', 48, 100
Senova, 198
Sensible Studios, 136
'Sex', 135
Shalit, Jonathan, 77–83, 88, 112, 127, 133,
    135, 149–50, 232
  and Barlow, 145
  'big strings' pulled by, 183
  Edwards represented by, 160
  introduces *Being . . . N-Dubz*, 167
Shield, Miss, 52
'Shoulda Put Something On', 154–5
Shystie, MC, 67, 110

Silverton, Kate, 80
Simply Deep, 216
Sinitta, 89, 188
Sixx, Aaron, 8
Size, Roni, 41
Skepta, MC, 190, 236
Skins, 232
'Skit featuring Fearless', 136
Sky Living, 222
Smith, Fraser T., 104, 131
'So Alive', 190
'So Macho', 188
So Solid Crew, 68
Solly (friend), 219
Spears, Britney, 23, 145, 192, 215
Spice Girls, The, 103
Spiceland Folk Group, 11
'Spit It Out', 108–9
Split Endz Vol. 1, 153
Spotlight, 149
Star in the Hood, 105–6
Star Search, 22, 215
'Stay Safe in Cyber Space', 119–20
Stennett, Justin, 67
Stilgoe, Richard, 12
Sting, 38, 78
Stockport County FC, 169, 172
Stone, Joss, 88
StreetDance 3D, 166
Streets, 67
'Strong Again', 101–2, 104, 130, 133, 167
  MOBO nomination for, 129
Stryder, Tinchy, 88, 90, 104–6, 123,
  129–30, 147
  Dappy's fallout with, 126
'Stryderman', 104
Studio Valbonne, 182
Subba-Cultcha, 100
Suede, 25
Sugababes, The, 88, 115
Sugar, 147, 159
Suggs, 51
Sun, 115, 117, 122, 127, 135, 154, 182, 201, 231
  Tulisa a guest columnist in, 156–8
Sunday Mirror, 19, 184–5, 208, 218
Sunday People, 169, 172
Sunday Times, 46, 53
Supremes, The, 216
Sutton, Mark, 73, 89
Sweeney, Claire, 80
swine flu, 127–8
Syco Records, 185

'Take Me Back', 104
Take That, 145, 181, 192
Takeover Entertainment, 106
Tammam, Lucy, 196

Tarantino, Quentin, 89
Tarbuck, Jimmy, 12
tattoos, 205–6
Taylor, Elizabeth, 187
The Dream, 230–31
'3', 145
36th Chamber of Shaolin, The, 37
Tibbs, Jade, 154
Timbaland, 101, 140
Timberlake, Justin, 23, 101, 215
Time Out, 84, 92
Times, The, 126–7
'Took It All the Way', 191
'Torn', 123
Total Film, 193–4
Towns and Bars, 8
True Colours, 109
Tula/Tulisa, *see* Contostavlos, Tulisa
Tulisa: My Mum and Me (BBC
  documentary), 13, 17, 29, 53, 55, 173
Tupac, 88
Twin B, 135
Twitter, 151–2, 158, 160, 171–2, 227, 229, 231
  Tulisa's 1.7 million followers on, 237
2-Shoes, 212
2-Step, 40, 42
Tydolla$ign, 230

U-God, 37
Ultra, *see* Edwards, Justin
'Unchained Melody', 188
Uncle B, *see* Contostavlos, Byron
Uncle B, 97, 99–101, 111, 144
  goes platinum, 103
  MOBO win for, 129–30
  release and chart success of, 99
  tour, 117, 123–5, 126–7
UnkleJam, 88, 90
Urban Development, 193
Urban Music Awards, 81
Urban Review, 96
Ustream, 153
U2, 130

Varey, Gareth, 166, 169–70, 175, 213, 228, 229, 230
  birthday celebration for, 227
  Jack introduced to Tulisa by, 232
  tattoo of, 229
Vassell, Kaye, 117–18, 126, 154–5, 159, 177
  Dappy suspected of assaulting, 213
  first son born to, 117
  reports of row between Tulisa and, 201
  second son born to, 181
Verrico, Lisa, 126–7
Viva Las Vegas, 68
Voice of an Angel, 79

Vondrau, Mel (stepmother), 16, 19, 23, 26–9, 46, 55, 208

WAC Performing Arts and Media College, 57–8
Wade, Rachel, 94
Walsh, Louis, 185, 195, 199, 208, 214–15, 217–18
Wanted, 229
War Child, 130–2
Ward, Joe, 100
Ward, Mark, 114
Warren, Diane, 230
Watson, Russell, 80
'We Dance On', 166
Welby, Aaron, 211–2
Welham, Jez, 64, 91
West, Kanye, 129, 148, 155
Westbound, 26
Westwood, Tim, 85, 132
'What Is the World Coming To . . .', 40
White, Vanessa, 228, 229
'Why Can't I Wake Up With You?', 146
Wiley, 105, 132, 153
Williams, Maureen, 27
Williams, Michelle, 216
Williams, Robbie, 146, 150, 205
Williams, Roy, 216
Willis, Matt, 80
Wiredradio, 94
Wireless Festival, 236
Wiseman, Rochelle, 150, 228, 229
Wix, Katy, 187
Wolfson, Sam, 99
Wootten, Dan, 56
Workers' Playtime, 10
'Wouldn't You', 106

Wright, Mark, 232
Wroldsen, Ina, 176
Wu-Tang Clan, The, 36–7, 67

X Factor, The, 44, 66, 126, 145, 184–9 *passim*, 190, 194–5, 202–5, 207–12, 214–22
final of, 223–5
manufactured acts on, 210
and 'Mishagate', 217–20
slickly edited, 202
Tulisa–Kelly rivalry on, 214, 217–19
Tulisa mentors groups on, 210
Tulisa signs for, 189
Tulisa's earnings from, 235
Tulisa's first appearances on, 198–9, 202
Tulisa's topless butler at auditions for, 200
wrap party of, 225
X Factor USA, The, 184, 189, 194
XL Bass, 153
XTC, 8
Xtra Factor, The, 183, 204–5

You, 209
'You Better Not Waste My Time', 60, 61–2, 68, 123, 191, 197
performed at MOBOs, 89
Polydor release, 91–2
votes cast for, 62
'Young', 230, 234, 250
Young Soul Rebels, 130–2
Young, Will, 64, 188
'Your Song', 203
YouTube, 26, 62, 91, 95, 100, 102, 153

ZeeTVD, 102, 133, 171, 175–6